THE SYMPHONY

MUSIC RESEARCH AND
INFORMATION GUIDES
(VOL. 14)

GARLAND REFERENCE LIBRARY
OF THE HUMANITIES
(VOL. 862)

MUSIC RESEARCH AND INFORMATION GUIDES

THE SYMPHONY
A Research and Information Guide
Volume I: The Eighteenth Century

Preston Stedman

GARLAND PUBLISHING, INC. • NEW YORK & LONDON
1990

Library of Congress Cataloging-in-Publication Data

Stedman, Preston, 1923–
    The symphony: a research and information guide / Preston Stedman.
      p. cm. — (Music research and information guides; vol. 14)
(Garland reference library of the humanities; vol. 862.)
    Contents: v. 1. The eighteenth century.
    ISBN 0–8240–4447–9 (alk. paper)
    1. Symphony—Bibliography. I. Title. II. Series. III. Series:
Garland reference library of the humanities; vol. 862.
ML128.S9S7 1990
016.78418′4—dc20   90–2927
                                                                         CIP
                                                                        M N

Printed on acid-free, 250-year-life paper
Manufactured in the United States of America

CONTENTS

III. National Activities

Contents   *vii*

ACKNOWLEDGMENTS

Several research grants from California State University, Fullerton, have underwritten a major portion of the effort required by this project. These were augmented by a grant from the university's School of the Arts. An initial award from the Graduate School of the University of the Pacific supported early research on Haydn. Some materials examined were obtained through the Interlibrary Loan Division of the University Library at California State University. The assistance of the latter unit was extremely valuable. Numerous scholars have also assisted. Polish materials, in part, were translated and evaluated by Dr. William Smialek. Niels Krabbe and Karsten Hatting of Copenhagen University provided assistance with Danish composers. Dr. Lovro Županović of Zagreb, Yugoslavia, gave information and insight on Ivancic's symphonies. The American Musicological Society provided translations of some materials. Jan LaRue supplied a description of his huge thematic index of 18th century symphonies. The author's research assistant and doctoral musicology student at U.C.L.A., Marissa Solomon, translated and/or abstracted several crucial articles on the symphony in Germany.

INTRODUCTION

Research on the history of the symphony has been a steady and ongoing evolution. Vogler's 18th century writings are peripherally associated with works of the Mannheim school while Burney's travel chronicles document symphonic activity throughout most of western Europe. In the 19th century, biographers of 18th century composers included information on their symphonies. Specific writings on the symphony, however, began in the late 19th century, the first coming from France (Fétis, Brenet, and Pierre). Riemann appears in 1902 as the first major symphony scholar in his editions of and writings on Mannheim works. His activities stimulated others, including Botstiber, Cucuel, Dwelshauvers, Fischer, Niecks, Torrefranco, Heuss, Flueler, Hase, Mennicke, and Saint-Foix.

Starting around 1920, another generation of scholars emerged, most notably Sondheimer and Tutenberg. They were followed in the 1930s and 1940s by Gradenwitz, Adler and Casella. The effects of World War II delayed further expansion until the 1950s, with most of this activity in the United States. The major scholars emerging in that period and in the 1960s include LaRue, Larsen and Brook, with LaRue and Brook both providing major stimuli through doctoral programs under their supervision. Mention should also be made of the contributions of Landon, Feder, Zaslaw, Cudworth, Churgin, and Wolf. There are also scores of other superb scholars emerging today. Their dissertations and other writings form the core of materials produced after 1970.

Since the findings of earlier scholars tend to be minimized by more recent research, many older writings gradually diminish in historical significance. In spite of this, most of the earlier research is included in this project so that those using this volume can gain perspective and insight not only into the symphony's history but also into the evolution of research on that history.

ABBREVIATIONS FOR PUBLICATIONS

ActaM	*Acta Musicologica*
ActaMo	*Acta Mozartiana*
AfMw	*Archiv für Musikwissenschaft*
AM	*Année Musicale*
AMz(Bln)	*Allgemeine Musik-Zeitung (Berlin)*
AnM	*Analecta Musicologica*
b	See *MGG* below.
BQ	*Brass Quarterly*
CM	*Current Musicology*
DaM	*Dansk Musiktidsskrift*
DM-Z	*Deutsche Musik-Zeitung*
DTB	*Denkmäler der Tonkunst in Bayern*, Denkmäler deutscher Tonkunst, 2. Folge. Brunswick, 1900-1938; rev. ed., Wiesbaden: Breitkopf & Härtel, 1962- .
DTOe	*Denkmäler der Tonkunst in Österreich.* Vienna: Österreichischer Bundesverlag, 1894-1959; Graz: Akadem Verlag, 1960- ; reprint, Graz: Akadem. Druck, 1959- .
Festschrift Abraham	*Slavonic and Western Music: Essays for Gerald Abraham,* ed. M.H. Brown and R.J. Wiley. Ann Arbor: UMI Research Press, 1985.
Festschrift Albrecht	*Studies in Musicology in Honor of Otto E. Albrecht,* ed. J.W. Hill. Kassel: Bärenreiter, 1977.
Festschrift Becker/60th	*Festschrift Heinz Becker zum 60. Geburtstag am 26. Juni 1982,* ed. J. Schläder and R. Quandt. Laaber: Laaber Verlag, 1982.
Festschrift Bernstein	*A Musical Offering: Essays in Honor of Martin Bernstein,* ed. E.H. Clinkscale and C. Brook. New York: Pendragon, 1977.
Festschrift Blume/70th	*Festschrift Friedrich Blume zum 70. Geburtstag,* ed. A.A. Abert and W. Pfannkuch. Kassel: Bärenreiter, 1963.

Festschrift Brook	Music in the Classic Period: Essays in Honor of Barry S. Brook, ed. A.W. Atlas. New York: Pendragon, 1985.
Festschrift Cudworth	Music in Eighteenth Century England: Essays in Memory of Charles Cudworth, ed. C. Hogwood and B. Luckett. Cambridge: Oxford Univ. Press, 1987.
Festschrift Deutsch/80th	Festschrift Otto Erich Deutsch zum 80. Geburtstag, ed. W. Gerstenberg, et al. Kassel: Bärenreiter, 1963.
Festschrift Engel/70th	Festschrift Hans Engel zum 70. Geburtstag, ed. H. Heusser. Kassel: Bärenreiter, 1964.
Festschrift Fellerer/60th	Festschrift Karl Gustav Fellerer zum sechzigsten Geburtstag am 7. Juli 1962, ed. H. Hüschen. Regensburg: G. Bosse, 1962.
Festschrift Fellerer/70th	Musicae scientiae collectanea: Festschrift Karl Gustav Fellerer zum siebzigsten Geburtstag am 7. Juli 1972, ed. H. Hüschen. Cologne: Arno-Volk-Verlag, 1973.
Festschrift Fischer/70th	Festschrift Wilhelm Fischer zum 70. Geburtstag überreicht im Mozartjahr 1956 (Innsbrucker Beiträge zur Kulturwissenschaft, Sonderheft 3), ed. H. Zingerle. Innsbruck: Sprachwissenschaftliches Seminar der Univ. Innsbruck, 1956.
Festschrift Fulda/200th	Von der Klosterbibliothek zur Landesbibliothek (Beiträge zum zweihundertjährigen Bestehen der Hessischen Landesbibliothek Fulda), ed. Artur Brail. Stuttgart: A. Hiersemann, 1978.
Festschrift Geiringer/70th	Studies in Eighteenth-Century Music: A Tribute to Karl Geiringer on His Seventieth Birthday, ed. H.C.R. Landon, in collaboration with Roger E. Chapman. New York: Oxford Univ. Press, 1970; Music Reprint Service, 1979.
Festschrift Hoboken/75th	Anthony von Hoboken. Festschrift zum 75. Geburtstag, ed. Joseph Schmidt-Görg. Mainz: B. Schott's Söhne, 1962.
Festschrift Kaufmann	Music East and West: Essays in Honor of Walter Kaufmann, ed. Thomas L. Noblitt. New York: Pendragon, 1981.
Festschrift Lang	Music in Civilization: Essays in Honor of Paul Henry Lang, ed. E. Strangchamps and

	M.R. Mariates, with C. Hatch. New York: Norton, 1984.
Festschrift Larsen/70th	*Festschrift Jens Peter Larsen 14. VI. 1902-1972*, ed. N. Schiorring, H. Glahn and C.E. Hatting. Copenhagen: W. Hansen, 1972.
Festschrift Riemann	*Riemann-Festschrift: Gesammelte Studien. Hugo Riemann zum sechzigsten Geburtstag*, ed. C. Mennicke. Leipzig: M. Hesse, 1909.
Festschrift Schmidt-Görg/70th	*Colloquium amicorum: Joseph Schmidt-Görg zum 70. Geburtstag*, ed. S. Kross and H. Schmidt. Bonn: Beethoven-Haus, 1967.
Festschrift Senn/70th	*Festschrift Walter Senn zum 70. Geburtstag*, ed. E. Fischer. Munich/Salzburg: Katzbicher, 1975.
Festschrift Schneider/80th	*Festschrift Max Schneider zum achtzigsten Geburtstag*, ed. W. Vetter. Leipzig: Deutscher Verlag für Musik, 1955.
Festschrift Vötterle/65th	*Music und Verlag: Karl Vötterle zum 65. Geburtstag am 12. April 1968*, ed. R. Baum and W. Rehm. Kassel: Bärenreiter, 1968.
Festschrift Wiora	*Festschrift Walter Wiora zum 30. Dezember 1966*, ed L. Finscher and C.-H. Mahling. Kassel: Bärenreiter, 1967.
Fontes	*Fontes artis musicae*
g	See *NGDMM* below.
GaSJ	*The Galpin Society Journal*
Haydn Studies	*Haydn Studies; Proceedings of the International Haydn Conference, Washington, D.C., 1975*, ed. J.P. Larsen, H. Serwer and J. Webster. New York: Norton, 1981.
HMYb	*Hinrichsen's Musical Year Book*
H-St	*Haydn-Studien*
HYb	*The Haydn Yearbook*
IRASM	*International Review of the Aesthetics and Sociology of Music*
JAMIS	*Journal of the American Musical Instrument Society*
JAMS	*Journal of the American Musicological Society*
JaP	*Jahrbuch der Musikbibliothek Peters*

JHW-HI	*Joseph Haydn Werke*, ed. Joseph-Haydn-Institut, Cologne, under direction of J.P. Larsen (1958-61) and G. Feder (1962-). Munich/Duisburg: G. Henle, 1958- .
JM	*The Journal of Musicology*
JMR	*Journal of Musicological Research*
JMT	*Journal of Music Theory*
Kongress Basel/1924	*Bericht über den musikwissenschaftlichen Kongress in Basel, 1924.* Leipzig: Breitkopf & Härtel, 1925.
Kongress Bonn/1970	*Bericht über den internationalen musikwissenschaftlichen Kongress, Bonn, 1970*, ed. C. Dahlhaus, H.J. Marx, M. Marx-Weber and G. Massenkeil. Kassel: Bärenreiter, 1971.
Kongress Buchen/1980	*Joseph Martin Kraus in seiner Zeit. Referate des zweiten internationalen Kraus-Symp. in Buchen, 1980*, ed. F.W. Riedel. München/Salzburg: Katzbichler, 1982.
Kongress Graz/1970	*Der junge Haydn. Wandel von Musikauffassung und Musikaufführung in der österreichischen Musik zwischen Barock und Klassik. Bericht der internationalen Arbeitstagung des Instituts für Aufführungspraxis der Hochschule für Music und darstellende Kunst in Graz, 29. 6.-2. 7. 1970*, ed. V. Schwarz. Graz: Akademische Druck- und Verlagsanstalt, 1972.
Kongress New York, 1961	*International Musicological Society. Report of Eighth Congress*, ed. J. LaRue. New York: American Musicological Society; Kassel: Bärenreiter, 1961.
Kongress Stockholm/1978	*Joseph Martin Kraus, ein Meister im gustavianischen Kulturleben. Bericht von einem Kraus-Symposium 1978.* Stockholm: Kungliga Musikaliska Akajemien, 1980.
Kongress Vienna/1956	*Bericht über den internationalen musikwissenschaftlichen Kongress Wien Mozartjahr 1956*, ed. E. Schenk. Graz/Köln: H. Böhlaus, 1958.
Kongress Vienna/1982	*Bericht über den internationalen Joseph Haydn Kongress Wien 1982*, ed. E. Badura-Skoda. München: Henle, 1986.

MbM	Musikbibliographische Monatshefte
Md'O	Musica d'Oggi
MGG	Die Musik in Geschichte und Gegenwart, ed. F. Blume. Kassel: Bärenreiter, 1949-79.
MMASM	Miscellanea musicologica: Adelaide Studies in Musicology
MMR	The Monthly Musical Record
Mozart Influences	Les Influences Étrangeres dans l'Oeuvre de W.A. Mozart, ed. A. Verchaly. Paris: Éditions de Centre National de la Recherche Scientifique, 1956.
Moz/Comp	The Mozart Companion, ed. H.C.R. Landon and D. Mitchell. New York: Norton, 1969.
MozJb	Mozart-Jahrbuch
MF(Da)	Musik og Forkning
Mf	Die Musikforschung
MQ	The Musical Quarterly
MR	The Music Review
MuGes	Musik und Gesellschaft
NGDMM	The New Grove Dictionary of Music and Musicians, ed. S. Sadie. London: Macmillan, 1980.
NMA-K	Wolfgang Amadeus Mozart: Neue Ausgabe sämtliche Werke, ed. E.F. Schmid, W. Plath and W. Rehm. Internationale Stiftung Mozarteum Salzburg. Kassel: Bärenreiter, 1955- .
NOHM	The New Oxford History of Music. London: Oxford Univ. Press, 1954- .
ÖMz	Österreichische Musikzeitschrift
PMTNA	Proceedings of the Music Teachers National Association
PRMA	Proceedings of the (Royal) Musical Association
PRPSG1	Proceedings of the Royal Philosophical Society of Glascow
RM	La Revue Musicale
RBM	Revue Belge de Musicologie
RMI	Revista Musicale Italiana
RM1	Revue de Musicologie
SAI	Studien zur Aufführungspraxis und Interpretation von Instrumentalmusik des 18. Jahrhunderts.
SIMG	Sammelbände der internationalen Musikgesellschaft

SMZuS   *Schweizerische Musikzeitung und Sänger-*
               blatt
StM1   *Studia Musicologica*
StMW   *Studien zur Musikwissenschaft*
SvTMf   *Svensk tidschrift för musikforskning*
Sym/Hill   *The Symphony, ed. R. Hill. Hammonds-*
               worth, 1949.
Symphony   *The Symphony, 1720-1840; A Comprehensive*
               Collection of Full Scores in Sixty
               Volumes, ed. Barry S. Brook. New York:
               Garland, 1979-86.
ZfM   *Zeitschrift für Musik*
ZfMw   *Zeitschrift für Musikwissenschaft*
ZhVfS   *Zeitschrift des historischen Vereins*
               für Schwaben
ZIMG   *Zeitschrift der Internationalen Musik-*
               gesellschaft

The Symphony

I. GENERAL RESOURCES
Bibliographies

1. Brook, Barry S., gen. ed. *RILM Abstracts of Music
    Literature.* New York: International RILM Center, 1967-
    ISBN 0033-6955   ML118 R2

    Contains abstracts of books, articles, essays, reviews,
    dissertations, catalogues, iconographies, etc. Four
    issues/year, fourth being subject-author index of entire
    year. Other issues have author index only. Covers
    publications in most languages. *RILM (Répertoire
    Internationale de Littérature Musicale) Abstracts*
    remains a major resource for writings about music.
    Issues appear to be published about two years later than
    the dates of the works covered.

2. Brook, Barry S. *Thematic Catalogs in Music: An Annotated
    Bibliography.* Hillsdale (New York): Pendragon, 1972.
    xxxvi, 347p. ISBN 0-918728-02-9 ML113 B86

    Locates existing indices of literally hundreds of
    composers. Index includes entries for composer and
    compiler, subjects (incl. classification and indexing,
    thematic catalogs, manuscripts and other related sub-
    jects). Introduction has excellent historical commentary
    on thematic catalogs. Detailed instructions on use of
    book.

3. Gerboth, Walter. *An Index to Musical Festschriften and
    Similar Publications.* New York: Norton, 1969. ISBN
    393-02134-3 ML128 M8G4

    Organized by periods (classical, romantic, post-romantic
    and modern. Other divisions include theory and analysis,
    performance practice and instruments and subheadings:
    Haydn, Mannheim School, Mozart. Author-subject index
    ("symphonies," etc.). Valuable bibliographical tool.

4. *RISM (Répertoire International des Sources Musicales).*
    Series A. 9 vols. Kassel: Bärenreiter, 1971-81.
    Series B. 15 vols. to date. Munich: Henle, 1960-80.
    Series C. 4 vols. to date. Kassel: Bärenreiter,
    1967-79.

    Originally presented listings from each cooperating
    nation of their holdings in manuscript and printed music
    by composers active before 1800 and books about music
    printed before 1801. Was expanded to include 18th
    century anthologies, books and bibliographies on special
    subjects (Hebrew writings on music, etc.) and a music
    library directory. Series A, volume I: printed music of
    most composers before 1800; volume II: manuscript
    holdings; series B, volumes 1 and 2: collections
    printed in 16th, 17th, and 18th centuries; series C:
    directory of research libraries.

5. Tyrrell, John, and Rosemary Wise. *A Guide to Interna-
    tional Congress Reports in Musicology, 1900-1975.* New
    York: Garland, 1979. xiii, 353p. ISBN 0-8240-9839-0
    ML113 T95

    Arranged chronologically with contents of each report
    listed (translated to English where required). Indices:
    places; titles, series and sponsors; authors and editors;
    subject.

    Histories of the Symphony

6. Beck, Hermann. "The Symphony: An Historical Survey." In
    The Symphony, edited by Ursula von Rauchhaupt, pp. 91-
    94. London: Thames and Hudson, 1973. ISBN 0-500-
    01099-4

    Very brief but accurate account of symphonic history
    by an established authority in field. General biblio-
    graphy for entire book.

7. Bengtsson, Ingar. "The Symphony in Scandinavia."
    Translated by Eugene Hartsell. In *The Symphony*,
    edited by Ursula von Rauchhaupt, pp. 247-56. London:
    Thames and Hudson, 1973. ISBN 0-500-01099-4

    Has coverage by countries and (within countries) by
    historical periods. Includes 18th century composers:

Weyse (Denmark), Roman (Sweden); 19th century: Lindblad
and Berwald (Sweden), Gade (Denmark), Svendsen (Norway).
Coverage of both Sibelius and Nielsen is both detailed
and stylistically oriented. Mentions several other 20th
century composers but with little about their works or
styles. Excellent pictorial illustrations. No bibliography. Author is a major Swedish scholar.

8. Botstiber, Hugo. *Geschichte der Ouverture und der freien
   Orchesterformen.* Kleine Handbücher der Musikge-
   schichte nach Gattungen, Bd. IX. Edited by Hermann
   Kretzschmar. Leipzig: Breitkopf & Härtel, 1913. 274p.
   Republication by Dr. Martin Sändig (Wiesbaden), 1969.

   Studies genre from early 17th through early 20th
   centuries. Advocates Vienna's role in the early symphony's emergence, suggesting that Viennese opera composers (in their overtures) wrote in a fairly advanced
   style in *allegro* first movements as early as the 1720s.
   Contains scores of several overtures: single examples by
   Donati, Rossi, Draghi, Lully, Conti and one anonymous
   composer; two examples by Scarlatti. Index. No bibliography except that in footnotes.

9. Cuyler, Louise. *The Symphony.* New York: Harcourt Brace
   Jovanovich, 1973. 236p. ISBN 0-15-585076-8 ML1255 C9

   A chronological history with three major subdivisions:
   "Mainstream..in Austria and Germany" (precursors through
   Mahler); "Tributary Streams, 1780-1914" (Berlioz, other
   French, Tchaikovsky, Dvorak, Sibelius, Ives; symphonic
   poems of Liszt, Strauss and Debussy); 20th Century
   (England, France, Germany and Austria, United States,
   Russia with "Some Perspectives" being a short discussion
   of Penderecki and Lutoslawski). US composers: Hanson,
   Piston, Harris, Barber and Copland. Includes summary of
   each composer's style and an analysis of at least one
   work (exceptions: Mozart, 3; Beethoven, 9; Schubert, 2;
   Brahms, 4; Berlioz, 2; Ives, 3). Brahms coverage is
   most detailed while Mahler and Bruckner sections are
   brief. Karl Geiringer was general editor of the series
   (Harbrace History of Musical Forms). Index and reading
   list.

10. Ferchault, Guy. "The Symphony in France." Translated by
    Eugene Hartsell. In *The Symphony,* edited by Ursula

von Rauchhaupt, pp. 217-26. London: Thames and Hudson, 1973. ISBN 0-500-01099-4

Brief history that encompasses major periods, listing important composers and representative works, concert activities, music schools and other symphonic genre of 20th century. Superb illustrations and short bibliography.

11.   Hill, Ralph T., ed. *The Symphony.* Harmondsworth, Middlesex: Penguin Books, 1949. 416p. Republ., Scholarly Press, 1978. ISBN 0-403-01578-2 ML1255 H498

Series of essays on 19 composers with opening comments on the symphony and its overall development by Hill. Composers (authors): Haydn (Cecil Gray), Mozart (Eric Blom), Beethoven (A.K. Holland), Schubert (William McNaught), Berlioz (J.H. Elliott), Mendelssohn (Dyneley Hussey), Schumann (Stephen Williams), Liszt (Humphrey Searle), Franck (Stanley Bayliss), Bruckner (Richard Capell), Brahms (Herbert Wiseman), Borodin (Hubert Foss), Tchaikovsky (Martin Cooper), Dvorak (Alec Robertson), Mahler (Geoffrey Sharp), Elgar (F. Bonavia), Sibelius (Julian Herbage), Vaughan Williams (Scott Goddard), Rachmaninov (Robin Hull), Bax (H.G. Sear). Each article covers several works after short introduction to composer's style. Musical examples accompany each analysis. Essays on Bax, Elgar and Vaughan Williams especially rigorous.

12.   Hoffmann-Erbrecht, Lothar. *The Symphony.* Translated by Robert Kolben. Cologne: Arno Volk, 1967. 144p. M2 M945 12 No. 29

Introduction (48p) is accurate but understates 20th century symphonists. Works quoted (Sammartini, Stamitz, Haydn, Mozart, Beethoven, Schubert, Brahms, Bruckner, Tchaikovsky and Schoenberg) are complete movements except for those after Haydn. Primarily a European bibliography with publishers not provided. LaRue and Brook only US scholars noted.

13.   Keldysch, Juri. "The Symphony in Russia." Translated by Eugene Hartsell. In *The Symphony,* edited by Ursula von Rauchhaupt, pp. 237-46. London: Thames and Hudson, 1973. ISBN 0-500-01099-4

Composers included: Glinka, Balakirev, Rimsky-Korsakov, Dargomyzhsky, Borodin, Tchaikovsky, Cui, Glazunov, Liadov, Kalinnikov, Rachmaninov and Scriabin, with Tchaikovsky getting detailed style discussion. Excellent photographic illustrations. Short bibliography, many in Russian.

14. Leuchter, Erwin. *La Sinfonía, su Evolución y su Estructura*. Rosario (Argentina): Dirección Municipal de Cultura, 1943. 149p.

Probably one of the earliest American chronicles of symphonic history. Encompasses antecedents, overall form, instrumentation and growth of genre, 1750-1900. Lengthy and interesting discography: W.F. Bach, C.P.E. Bach, J.C. Bach, Boyce, Wagenseil, Leopold Mozart, Cannabich, Juon, Atterberg, Holbrooke, Sowerby, Hanson, Harris, Still, Creston, Chavez and Harl McDonald. No bibliography.

15. Marmontel, Antoine-François. *Symphonistes et Virtuoses*. Paris: Chaix, 1881.

Treats selected composers, including Haydn, Mozart, Beethoven and Mendelssohn, with brief comments on either their orchestral talents or their symphonies. In spite of book's title, does not emphasize the symphony.

16. Moore, Earl V., and Theodore E. Heger. *The Symphony and the Symphonic Poem*. 6th rev. ed. Ann Arbor: Ulrich's Books, Inc., 1974. 287p. ISBN 0-914004-01-5 MT125 M7 1974

Originally issued in 1949 as text for symphonic literature courses at the University of Michigan and subtitled "Analytical and Descriptive Charts of the Standard Symphonic Repertory," is organized alphabetically by composer. Charts are quite detailed with musical quotations and intricate form details included. Modern works slighted; one each by Prokofiev, Vaughan Williams, Sibelius, Shostakovich, Bartok, Hindemith, Holst, and Scriabin. Table of contents. No index.

17. Nadeau, Roland. *The Symphony: Structure and Style*. Boston: Crescendo, 1974. iv, 241p. ISBN 0-87597-089-3 MT125 N17S9

Designed as text for non-music majors at Northeastern
University, approaches standard repertoire chronologically. Deemphasizes style. Inserts many musical examples.

18. Nef, Karl. *Geschichte der Sinfonie und Suite*. Leipzig:
Breitkopf & Härtel, 1921. 344p. Republication by Dr.
Martin Sändig (Wiesbaden), 1970. ISBN 3-500-21630-7

Gives 65% of space to symphony with ample musical
quotations; preclassic examples especially valuable.
Coverage of the genre in Scandinavia, France and
Russia, unusual for 1921. Includes full score of
Sammartini *sinfonia* plus single complete examples by
Ghro, Christenius, Horn (suite). Footnoted. Index
and table of contents.

19. Newman, Ernst. *More Essays from the World of Music*.
*Essays from the "London Times" selected by Felix
Aprahamian*. London: John Calder, 1958. 268p. ISBN 0-
306-77520-4 ML60 N49

Articles on symphonies (Bruckner, Holst, Mozart,
Schubert and Sibelius) show insight into symphonic
writing.

20. Petersen, Peter. "The Symphony in Czechoslovakia and
Other Eastern Countries." Translated by Eugene
Hartsell. In *The Symphony*, edited by Ursula von
Rauchhaupt, pp. 227-36. London: Thames and Hudson,
1973. ISBN 0-500-01099-4

Coverage: Dvorak, Janáček, Martinů, Bartok, Kodály,
Szymanowski, Lutoslawski, Enesco. Contains good illustrations. Bibliography.

21. Rauchhaupt, Ursula von. "A History of Music and the
Symphony in Selected Dates, 1730-1930." In *The
Symphony*, edited by Ursula von Rauchhaupt, pp. 85-89.
London: Thames and Hudson, 1973. ISBN 0-500-01099-4

Comprised of charts arranged by decades. Matches dates
of major music events with important symphonic mile-
stones. Bibliography by categories.

22. Rauchhaupt, Ursula von, ed. *The Symphony*. London:
Thames and Hudson, 1973. 324p. ISBN 0500-01099-4

Originally published in German (Hamburg: Polydor, 1972) as DGG 75th anniversary promotional volume. Covers many aspects of symphonic history and symphony performance: concert halls, music criticism, recording, plus variety of essays in history, many written by known scholars (LaRue, Mahling, Beck, Salter, Bengtsson, Watanabe, etc.) Index. Handsomely illustrated. See author entires under proper period and country.

23. Salter, Lionel. "The Symphony in England." In *The Symphony*, edited by Ursula von Rauchhaupt, pp. 207-116. London: Thames and Hudson, 1973. ISBN 0-500-01099-4

Avoids generally any discussion of style but lists major composers, making style summaries for Bax, Walton and Rubbra. Illustrations show Vauxhall Gardens. Hanover Square Rooms and Queen's Hall.

24. Simpson, Robert, ed. *The Symphony*. 2 vols. Harmondsworth: Penguin, 1966, 1967. 382p, 282p.

Volume 1: Haydn-Dvorak; volume 2: Elgar to present day. Mennin is most recent composer. Is series of essays by various authors (Searle, Cooke, Ottoway, Layton, etc.) on individual composers with general style discussion and analysis of at least one work. Coverage broad, including Nielsen, Martinů, Holmboe, Schmidt, Brian, Rubbra, Tippett, Riegger and Toch. Examples with each analysis. Index of proper names. No bibliography.

25. Stedman, Preston. *The Symphony*. Englewood Cliffs (NJ): Prentice-Hall, 1979. 429p. ISBN 0-13-88062-6 ML1255 S83

Offers chronological treatment of genre with emphasis on period and individual composer styles. Detailed analysis (themes and form diagrams) for at least one work by each composer. Final chapter lists 20th century composers (grouped by nationality) with output. Contains limited bibliographical data. Detailed index. Glossary of terms. Second edition in preparation, with publication expected in 1990.

26. Ulrich, Homer. *Symphonic Music: Its Evolution since the Renaissance*. New York: Columbia University Press, 1952. ix, 352p. ISBN 0-231-01908-4 ML1200 U4

Scope includes symphony, concerto, overture, symphonic poem, suite, incidental music, divertimento, serenade, ballet, variations and concerto grosso. Coverage of symphony after Beethoven becomes less specific. Broadest and most detailed essays: Bach, Haydn, Mozart and Beethoven. Lengthy bibliography and extended index.

27.   Wohlfahrt, Frank. *Geschichte der Sinfonie.* Hamburg: Sikorski, 1966. 203p. ML1255 W64

Has careful analysis of major works by most composers Coverage: preclassic (2 pages), Haydn (14), Mozart (19), nine works by Beethoven, three by Schubert, one by Schumann, Brahms' four, one by Mendelssohn, Bruckner's nine (extensive and in great detail) and a two-page summary of the form after Bruckner. No examples but supplies scores' measure numbers. No bibliography.

28.   Young, Percy. *Symphony.* Phoenix Music Guide No. 2. London: J.D. Dent, 1968. 155p. Republication by Crescendo (Boston), 1968. ISBN 87597-018-4

For "the music lover, modest, perhaps, in his attainments." Topics: symphony today, symphony yesterday (Vaughan Williams. Elgar, Bax, Walton, Sibelius, Nielsen), Beethoven, his predecessors (Boyce, Arne, J.C. Bach, Mozart, Haydn), his successors (Tomášek, Clementi, Spohr, Schubert, Mendelssohn, Schumann, Brahms) and expanding tradition (Bizet, Franck, Tchaikovsky, Borodin, Dvorak, Bruckner, Mahler). No musical examples.

Orchestral History and Orchestration

29.   Becker, Heinz. "(Orchester B.) Das neuere Orchester." In *MGG,* vol. 10, cols. 172-94.

Encompasses development from Monteverdi to modern orchestra. Table documents instrumentation of many important orchestras, 1550-1961, arranged alphabetically by nationality. Demonstrates gradual expansion of wind sections and overall size of orchestra in nineteenth century. Bibliography.

30.   Bekker, Paul. *The Orchestra.* New York: Norton, 1963. 320p. Originally published in 1936 as *The Story of the Orchestra.*

Is blend of orchestral and orchestration histories from Haydn to Stravinsky but somewhat lacking the stylistic insight of Carse (see entry 32 below). No music examples, footnotes nor bibliography.

31. Brown, Howard, Jack Westrup, and G.W. Hopkins. "Orchestration." In *NGDMM*, vol. 13, pp. 691-700.

Careful and explicit study of development of style in orchestration. Good insight into orchestration as essential ingredient in symphonic composition. Valuable: major features of Baroque style (ensemble compactness, contrast and keyboard presence), expanding instrumental rosters in 18th century and Wagner's influence in 19th century. No examples. Bibliography.

32. Carse, Adam. *History of Orchestration*. London: Kegan Paul, Trench, Trubner, 1925. xiii, 348p. Republication by Dover (New York), 1964. ISBN 0-486-21258-0 ML455 C32

Shows (in tables) sizes of orchestras in European centers (La Scala, Mannheim, etc.) with lucid account of orchestral style development. Musical examples illustrate style devices. Modern styles: Strauss, Elgar, Debussy. Footnotes; lacks bibliography.

33. Carse, Adam. *Musical Wind Instruments*. New York: Da Capo, 1965. xi, 381p. ISBN 0-306-80005-5 ML950 C38m

Is republication of 1938 edition with introduction and enriched bibliography by Hymie Voxman. Treats history of each instrument, minimizing orchestral usages. Footnotes, illustrations (photographs and drawings). Coverage of instruments in *NGDMM* or *MGG* is more thorough.

34. Del Mar, Norman. "Confusion and Error (I)," *Score* 21 (October, 1957): 14-29.

Suggests changes in scoring (based on author's research) in symphonies by Beethoven, Mozart, Haydn, Mahler, Hindemith, Prokofiev and Schubert. Suggests as many as 17 changes in Mozart *Prague Symphony*. Includes other orchestral genre (concerto, overture, etc.) also.

35. Del Mar, Norman. "Confusion and Error (II)," *Score* 22 (February, 1958): 28-40.

Contains error correction in symphonies by Haydn,
Mozart, Liszt and Schoenberg and in other forms also.
Locates 22 errors in Liszt's *Faust Symphony*.

36. Del Mar, Norman. *Orchestral Variation - Confusion and
     Error in Orchestral Repertoire.* London: Eulenberg,
     1981. xiv, 240p. ISBN 0-093873-37-0 ML1200 D46

     Additional score correction, including symphonies by
     Bruckner, Dvorak, Mozart, Schubert and Sibelius. In
     spite of title, is not on variation form.

37. Fitzpatrick, Horace. *The Horn and Horn-Playing and the
     Austro-Bohemian Tradition from 1680 to 1830.* London:
     Oxford University Press, 1970. xiv, 256p. SBN 19-
     318703-5 ML955 F5

     Emphasizes evolution in construction and performance.
     Includes registries of players (1680-1760, 1750-1830).
     Explains chromatic playing on natural horns in relation
     to symphonic works of era and underscores horn's regional
     history in Europe.

38. Mahling, Christoph-Hellmut. "The Orchestra." In *The
     Symphony*, edited by Ursula von Rauchhaupt, pp. 39-57.
     London: Thames and Hudson, 1973. ISBN 0-500-01099-4

     Incorporates orchestral history from 1700 to 1850,
     adding a chronology of orchestra foundings from ca. 1400
     to 1967. Details size and complement of many orchestras.
     Illustrations (some in color) and bibliography.

39. Peyser, Joan, ed. *The Orchestra: Origins and Transfor-
     mations.* New York: Scribner, 1986. xvii, 652p. ISBN
     0-684-18068-5 ML1200 O75 1986

     Consists of numerous essays on broad spectrum of
     subjects: history, development of instruments, forms of
     orchestral music, use of orchestra in opera and ballet,
     texture and orchestration and others. Spans beginnings
     through 20th century. Each essay has excellent biblio-
     graphy. Book emphasizes scholarship and historical
     accuracy.

40. Raynor, Henry. *The Orchestra.* New York: Scribner,
     1978. 207p. ISBN 0-684-15535-4 ML1200 R33

Comprehensive history of the medium, noting size and disposition of evolving ensembles, concert activities and locations. Also covers: Beethoven orchestral style, 20th century styles and opera orchestras. Examples, index.

41. Westrup, Jack, with Neal Zaslaw. "Orchestra," In *NGDMM*, vol. 13, pp. 679-91.

Starts with early 17th century beginnings in France and England and covers redesigned wind instruments (ca. 1670-80), rise of court orchestras, early 18th century wind expansion, four-voice string ensemble, Wagner's orchestra, 19th century expansion and the 20th century models. Table (by Eleanor Selfridge Field) of 39 orchestras, 1607-1974, including *24 Violons du Roi*, London King's Theatre, Dresden court, *Concert Spirituel*, Hanover Square Rooms, La Scala (1814), Gewendhaus (1839 and 1865), Bayreuth Festspielhaus and many others.

Descriptions of Orchestral Music

42. Bagar, Robert, and Louis Biancolli. *The Complete Guide to Orchestral Music* (*The Concert Companion*). New York: Grosset & Dunlap, 1947. 868p. MT125 B15 1955

Both authors served for many years as program annotators for the New York Philharmonic. Contains many notes by composers of works performed by Philharmonic, including: Samuel Barber (*First Symphony*), Bela Bartok (*Concerto for Orchestra*), Robert Russell Bennett (*Brooklyn Dodger Symphony*), Benjamin Britten (*Sinfonia da Requiem*), Aaron Copland (*El Salon Mexico*), Paul Creston (*Second Symphony*), David Diamond (*Symphony No. 2*), and others. Historical material appears accurate. Lacks musical quotations and any involved data on style or structure.

43. Bookspan, Martin. *101 Masterpieces of Music and Their Composers*. Garden City: Dolphin Books (Doubleday), 1973. vii, 466p. ISBN 0-385-05721-0 MT6 B695 O5 1973

Collection of author's *Stereo Review* record reviews, augmented with biographical and additional analytical data. Symphony coverage uneven (all by Beethoven and Brahms but only one each for Schumann and Prokofiev and two for Schubert). Includes glossary of terms and very detailed index.

44.   Ferguson, Donald N. *Masterpieces of the Orchestral
       Repertoire - A Guide for Listeners.* Minneapolis:
       University of Minnesota Press, 1954. 662p. MT125 F4

       Incorporates most of traditional symphonic literature
       (J.S. Bach to William Walton) with emphasis on analysis
       of each work. Very few musical examples. Served as Min-
       neapolis Symphony's program annotator while on faculty at
       Univ. of Minnesota. Index.

45.   Frankenstein, Alfred. *A Modern Guide to Symphonic Music.*
       New York: Meredith, 1966. 667p. MT125 F83

       Based in part on program annotations for San Francisco
       Symphony. Most major symphonists represented (also:
       Wallingford Riegger). Profusely illustrated with music
       examples, including developmental passages. No index.

46.   Gilman, Lawrence. *Orchestral Music: An Armchair Guide.*
       New York: Oxford, 1951. 484p. MT125 G53

       Compilation of program notes without music examples.
       Emphasizes biographical and historical data. Author for
       many years was program annotator for Philadelphia and New
       York Philharmonic orchestras. Index.

47.   Hopkins, Antony. *Talking about Symphonies.* Belmont
       (Ca.): Wadsworth, 1964. 157p. MT125 H67

       Composers discussed: Haydn (1 work), Mozart (1),
       Beethoven (2), Berlioz (1), Berwald (1), Brahms (1),
       Sibelius (1) and Stravinsky (1). Offers commentary
       with many musical examples rather than analysis. Book
       titled derived from name of author's weekly radio
       broadcasts in London, popular for over 20 years.

48.   Morrden, Ethan. *A Guide to Orchestral Music; A Handbook
       for Non-Musicians.* New York: Oxford, 1980. 579p.
       ISBN 19-502686-1 MT125 M72

       Approach is general with 52 composers (Vivaldi to
       Werner Henze) offered. Focuses on newer music: Carter
       (4 works), Sessions (4), Stravinsky (18), Webern (4),
       Schuman (4) and others. Conversely, also includes 41
       works by Mozart, 10 Mahler and 7 Bruckner symphonies.
       Glossary of terms and index of works.

II. THE SYMPHONY IN THE EIGHTEENTH CENTURY
Bibliographies

49. Hill, George Robert. *A Preliminary Checklist of Research on the Classic Symphony and Concerto to the Time of Beethoven (excluding Haydn and Mozart).* Hackensack: Boonin, 1970. vii, 58p. ISBN 0-913574-02-3 ML128 O5 H44

    Listings grouped in two categories (symphony, concerto) under nationalities (England, France, Italy, Mannheim, North Germany [includes Scandinavia] and Vienna). Opens with general bibliography (symphony and concerto) and then lists composers covered at beginning of each national section before detailed bibliography ensues. Based in part on LaRue's extensive files and on sources by Brook, Carse and Cudworth. Valuable research tool.

50. Wolf, Eugene K., and Jan LaRue. "A Bibliographical Index to Robert Sondheimer's *Die Theorie der Sinfonie.*" *ActaM* 37 (1965): 79-86.

    An exhaustive effort that includes sources used in footnotes and on composers, forms, genres, style characteristics and periodicals. Marks (*) entries on contemporary comments on 18th century symphonists, the most valuable feature of Sondheimer's book. Further, "...have added fuller references...even when details.. missing from Sondheimer's text." Resulted from NYU seminar (LaRue). Extremely valuable. See also entry 112.

Form Studies

51. Bartha, Denes. "Liedform Probleme." In *Festschrift Larsen/70th,* pp. 317-37.

Works analyzed include Haydn, *Symphony No. 103*, ii;
Symphony No. 92, ii; and Mozart, *Symphony No. 40*, iv.

52.   Blom, Eric.   "The Minuet-Trio."   *ML* 23 (1941): 162-80.

Examines element of contrast between minuet ("aristocracy") and trio ("rustic").   Traces form's history with
good documentation.   Feels French revolution spelled end
of minuet as a viable form.

53.   Cudworth, Charles L.   "Cadence Galante; the Story of a
      Cliche.".   *MMR* 79 (1949): 176-78.

Identifies a specific cadence typical of many *galant*
works, including symphonies of J.C. Bach, C. Stamitz,
Cannabich, Haydn and Mozart.

54.   Cole, Malcolm S.   "The Development of the Instrumental
      Rondo Finale from 1750 to 1800."   2 vols.   Ph.D. dis-
      sertation, Princeton Univ., 1964.   279, 120p.

Sums up 18th century writings on the form, establishes
form's definition for France, Germany and Italy.   Concentrates on works by Clementi, Mozart, Haydn and Beethoven
while including those by C.P.E. Bach, Wagenseil, Rosetti
and others.   Appendix I contains translations of 18th and
early 19th century writings on the form, including 45
quotes from Brossard (1703) to Koch (1865).   Table 3 is
17-page listing of all rondo movements by composers in
the period defined.

55.   _____.   "Rondos, Proper and Improper."   *ML* 51 (1970):
      388-99.

Proper means refrain returns in tonic key; improper is
recurrence in key other than tonic.   Summarizes writings
from all periods about the form (Kollmann, Forkel, Cramer
and others).   Sonata-rondo defined.   Many rondo examples
drawn from Haydn symphonies.

56.   _____.   "Sonata-Rondo, the Formulation of a Theoretical
      Concept in the Eighteenth and Nineteenth Centuries."
      MQ 55 (1969): 180-92.

Examines recent writings on subject and 18th and 19th
century definitions.

57. _____. "The Vogue of the Instrumental Rondo in the Late
    Eighteenth Century." *JAMS* 22 (1969): 425-55.

    Documents increase in popularity of form through exami-
    nation of 18th century writings and statistical study of
    rondo output, 1773-1786. Notes Haydn's use of form in
    the symphonies. Attributes form's prominence in part to
    18th century *opera buffa* craze.

58. Hatmaker, John Edward. "A Theory of Timbre in the Late
    Classical Symphony." Ph.D. dissertation, Univ. of
    Iowa, 1985. 87p.

    Theorizes that timbre "events" (instrumentations less
    than *tutti*) progress toward important *tutti* "arrivals."
    Proposes also that timbre and tonal movement are related
    in Haydn symphonic style.

59. Heimes, K.F. "The Ternary Sonata Principle before 1742."
    ActaM 45 (1973): 222-48.

    Details gradual evolution of instrumental binary form
    into ternary outline of incipient sonata-allegro form.
    Shows that restatement of principal material at the out-
    set of third section occurs in works composed in years
    1712-1740.

60. Klinkhammer, Rudolf. *Die langsame Einleitung in der
    Instrumentalmusik der Klassik und Romantik. Ein
    Sonderproblem in der Entwicklung der Sonatenform.*
    Kölner Beiträge zur Musikforschung, edited by Heinrich
    Hüschen. Regensburg: Gustav Bosse, 1971. 206p. ISBN
    3-7649-2574-4 ML5 K6 v.65

    Includes study of slow introductions by Boccherini,
    Haydn, Mozart and Beethoven and 19th century works by
    Schubert, Mendelssohn, Schumann, Brahms, Bruckner,
    Dvorak and Tchaikovsky. Introduces Haydn's usages with
    extended quote from Menk's dissertation (see entry 279).
    Based on all slow introductions by above composers, with
    symphonies included. Extensive bibliography.

61. Krabbe, Niels. "A Critical Review of Fritz Tutenberg's
    Theory of First-Movement Form in the Early Classical
    Symphony." In *Haydn Studies*, pp. 487-93.

Reviews Tutenberg's 1926 article, summarizes his typology of sonata-allegro forms (Mannheim *ritornello*, etc.) and applies forms to works by Haydn and J.C. Bach.

62. Larsen, Jens Peter. "Sonata Form Problems," In *Handel, Haydn, and the Viennese Classical Style*. Translated by Ulrich Krämer, pp. 269-79. Ann Arbor: UMI Research Press, 1988. ISBN 0-8357-1851-4 ML195 L13 1988

Traces theories of sonata-allegro form through various authorities (Marx, Westphal, von Tobel and others), finally arriving at a somewhat flexible definition. Stresses that concept of form originates in theoretical writings around 1840 and that judging works written before 1840 is historically inaccurate. Larsen's concluding definition is for exposition only. Article originally published in Blume *Festschrift* (Kassel: Bärenreiter, 1963).

63. LaRue, Jan. "Significant and Coincidental Resemblance between Classical Themes." *JAMS* 14 (1961): 224-34.

Advocates greater dependence on styles analysis of melodic contour, rhythmic function and tonal and harmonic background in the science of thematic attribution. Systematically dissects and rejects thematic borrowings advocated or "discovered" by other historians.

64. Longyear, Rey M. "Binary Variants of Early Classic Sonata Form." *JMT* 13 (1969): 162-83.

Establishes eight factors in the determination of binary quality in early sonata form.

65. Nicolosi, Robert Joseph. "Formal Aspects of the Minuet and *Tempo di Minuetto* Finale in Instrumental Music of the Eighteenth Century." Ph.D. dissertation, Washington Univ., 1971. 195p.

Shows broadening of minuet style to include finales in variety of forms, including bipartite and tripartite sonata form. First chapter discusses form's transition from Baroque suite movement to Classic minuet. Many examples drawn from symphonies of period.

66. Ratner, Leonard G. "Harmonic Aspects of Classic Form."
    Ph.D. dissertation, Univ. of California (Berkeley),
    1947. 184p.

    Examines form-harmony relationship (classic harmony,
    18th century theories of form, harmony-period-theme rela-
    tionships). Studies preclassic form in first movements
    of symphonies by Wagenseil, Stamitz and J.C. Bach and
    keyboard works of other composers. Postulates that style
    maturity in part results from manipulation of harmony and
    phrase structure.

67. Ratner, Leonard G. "Harmonic Aspects of Classic Form."
    JAMS 2 (1949): 159-68.

    Focuses on sonata form and period structure and argues
    that classic form is created through manipulation of
    harmony and key structure. Appendix lists 18th and 19th
    century theoretical writings that deal with form.

68. Schwartz, Judith Leah. "Phrase Morphology in the Early
    Classic Symphony, c.1720-c.1765." Ph.D. dissertation,
    New York Univ., 1973. 367p.

    Relates growth of classical form to phrase evolution
    through study of first movements of 204 symphonies by
    composers from Italy, Germany, France and Austria. Shows
    that "basic classic vocabulary and rhetoric" was achieved
    before appearance of mature styles of Haydn and Mozart.
    Demonstrates interrelation of phrase structure with
    basic elements (harmony, rhythm, etc.), with phrase con-
    tinuity and with increase in phrase length. Applies
    study's principles to J.A. Hasse's phrase style over a
    period of 35 years.

69. Sondheimer, Robert. "Die formale Entwicklung der vor-
    klassischen Sinfonie." *AfMw* 4 (1922): 85-99, 123-
    39 (examples).

    Distinguishes between emerging preclassicism (typified
    by *kleinformal Technik* or basic ingredients of rhythm,
    harmony and texture) and larger formal elements (*gross-
    formaler Aufbau*). Asserts that basic changes in musical
    language must occur before larger designs can be put in
    place. Perceives that homophonic style of 18th century
    sinfonia established foundation for changes in overall
    form developing in the new style.

70.   Stedman, William Preston. "Form and Orchestration in the
        Pre-Classical Symphony." 2 vols. Ph.D. dissertation,
        Eastman School of Music of the Univ. of Rochester,
        1953. 214, 222p (scores, examples, thematic index).

        Studies 264 multi-movement preclassical symphonies
        written between 1730 and 1777. Examines formal and orch-
        estral growth in three phases: 1730-40, 1740-50 and 1750-
        60, finding expansion of first movements from binary to a
        more ternary design was steady and gradual change.
        Classifies as antecedents: *sinfonia*, French overture,
        concerto, suite and trio sonata. Focuses on wind role as
        vital factor in orchestral maturity. Includes critical
        editions of six works (G.M. Alberti, Arne, J. Stamitz,
        Filtz, A.G. Solnitz and Abel). Includes thematic index
        of all works studied.

71.   Tobel, Rudolf von. *Die Formenwelt der klassischen Inst-
        rumentalmusik*. Bern: Paul Haupt, 1935. xvi, 357p.

        Concentrates on sonata-allegro, rondo, variation, ter-
        nary, binary and smaller aspects (phrase, period, rhythm,
        etc.). Examples drawn from works by composers of 18th
        and 19th centuries. Valued as an essential form study.

72.   Tutenberg, Fritz. "Die Durchführungsfrage in der vorneu-
        klassischen Sinfonie." *ZfMw* 9 (1926-27): 90-94.

        Identifies four first-movement formal types: suite
        symphony (overture from *opera seria*), song symphony (from
        opera buffa), Mannheim *ritornello* symphony (from Tessa-
        rini concerto form) and Vienna *ritornello* symphony (from
        Tartini concerto form). Applies types to selected sym-
        phonies of Haydn and J.C. Bach.

Historical Studies

73.   Abraham, Gerald. "Eighteenth Century Music and the Prob-
        lems of Its History." *CM* 9 (1969): 49-51.

        Describes problem as many composers as yet unknown and
        many works of known composers still unexplored.

74.   Apfel, Ernst. *Zur Vor- und Frühgeschichte der Symphonie*.
        Baden-Baden: Koerner, 1972. 133p. ISBN 3-87320-556-4

Has three main sections: early history of symphony, general development of symphony (up to Viennese classical) and number of voices (studied in phases, starting with preclassic and moving through various geographical schools). Central concept is progressive composition in which main design of work was developed in traditional three or four-voice texture and, through orchestration, *ad libitum* voices added, these tending to obscure main concepts of composer. No musical examples.

75.   Blume, Friedrich. *Classic and Romantic Music.* Translated by M.D. Herter. New York: Norton, 1970. 213p. SBN 393-02137-8 ML60 B688.

Originally published in *MG&G* as articles on classic and romantic music. Includes classic style details (rhythm, meter, tempo, harmony, tonality, motive, theme and thematic development, forms and genres) plus sections on orchestra, classic concept of sound (pp. 75-82) and the public concert and the role of the musician. Article on romanticism presented in same general format. Bibliography.

76.   Brook, Barry S. "Symphonie concertante." In *NGDMM,* vol. 18, pp. 433-38.

Encompasses definition and description of genre, terminology, history, social basis for the form and post-1800 development. Indicates greatest difference from symphony is its "lighthearted character" when compared to symphony's more "intense and profound emotion." Author is foremost scholar on subject. Bibliography.

77.   Burney, Charles. *Dr. Burney's Musical Tours of Europe.* Vol. 1: *An Eighteenth-Century Musical Tour of France and Italy.* Vol. 2: *An Eighteenth-Century Musical Tour of Central Europe and the Netherlands.* Edited by Percy A. Scholes. London: Oxford University Press, 1959. 328p., 268p. ML195 B96

Is modern edition of original 1773 London version. Comments on musical events and genres, including Mannheim orchestra (II, 34), Sammartini's symphonies (I, 73) and many of major composers of period. Index by Scholes located in second volume and is very detailed. AMS Press issued another single-volume version in 1978

with editor Cedric Howard Glover's treatment of 1927
one-volume summary published in London by Blackie.

78.   Bücken, Ernst. "Der galante Stil: Eine Skizze seiner
      Entwicklung." *ZfMw* 6 (1923/24): 418-30.

      Evolves an emergence theory for the style while sum-
      marizing writings (18th century and later) and isolating
      specific style features.

79.   Carse, Adam. "Early Classical Symphonies." *PRMA* 62
      (1935-36): 39-55.

      Discusses origins of concert symphony, form of move-
      ments, thematic material and its treatment and orchestra-
      tion. Lists generations of composers: those born before
      1730 and those born between 1730 and 1750.

80.   Carse, Adam. "Early Overtures." *MMR* 51 (1921): 3-4,
      53-54.

      Discusses overture from 1600 through 1721, including
      works by Monteverdi, Rossi, Legrenzi, Cavalli, Cesti,
      Draghi, Lully, Scarlatti, and Purcell.

81.   Carse, Adam. *18th Century Symphonies: A Short History*.
      London: Augener, 1951. 75p. Hyperion Press (Westport,
      Conn.) issued reprint in 1979. ISBN 0-88355-731-2
      ML1255 C3 1979

      Accurate if general history of preclassical symphony.
      Analyzes symphonies by Arne, Filtz, Gossec, Maldere,
      Holzbauer, Toëschi, J.C. Bach, Schwindl, Dittersdorf and
      Pleyel and overtures by Handel, Gretry, Linley, Philidor
      and Cimarosa. Adds two composers lists: one showing num-
      bers of works, another detailing unpublished composers.

82.   Combarieu, Jules. "Les origines de la symphonie." *La
      Revue Historique et de Critique Musicale* (1903): 335-
      58, 459-64, 539-42.

      Only first segment was available for study. Focuses on
      philosophical and sociological examination of 17th cen-
      tury roots of symphony.

83.   Dickinson, A.E.F. "The Founders of the Symphony." *MMR*
       77 (1947): 227-32; 78 (1948): 4-10, 42-48, 92-97.

       Has four sections: beginnings of symphony and its evo-
       lution from three to four movements; Vienna and Mannheim
       (analyzes works by Monn, Wagenseil, Beck and J. Stamitz);
       "Characteristic Composition" (covers in detail K. Stamitz
       and mentions Rosetti, Filtz, Gossec and Dittersorf);
       "Test of Tradition" (offers Mozart as more important than
       Haydn as bearer of symphonic history).

84.   Dwelshauvers, Victor Félix. "La Symphonie préhaydn-
       ienne." *Revue de Belgique* 40 (1908): 146-67.

       Emphasizes growth of sonata-allegro, allying dualism
       with fugue countersubject concept. Suggests that other
       composers shared early symphonic progress with Stamitz
       and that Mozart predates Haydn as symphony pioneer.

85.   Engel, Hans. "Die Quellen des klassischen Stils." In
       Kongress New York/1961. I: 285-304, II: 135-39 (panel
       discussion).

       Article covers Italian sonata and opera as important
       sources but focuses on evolving symphonic style, marking
       growth of first-movement form as of greatest import.
       Also details briefly evolution of other movement forms.
       Discussion (in English) by Jens Larsen, F. Blume, Erich
       Hertmann, Charles Cudworth, Gerald Abraham, Jan LaRue,
       Barry Brook, William Newman, Murray Barbour, Eduard
       Reeser, Denés Bartha and Georg Reichert.

86.   Fischer, Wilhelm. "Instrumentalmusik von 1750-1828." In
       Handbuch der Musikgeschichte, edited by Guido Adler,
       pp. 795-833. Berlin: Heinrich Keller, 1930. Photo re-
       print, 1961.

       Establishes early roots in Italian tradition and sets
       four sub-periods: preclassic transition (up to 1760),
       early classic (ca. 1760-1780), high classic (ca. 1780-
       1810) and early romantic (ca. 1810-1828). Numerous
       examples drawn from symphonies of period.

87.   Fischer, Wilhelm. "Zur Entwicklungsgeschichte des wiener
       klassischen Stils." *StMW* 3 (1915): 24-84.

Traces style's origins to art and folk music in Vienna area while noting influences of C.P.E. Bach, J.C. Bach, Mannheim and Pergolesi. Makes distinction between "aria" and "dance" styles in emerging style. Identifies two types of instrumental melodies: *Fortspinnungstypus* (more "spun-out" and freely-developed asymmetrical melody) and *Liedtypus* (traditional and symmetrical with clearly defined sections of two, four and/or eight measures, emphasizing cadences, etc.). Remains one of best such discussions available.

88.   Gerritt, Reid Paul. "The Development of the Sinfonia to 1715: A Chronological Discussion with Emphasis on Selected Sinfonias of Johann Rosenmüller, Georg Muffat and Alessandro Scarlatti." Master of Music in Music Education thesis, Oklahoma City Univ., 1977. 95p.

Incorporates thorough discussion of sinfonia history and shows gradual evolution of form. Includes full score of *sinfonia* to Scarlatti's opera *Eraclea*.

89.   Gradenwitz, Peter. "Mid-eighteenth Century Transformations of Style." *ML* 18 (1937): 265-75.

Attempts "to characterize the centers of development in the mid-eighteenth century and to show the respective contributions of Mannheim and the south-German circle, of Vienna, of Italy, and of northern and central Germany to the evolution of a style that led to..." Viennese classicism. More philosophical than stylistic.

90.   Gradenwitz, Peter. "New Trends about 1750: Mannheim, Berlin, Hamburg." In *Of German Music*, edited by Hans-Hubert Schönzeler, pp. 71-87. London: Oswald Wolff and New York: Barnes and Noble, 1976. ISBN 0-06-496113-3 ML275.1 O4

Explains social, political and philosophical factors (ca. 1750) and their relation to newly emerging style. Notes strong influence of Italian music on new instrumental style and comments on the dualism-Jesuitism connection theory. Includes Mannheim school, a detailed section on Stamitz's style and North Germany (C.P.E. Bach).

91.   Hoffman-Erbrecht, Lothar. "Der 'Galante Stil' in der Musik des 18. Jahrhunderts; Zur Problematik des Begriffs." *StMW* 25 (1962): 252-60.

Regroups all earlier theories on style and proposes that style existed primarily between 1730 and 1750 in music of simple design and prominent melody (as opposed to more complex and intellectual style of contrapuntal music). Infers that application of term to the entire mid-18th period is inaccurate. Excellent documentation and bibliography.

92.   Kamien, Roger. "Style Changes in the Mid-18th Century Keyboard Sonata." *JAMS* 19 (1966): 37-58.

Isolates unique style features in early (1742-1759) and late (1760-1774) sub-periods. Concentrates on sonata-allegro movements. Is relevant to symphony.

93.   Kirby, F.E. *Music in the Classic Period; An Anthology with Commentary.* New York: Schirmer, 1979. 928p. ISBN 0-02-870710-9 ML2 M633

Includes symphony scores by Sammartini, Stamitz, Haydn, Mozart (2) and Beethoven with brief formal analysis and concise style descriptions.

94.   Kolneder, Walter. "Orchestral Music in the Early Eighteenth Century." In *NOHM*, vol. 6, pp. 233-301.

Asserts founding of court orchestras and continuance of fine church ensembles was basis for emergence of symphony. Covers constitution of groups, expanding output, orchestral suites, opera and non-operatic overtures, concerto grosso and church use of orchestral music. Notes *sinfonia*'s transitional nature, birth of a new melodic style and gradual merging of high level of orchestral activity into a true symphonic genre. Bibliographies: modern editions of music, topics, composers.

95.   _____. "Music for Instrumental Ensemble, 1630-1700." In *NOHM*, vol. 6, pp. 186-230.

Includes sections on contrast principle origins, opera overture, French overture, orchestra in church music and three-movement sinfonia. Bibliography.

96.   Lam, Basil. "The Classical Symphony: Haydn-Mozart-Beethoven." In *Of German Music*, edited by Hans-Hubert Schönzeler, pp. 88-123. London: Oswald Wolff and New

York: Barnes and Noble, 1976. ISBN 0-06-496113-3
ML275.1 O4

Emphasizes period's overall stylistic evolution with
negligible emphasis on symphonies.

97.   Landon, H.C. Robbins. *Essays on the Viennese Classical
Style.* New York: Macmillan, 1970. ML60 L225 E9 1970b

Says present articles are "designed at...the popular
level" but includes coverage of bogus Beethoven "Jena"
symphony and its rightful attribution to Friedrich Witt.
Places symphony data in opening section on period style.
Surprising bonus: radio script, "The Decline and Fall of
Wolfgang Amadeus Mozart."

98.   _____, with Roger E. Chapman, editors. *Studies in
Eighteenth-Century Music: A Tribute to Karl Geiringer
on his Seventieth Birthday.* New York: Oxford Univ.
Press, 1970, and Music Reprint Service, 1979. 425p.
ISBN 0-306-79159-1 ML55 G24 S8 1970b

Symphony-related articles: Polish symphonies (Gerald
Abraham) and similarities in Haydn works (Georg Feder).
See authors in appropriate sections of this book. Con-
cludes with interesting Geiringer bibliography. Index.

99.   Larsen, Jens Peter. "The Viennese Classical Period: A
Challenge to Musicology." *CM* 9 (1969): 105-12.

Is sequel to author's article ("Some Observations on
Viennese Classical Instrumental Music," *Studia Musicology* 9, 115-39); comments on sonata-allegro form in
evolving symphony. Gives steps needed for study of the
style, inadequately represented in printed research.

100.   Larsen, Jens Peter. "Der musikalische Stilwandel um 1750
in Spiegel der zeitgenössischen pariser Verlagskata-
loge." In *Festschrift Vötterle/65th*, pp. 410-23.

Studies Parisian publishers' catalogs as reflection of
the developing instrumental style, especially symphonic.
Notes greater frequency of orchestral and string quartet
publications starting in early 1760s.

101.   LaRue, Jan. "The Background of the Classical Symphony."
In *The Symphony*, edited by Ursula von Rauchthaupt, pp.

98-110. London: Thames and Hudson, 1973. ISBN 0-500-01099-4

Provides detailed account of early symphony, stressing important composers and symphonic style. Attractive illustrations, some in color. Bibliography in geographical areas. Includes European map, isolating areas of symphonic activity (including religious communities).

102. LaRue, Jan. "Sinfonia 2. After 1700." In *NGDMM*, vol. 17, pp. 336-37.

Covers general style, *da capo* sinfonia and evolution of single-movement form that characterized late 18th and early 19th century Italian opera. Notes surviving features of 18th century genre in Rossini overtures.

103. LaRue, Jan. "Symphonie" (Die Entwicklung der Symphonie im 18. Jahrhundert: Italien, Wien, Mannheim, Nordeutschland, Einzelne Komponisten). In *MGG*, vol. 12, cols. 1803-23.

More or less parallels author's *NGDMM* 18th century entries, noting the latter's tendency to shorten the original coverage. *NGDMM* benefits from fifteen years of research subsequent to *MGG* volume.

104. LaRue, Jan. "Symphony I. 18th Century." In *NGDMM*, vol. 18, pp. 438-53.

Has subdivisions: introduction, sources, form, Italy, North Germany, Vienna, Mannheim, Paris, London and other centers, Haydn and Mozart. Is detailed, accurate and comprehensive. Indicates widespread popularity of emerging genre and "uninterrupted continuity of (its) development" makes symphony best vehicle for study of Classical style. Treatment of Italy brings together facts essential in understanding roots of genre. Extended bibliography listed in chronological order.

105. Lazarevich, G. "The Role of the Neapolitan Intermezzo in the Evolution of Eighteenth Century Musical Style, 1685-1775." Ph.D. dissertation, Columbia Univ., 1970. 418p.

Proposes that style of intermezzo (melody, harmony, texture, etc.) was important in establishing basic

style of late *sinfonia* and preclassical symphony. Says
that outline of sonata-allegro possibly originated in
aria form and that "comic spirit of the genre became the
spirit of the (18th century) Italian *sinfonia*."

106. Longyear, Rey M. "The minor mode in the Classic Period."
      MR 23 (1971): 27-35.

      Based on study of 18th century catalogs; incorporates
      data on symphonies, string quartets, concertos and
      opera (brief study of latter).

107. Mahling, Friedrich. "Die deutsche vorklassische Sin-
      fonie." In *Klangbilder aus der deutschen Musikge-
      schichte* (Deutsche Grammophon GmbH). Berlin: Otto
      Stollberg, 1940. 24p.

      As monograph accompanied DGG recordings of five pre-
      classical symphonies (Wagenseil, J. Stamitz, Cannabich,
      J.C. Bach and L. Mozart). Presents style resume and
      analysis of each recorded work. Sources for scores
      given. Print available at Library of Congress.

108. Newman, William S. *The Sonata in the Classic Era*. New
      York: Norton, 1972 (paper). xxiii, 917p. SBN 393-
      00623-9

      Valuable aid to symphony research because of excellent
      documentation and bibliography, its well-founded discus-
      sion of early sonata's development and its assimilation
      into the main body of the volume of most of the signifi-
      cant research on the sonata's history. Bibliography is
      exhaustive, containing much that is germane to symphony.
      Treatment of all composers is excellent, including Mann-
      heim School (encompassing symphonies).

109. Pauly, Reinhard G. *Music in the Classic Period*. 3d ed.,
      rev. Englewood Cliffs (NJ): Prentice-Hall, 1988.
      265p. ISBN 0-13-607623-8

      Devotes one chapter (pp. 37-69) to preclassical sym-
      phony, reflecting recent research. More Mozart emphasis
      (Haydn and Mozart, pp. 105-21) than in many texts.

110. Ratner, Leonard G. *Classic Music: Expression, Form, and
      Style*. New York: Schirmer, 1980. xvii, 475p. ISBN
      0-02-872-690-1 ML195 R38

Based on study of 18th and 19th century writings on classic music, with linking of those comments to musical features author feels might apply. Under "expression" groups concepts such as singing style, Turkish music. French overture, storm and stress, learned style, etc. Other major divisions: rhetoric (melody, harmony, etc.), form (larger forms), and style perspectives (national styles). Bibliography, index and examples.

111. Rosen, Charles. *The Classical Style: Haydn, Mozart, Beethoven.* New York: Norton, 1971. 467p. ISBN 0-393-00653-0 ML195 R68 (Paper reprint, with corrections, of 1971 Viking Press edition.)

Contains good technical definition of style and application of definition to works of the three composers. Five Haydn symphonies analyzed (46, 47, 75, 81 and Oxford). Is not survey of period's music. Limited footnotes. Index of names and works. No bibliography. See review by Ian M. Bruce in *Haydn Year Book IX* (1975), pp. 359-61.

112. Sondheimer, Robert. *Die Theorie der Sinfonie und die Beurteilung einzelner Sinfoniekomponisten bei des Musikschriftstellern den 18. Jahrhunderts.* Leipzig: Breitkopf & Härtel, 1925. 99p.

Quotes from 18th century writings on genus and presents more balanced view of early symphony than does Riemann. Enhanced by 1965 bibliographical index prepared by Eugene Wolf and Jan LaRue. See entry 50.

113. Tutenberg, Fritz. "Die Opera buffa-Sinfonie und ihre Bezeihungen zur klassischen Sinfonie." *AfMW* 8 (1926): 452-72.

Proposes linkages between *buffa sinfonia* and classical symphony: appearance of second theme; melody, harmony, dynamics (especially *crescendo*); similarity of early *sinfonia* (Jommelli and others) to classic symphony.

114. Weimer, Eric D. *Opera Seria and the Evolution of Classical Style, 1755-1772.* Ann Arbor: UMI Research Press, 1984. 331p. ISBN 8357-1581-7 ML1704 W44 1984

Includes Haydn's symphonies of the 1770s in substan-
tiating pervasiveness of style changes noted in opera
arias of same period. "...Haydn adopted many of the same
bass patterns and accompanimental rhythms and contours
that appeared contemporaneously in the operas of Jommelli
and J.C. Bach. Significantly, the new style affected all
symphonies of the early 1770s...." Also studies orchestration of *opera seria*. Is revision of author's 1982
University of Chicago dissertation.

115. Wellesz, Egon, and Frederick W. Sternfeld.   "The Early
      Symphony." In *NOHM*, vol. 7, pp. 366-433.

Gives broad, detailed, stylistic, and analytical coverage of some depth. Includes Galuppi and Jommelli,
later Italian opera overtures, Sammartini, Graun brothers and Hasse, C.P.E. Bach (form in symphonies), the
Viennese "school" (Monn, Wagenseil, Gassmann, Ordonez,
Hofmann, Dittersdorf, Vaňhal and Michael Haydn), Mannheim composers, French composers, the *symphonie concertante* and the *symphonie periodique*, German symphonists
in England, and native English symphonists. Was "prepared on the basis of material provided by Jan LaRue
(with) the editors responsible for its presentation."
Good synopsis of period. Short bibliography. Examples.

Collections of Symphonies

116. Breitkopf, Johann Gottlob Immanuel, ed.   *Raccolte delle
      megliore sinfonie di piu celebri compositori di nostro
      tempo, accomodate all'clavicembalo.* 4 vols. Leipzig:
      Breitkopf, 1761-1762.

A collection of 18th century symphonies, arranged for
keyboard by parties unknown. Contains 24 works by 19
composers: J. Adam, C.P.E. Bach, G. Benda, ETPA (Prin-
cess Maria Antonia Walpurgis, Electress of Saxony), J.G.
and K.H. Graun, G. Harrer, J.A. Hasse (4 works), J.A.
Hiller, L. Hofmann, Holzbauer, Kirnberger, L. Mozart,
G.F. Müller, J.K. Rodewald, J.H. Rolle, SM di RE di
Prussia (Frederick the Great), Wagenseil (3 works), and
Wiedner. At least two sets reside in US: Sibley library
(Eastman) and Library of Congress. John Kucaba placed
thematic index of *raccolte* in his edition of Wagenseil
symphonies (entry 448).

117.   Brook, Barry S., ed.   *The Symphony, 1720-1840; A Com-*
       prehensive Collection of Full Scores in Sixty Volu-
       mes.   New York: Garland, 1979-1986.

       Organized in six series (A. Italy; B. Austria, Bohe-
       mia, Slovakia, Hungary; C. Germany: Mannheim, So. and
       No. Germany; D. France and Low Countries; E. Gr. Brit-
       ain; F. Scandinavia, Iberia, Slavic Countries, Ameri-
       cas).   Each segment of collection has introduction,
       generally a thematic index (some in reference volume),
       bibliography and number of full scores. All composers
       included in series are listed individually in this
       volume (Stedman) under countries of major activities.
       See index. Reference volume has introduction, lists
       contents of volumes and adds thematic indices not in
       original books. Brook included most of current 18th
       century symphony scholars as editors of collection.

                        Authenticity Studies

118.   Brook, Barry S.   "Piracy and Panacea in the Dissemi-
       nation of Music in the Late Eighteenth Century."
       PRMA 102 (1975-1976): 13-36.

       Excessive piracy resulted from insatiable demand for
       new music. Created attribution of spurious music to
       masters and scoundrels alike.

119.   Landon, H.C. Robbins.   "Problems of Authenticity in
       Eighteenth-Century Music." In *Instrumental Music; A*
       Conference at Isham Memorial Library May 4, 1957,
       edited by David G. Hughes, pp. 31-56. Cambridge:
       Harvard Univ. Press, 1959. Republished by Da Capo,
       1972. ISBN 0-306-70273-8 ML38 C17 I8

       Emphasizes hazards in stylistic research as tool for
       identifying of unknown works. Ends with discussion by
       Downes, Geiringer, LaRue and Strunk

120.   LaRue, Jan.   "Die Datierung von Wasserzeichen in 18.
       Jahrhundert." *Kongress Vienna/1956*, pp. 317-21.

       Advocates use of watermarks in establishing dates of
       works.

121. LaRue, Jan. "Major and Minor Mysteries of Identifi-
      cation in the Eighteenth Century Symphony." *JAMS* 13
      (1960): 181-96; 15 (1961): 224-34.

      Problems isolated: variant spelling of proper names,
      printing error of name spelling, interchange of vowels,
      conversion of umlaut, rearrangement of compound names,
      unscrupulous publishers (filling out set of six by
      adding spurious works and attributing all to primary
      composer), mixed assortment of composers in single set,
      vague title pages and exaggerated authorship of works
      belonging to others. Lists (with incipits) conflicting
      attributions of works by Pokorny in Regensburg library.

122. Wolf, Eugene K. "Authenticity and Stylistic Evidence
      in the Early Symphony: A Conflict in Attribution be-
      tween Richter and Stamitz." In *Festschrift Bern-
      stein*, pp. 275-94.

      Makes strong case for increased emphasis on quantita-
      tive measurements in style definition. Stresses use of
      three types of evidence: documentary, stylistic and
      statistical (quantitative). Examples support argument.

Orchestra and Orchestration

123. Becker, Heinz. "Zur Geschichte der Klarinette in 18.
      Jahrhundert." *Mf* 8 (1955): 271-92.

      Is accurate and concise history of clarinet in form-
      ative years, tracing history to ca. 1712. Summarizes
      recent (to 1955) writings on that history. Focuses on
      Chalumeau as a precursor. Shows early fingering
      charts. Impressive documentation.

124. Bowles, Edmund A. "Music Ensembles in Eighteenth-Cen-
      tury Festival Books in the New York Public Library."
      In *Festschrift Brook*, pp. 1-42.

      Contains data on festivals' orchestral instruments.
      Original pictures (from which information taken) shown.

125. Broder, Nathan. "The Beginnings of the Orchestra."
      JAMS 13 (1960): 174-80.

      Chronicles growth of orchestral ensembles from 1414
      to 1594 and attributes formulation of the modern or-

chestra in part to French promotion of use of modern violin. Good documentation.

126.   Broyles, Michael. "Ensemble Music Moves out of the Private House: Haydn to Beethoven." In *The Orchestra: Origins and Transformations*, edited by Joan Peyser, pp. 97-122. New York: Charles Scribner's Sons, 1986. ISBN 0-684-18068-5 ML1200 075 1986

Reviews demise of court orchestras and beginning of public orchestras in major population centers (London, Paris, Berlin, Vienna, etc.) plus political and social disintegration of monarchies and its effect on private support of orchestras. Includes detailed facts on concert halls, especially those in London. Bibliography.

127.   Carse, Adam. *The Orchestra in the XVIIth Century*. Cambridge: Heffer, 1940. Republished by Broude (New York), 1969. vii, 176p. ML467 C37

Focuses on working conditions; strength and condition of 91 orchestras (from Anhalt-Zebst to Weimar ducal group, 1690-1799); reputation, personnel and status; conductor; score and parts (publishers listed with general comments on orchestral style).

128.   Mahling, Christoph-Hellmut. "The Composition of the Orchestra in Haydn's Time." In *Haydn Studies*, pp. 188-90.

Brief remarks drawn from earlier writings on personnel lists, performance of solo concertos, relationships of locale (court, church. etc.) to resources, and doubling of wind instruments.

129.   Reese, William Heartt. *Grundsätze und Entwicklung der Instrumentation in der vorklassichen und klassichen Sinfonie*. Gräfemhainichen: C. Schulze, 1939. 179p.

Establishes background in Baroque orchestral style but primarily emphasizes classic orchestral technique (strings, woodwinds, brass and tutti) and effects (tremolo, brass distribution, etc.). Illustrated by examples from symphonic literature. Publishes author's dissertation (Friedrich-Wilhelm Univ., Berlin).

130.   Spitzer, John, and Neal Zaslaw. "Improvised Ornamen-
        tation in Eighteenth-Century Orchestras." *JAMS* 39
        (1986): 524-77.

        Exhaustive documentary study, based on writings of
        Quantz, Mozart, Scheibe, Sulzer, Reichardt, Turk, Pot-
        ter, North, Bremner, Parke, Bourdelot, Muffat, Rous-
        seau, Marcello, Mendelssohn, and Spohr and others.
        Practice in general condemned and attributed to "vil-
        lage fiddler" traditions. According to Mendelssohn,
        practice made Italian orchestras of early 19th century
        "worse than could be believed." Bibliography.

131.   Stauffer, George B. "The Modern Orchestra: A Creation
        of the Late Eighteenth Century." In *The Orchestra:
        Origins and Transformations*, edited by Joan Peyser,
        pp. 37-68. New York: Charles Scribner's Sons, 1986.
        ISBN 0-684-18068-5 ML1200 O75 1986

        Covers standardization and refinement of instrumen-
        tation (with table of instrumentations of major court
        orchestras), rise of public concerts and music publish-
        ing (with sample programs) and emergence of classical
        orchestration style with comments on Haydn and Mozart
        symphonies. Feels Haydn's great orchestral contri-
        bution was in symphonies' *concertante* scorings. Says
        Mozart's technical demands on orchestral players were
        higher than those by Haydn. Bibliography.

132.   Todd, R. Larry. "Orchestral Texture and the Art of Or-
        chestration." In *The Orchestra: Origins and Trans-
        formations*, edited by Joan Peyser, pp. 191-226. New
        York: Charles Scribner's Sons, 1986. ISBN 0-684-
        18068-5 ML1200 O75 1986

        Discusses early orchestration treatises. Describes
        classical orchestral style and use of orchestral tex-
        ture as structural device, illustrating with Mozart and
        Haydn symphony examples. Bibliography.

133.   Weaver, Robert L. "The Consolidation of the Main Ele-
        ments of the Orchestra: 1740-1768." In *The Orches-
        tra: Origins and Transformations*. Edited by Joan
        Peyser, pp. 1-35. New York: Charles Scribner's Sons,
        1986. ISBN 0-684-18068-5 ML1200 O75 1986

Identifies orchestral complements from Baroque strings and *colla parte* winds to four types of early orchestration. Includes 18th century symphonic style, public concerts and extensive bibliography. Contains impressive insights into 18th century orchestration.

134. Westrup, Jack. "Orchestration 3. 1750 to 1800." In *NGDMM*, vol. 13, pp. 694-6.

Covers in some detail development of orchestral style, introduction of new instruments and devices, ensemble scoring, Mozart's orchestral sensitivity, orchestral *crescendo*, etc. Allies change in orchestral style around 1750 to popularity of Italian opera's homophonic texture. Many symphonic examples.

135. Zaslaw, Neal. "The Size and Composition of European Orchestras, 1775-1795." In *Haydn Studies*, pp. 186-88.

Summarizes author's research on orchestra, showing problems in knowing well the exact history of orchestral resources. Notes Haydn's preference for bass line of one cello, one bass and one bassoon over one of three cellos and six double basses "because (the bass line) is difficult to hear clearly" in the latter scoring (as per 1768 Haydn letter).

136. _____. "Towards the Revival of the Classical Orchestra." *PRMA* 103 (1976-1977): 158-87.

Provides insight into performance practices of early concert symphony with summary of orchestral resources in some sixty locations in western Europe and United States (Bethlehem, Pa.). Has data on instruments and playing techniques (notably bows and bowing), interpretation, seating charts (opera, church, concert), performance standards, repertoire, and wind-string ratios (based on 18th century practices). Bibliography.

Thematic Catalogs

137. Brook, Barry S., ed. *The Breitkopf Thematic Catalogs: The Six Parts and Sixteen Supplements, 1762-1787.* New York: Dover, 1966. 888p. ISBN 0-918728-92-4
ML145 B82115

Offers facsimile edition of original with corrections
by editor. Editor's introductory essay explains importance of collection. Outlines catalog's contents and
gives index of texts (first line) plus a general index
of names and topics (titles, categories, etc.). Contains about 15,000 musical *incipits* from works of about
1,000 composers.

138.   Dearling, Robert. "Annotations to the Breitkopf Thematic Catalogue and Supplement, Part One." *HYb* IX
(1975): 256-302.

Annotates instrumental works (symphonies, chamber
works and overtures) with references to "one or more of
the standard reference works on the composer."
Enhances value of Dover reprints by Barry S. Brook.

139.   Duckles, Vincent, and Minnie Elmer. *Thematic Catalog
of a Manuscript Collection of Eighteenth-Century
Italian Music in the University of California, Berkeley.* Berkeley: Univ. of California Press, 1963.
403p.   ML128 I65 C32

Primarily music of Tartini school in Padua (about 990
works by 82 composers), includes *sinfonias* by Stratico,
Wenzel, Brioschi, Kozeluh, Marcello and Tartini.

140.   LaRue, Jan, and Mary Rasmussen. "Numerical Incipits
for Thematic Catalogs." *Fontes* 9 (1962): 72-75.

Explains numerical system for encoding incipits in
LaRue's thematic indices at New York University (Union
Thematic Catalog of 18th-Century Chamber Music and Con-
certos and Union Thematic Catalog of 18th Century Sym-
phonies). Defines pitch more minutely than rhythm.
Will help computerize indices.

141.   LaRue, Jan. "Ten Rediscovered Sale-Catalogs: Leukart's
Supplements, Breslau 1787-1792." In *Festschrift
Vötterle/65th*, pp. 424-32.

Franz Ernst Christoph Leukart (1748-1817) started
publishing in Breslau in 1784. LaRue, who found early
(1787) catalogs at Gniezno (Poland) cathedral, reports
on catalogs' contents. Listings include symphonies.

142. LaRue, Jan. *A Thematic Identifier Catalog of 18th-Century Symphonies.* Computerized files, New York Univ.

Lists nearly 14,000 symphonies (ca. 1720–ca. 1810) in two interrelated files arranged (1) alphabetically by composer and (2) melodically by incipit (violin I opening bars). Original format (two card catalogs) is computerized on database that records signature, instrumentation, number and keys of movements, location of catalog listings and sources, opera overture usage, dates of composition and/or performance, and conflicts in attribution. Part 2 (Thematic Identifier) is being published. Issued to date: vol. 1 (Bloomington: Indiana Univ. Press, 1988; ISBN 0-253-31363-5). Helps identify hundreds of anonymous works and exposes conflicts in attribution, with "one battle-scarred symphony (having) been attributed...to seven different composers." LaRue provided above, edited with apologies.

143. LaRue, Jan. "A Union Thematic Catalog of Eighteenth Century Symphonies." *Fontes* 6 (1959): 18-20.

Describes derivation and organization of catalog and need to computerize process. See also entry 142.

Theoretical Writings

144. Barford, Philip. "The Sonata Principle: A Study of Musical Thought in the Eighteenth Century." *MR* 13 (1952): 255-63.

Provides overview of how sonata form became a vital structure.

145. Broyles, Michael. "The Two Instrumental Styles of Classicism." *JAMS* 36 (1983): 210-42.

Through study of 18th century writings identifies two distinct styles: sonata or solo style (expressively flexible vocal style, personal in emotional content) and symphony style (expressive, grand, exalted). Analyzes excerpts in applying theory.

146. Churgin, Bathia. "Francesco Galeazzi's Description (1796) of Sonata Form." *JAMS* 21 (1968): 181-99.

While endorsing 18th century concepts, dwells on
thematic function and usage, illustrating concepts with
excerpts. Reveals 18th century view of the form. Includes translation of Galeazzi's short treatise.

147. Churgin, Bathia. "The Symphony as Described by J.A.P.
Schultz (1774): A Commentary and Translation." *CM* 29
(1980): 7-16.

Identifies three types: chamber, theatre and church.
Defines *allegro* movement and comments on textual diversity. Schultz' writings are more on the affective
level than the prescriptive.

148. Jones, George Paul. "Heinrich Christoph Koch's Description of the Symphony and a Comparison with Selected Symphonies of C.P.E. Bach and Haydn." M.A.
thesis, University of California (Los Angeles), 1973.
110p.

Compares Koch's definition with music of period.
Koch detailed both phrase structure and larger formal
dimensions, referring to examples by Haydn and others.
Jones concludes that Haydn and Bach used symphonic form
differently: Haydn's tonalities tend to clarify form
while Bach's expressive harmonic style made form less
clear. Includes translation of Koch's writings.

149. Newman, William S. "About Carl Czerny's Op. 600 and
the 'First' Description of 'Sonata Form'." *JAMS* 20
(1967): 513-15.

Updates author's earlier article (1941) on 18th and
19th century theories of sonata form.

150. Newman, William S. "The Recognition of 'Sonata Form'
by Theorists of the Eighteenth and Nineteenth Centuries." *PMTNA* 36 (1941): 136-45.

Summarizes writings about form, asserting that
Czerny's description of the form was the earliest
despite Koch's explanation of the symphony's first
movement in 1793.

151. Ratner, Leonard G. "Eighteenth Century Theories of
Musical Period Structure." *MQ* 42 (1956): 439-54.

Reviews most writings from period. Delineates elements of *galant* and early classical styles: firm harmonic logic, rigidly regular phrase structure and consistent melodic style. Notes Koch's distinction between orchestral and quartet styles.

152. Ritzel, Fred. *Die Entwicklung der Sonatenform im musiktheoretischen Schriftum des 18. und 19. Jahrhunderts.* Wiesbaden: Breitkopf & Härtel, 1968. 298p. ML1156 R58

Covers most (if not all) writings, dividing these into three epochs: 1700-1750, 1750-1800 and 1800-1900. In second chapter, uses conceptual approach in treatment of subject, contrast, reprise and other aspects of the form. Bibliography lists primary and secondary sources, adding a chronology of primary sources.

153. Stevens, Jane. "Georg Joseph Vogler and 'Second Theme' in Sonata Form." *JM* 2 (1983): 278-304.

Proposes, through analysis, that Vogler's statements about second theme implied "elements of a two-part opening theme" and represented more an "observation of musical effect" rather than a "description of structure." Excellent bibliography and quotations from authorities.

III. NATIONAL ACTIVITIES
Austria

General

154. Adler, Guido. "Die wiener klassische Schule." In
     Handbuch der Musikgeschichte, edited by Guido Adler,
     pp. 768-95. Berlin: Heinrich Keller, 1930.

     Shows evolution of style in works of Mozart, Haydn,
     Beethoven and Schubert. Locates roots of style in
     works of Italian composers in Vienna, Mannheim, etc.

155. Bennett, Lawrence. "The Italian Cantata in Vienna,
     ca. 1700-ca. 1711." Ph.D. dissertation, New York
     Univ., 1980. 660p.

     Documents strong, perhaps dominating, Italian pres-
     ence in Vienna in early 18th century. Orchestral writ-
     ing in relatively few cantatas indicates transfer of
     Italian instrumental style to Vienna, establishing
     foundation for symphonies a generation later. Also
     concentrates on watermarks and copyists' styles in
     manuscript holdings in Viennese libraries.

156. Brown, A. Peter. "Notes on some Eighteenth Century
     Viennese Copyists." *JAMS* 34 (1981): 325-38.

     Sums up existing writings and identifies additional
     copyists active in Vienna during spread of 18th century
     symphony. Illustrations. Bibliography.

157. Chenevey, Paul Robert. "The Introduction as an Inte-
     gral Part of the Viennese Symphony." D.M.A. thesis,
     Univ. of Cincinnati, 1976.

     Broad approach based on study of works of J. Haydn,
     M. Haydn, Mozart and Beethoven. Modest bibliography.

158. Fischer, Wilhelm, "Wiener Instrumentalmusik im 18. Jahrhunderts." Intro. to *DTÖe* XV/2, pp. vii-xxiv.

    Author heralded Viennese school as Mannheim's equal in providing foundation for the classical symphony, thus challenging Riemann's support of Mannheim as that foundation. Volume has Monn's four-movement symphony.

159. Freeman, Robert N., ed. *Austrian Cloister Symphonists* in *Symphony*, series B, vol. VI. 336p.

    Contains editor's scores of symphonies by Zechner, Aumann, Albrechtsberger, Schneider and Paradeiser. See entries below. Introduction covers role of Austrian monasteries in late 18th century symphonic growth. Cloister orchestras, mostly amateur, were active symphony consumers and amassed huge collections in some monastery libraries. Identifies specific locations and composers active in each. See Landon's review in *HYb* XV (1984), pp. 233-39. Bibliography.

160. _____. "The Practice of Music at Melk Monastery in the Eighteenth Century." Ph.D. dissertation, Univ. of California (Los Angeles), 1971. 514p.

    Chapter 2 inventories monastery music positions and lists chronologically men in those positions. Chapters 3 and 4 discuss music activities (church, chamber, opera). Chapter 5 gives biographies of Robert Kimmerling, Franz Schneider, Johannes Georg Albrechtsberger and Maxmilian Stadler. List of works in appendix.

161. Ewen, David. "Early Viennese Music." *MMR* 69 (1939): 167-73.

    City was saturated with Italian style through importation of Italian musicians. Absorbed efforts of Gluck and Fux but resisted formation of a more idiomatic Viennese style until appearance of Monn, Wagenseil, Gassmann, Starzer, Mann, Vaňhal, Hofmann, Dittersdorf, and Haydn and Mozart later. Comments on symphonic styles of Monn and Wagenseil.

162. Henrotte, Gayle A. "The Ensemble Divertimento in Preclassic Vienna." 2 vols. Ph.D. dissertation, Univ. of North Carolina, 1967. 301, 504p.

Works of Porsille, Monn, Mann and Aspelmayr show
transition from Baroque to Classic, exhibiting foundation for mature works of Haydn, Mozart and Beethoven.
Promotes understanding of evolution of forms used in
symphony. Impressive bibliography with list of music
catalogs from period.

163. Larsen, Jens Peter. "Concerning the Development of the
Austrian Symphonic Tradition (circa 1750-1775)." In
Handel, Haydn, and the Viennese Classical Style,
translated by Ulrich Krämer, pp. 315-25. Ann Arbor:
UMI Research Press, 1988. ISBN 0-8357-1851-4 ML195
L13 1988

Examines Viennese symphonic activity and relates it
to established non-symphonic forms (*sonata da chiesa*,
etc.) Feels that Haydn "adapted a tradition...rooted in
the Austrian Baroque of Fux and Caldara, and...developed
further by the composers of the intermediate generation
about 1750 - Wagenseil, the two Monns, Holzbauer, Tuma,
Birkh, Schlöger, etc." Originally appeared as "Zur
Entstehung der österreichischen Symphonietradition
(ca. 1750-1775)" in *HYb X* (1978), pp. 72-80.

164. _____. *Handel, Haydn, and the Viennese Classical Style*.
Translated by Ulrich Krämer. Ann Arbor: UMI Research
Press, 1988. xii, 332p. ISBN 0- 8356-1851-4 ML195
L13 1988

Has 25 articles (8 on Handel; 9, Haydn; 9, Viennese
classical style) from various periods in author's life,
most translated from original German. Symphony and
Viennese style entries listed elsewhere this volume.

165. _____. "Some Observations on the Development and
Characteristics of Viennese Classical Music." *StMl* 9
(1967): 115-39. See entry 164, pp. 227-49, for
reprint.

Sums up studies on evolution of Classic style, including positioning of various scholars in their dis-
coveries of pioneers of style (e.g., Riemann and Stamitz, etc.). Identifies Fischer's article ("Zur Entwicklungsgeschichte des Wiener klassischen Stils,"
entry 87 this volume) as turning point toward a clearer
understanding of growth of new style. Larsen sets
periods in style growth: late Baroque, midcentury,

Classic, and early Romantic, each illustrated with
examples. Says Baroque influence in Haydn works makes
his handling of sonata-allegro differ from Mozart's.

166. Monk, Dennis Craig. "Style Changes in the Slow Movements of the Viennese Symphony, 1740-1770." 2 vols.
Ph.D. dissertation, Univ. of California (Los Angeles),
1971. 280, 147p.

Studies 275 works by Birck, Bonno, Gassmann, Hofmann,
Monn, Ordonnez, Predieri, Wagenseil, Reutter, Tuma,
Vaňhal, and first 50 symphonies of Haydn. Detailed
history of genre in Vienna precedes careful study of
style of above works. Defines instrumentation and
textural categories in shift from two-voice string
texture to four-voice orchestral texture. Also focuses
on harmony and tonality. Sees melody in four types:
fortspinnungs, *Lied*, *motif*-repetition or period. Finds
many movement-form options and much flexibility in
formal application. Results from Viennese study
compared with Haydn works in same period. Thematic
index plus scores of 45 movements.

167. Vinton, John. "The Development Section in Early Viennese Symphonies: A Re-valuation." *MR* 24 (1963): 13-
22.

Notes Baroque influence in Monn's works and more progressive style in Wagenseil's opera and oratorio overtures than in symphonies. Early Haydn symphonies (1,
3, 17, 16 and 4) show "spectacular" contrast to works
by Monn and Wagenseil in development quality.

Austrian Composers

Anton Cajetan Adlgasser (1729-1777)

168. Rainer, Werner, ed. *Anton Cajetan Adlgasser: Four Symphonies* in *Symphony*, series B, vol. VIII (Salzburg,
Part 2), pp.xxxiii-l, 57-175.

Contains biography and discussion of symphonic style.
Bibliography and thematic index of 10 authentic and 2
spurious works. Text translated by Bruce C. MacIntyre.

169. Rainer, Werner. "Verzeichnis der Werke A.C. Adlgas-
      sers." *Mozart-Jahrbuch* (1962-3): 280-91.

      Lists 11 symphonies and 1 symphony movement.

Franz Asplmayr (1728-1786)[g,b]

170. Monk, Dennis, ed. *Franz Asplmayr: Three Symphonies* in
      Symphony, series B, vol. VII, pp. xv-xxi, 1-63.

      Includes well-documented biography, restrained discus-
      sion of symphonic style and analysis of three edited
      symphonies. Notes that Asplmayr possibly wrote as many
      as 45 symphonies but level of authenticity so low pre-
      cludes developing thematic index.

Johann Georg Albrechtsberger (1736-1809)[g,b]

171. Freeman, Robert N., ed. *Johann Georg Albrechtsberger:
      Symphonies 4, 5, 6, 7, 8* in *Symphony*, series B, vol.
      VI (Austrian Cloister Symphonists), pp. xxii-xxxiii,
      xlix-lii, 57-251.

      Well-documented biography precedes discourse on
      sources and style. Analyzes edited symphonies (5).
      Thematic index lists 4 authentic overtures, 4 authentic
      symphonies, 6 questionable and 11 spurious works.
      See Landon review in *HYb XV* (1984), pp. 233-39.

Franz Joseph Aumann (1728-1797)[g,b]

172. Freeman, Robert N., ed. *Franz Joseph Aumann: Symphony
      1* in *Symphony*, series B, vol. VI (Austrian Cloister
      Symphonists), pp. xx-xxii, xlvii-xlviii, 33-55.

      Short discussion of style and symphonic output pre-
      cedes analysis of an "early provincial church symphony"
      edited for volume. Thematic index identifies 1 authen-
      tic and 3 questionable symphonies. Bibliography.

Antonio Caldara (ca. 1682-1732)[g.b]

173. Toscani, Bernard, ed. *Antonio Caldara: Six Introduz-
      ioni and One Symphony* in *Symphony*, series B, vol. II
      (Italians in Vienna), pp. xxxvii-xlviii, 97-157.

Opens with lengthy biography, detailing Caldara's reputation in Vienna. Most works analyzed are *intro-duzioni* (overtures) and overtures to operas and probably survive in multi-movement format because of the addition of spurious movements. One work is early *sinfonia concertante*. Bibliography but no thematic index.

Francesco Bartolomeo Conti (1682-1732)[g,b]

174. Williams, Hermine W., ed. *Francesco Bartolomeo Conti: Nine Sinfonie* in *Symphony*, series B, vol. II (Italians in Vienna), pp. xiii-xxxvi, 1-95.

Discusses Conti's works in great detail and briefly analyzes nine works edited (most are opera *sinfonias*). Shows how works anticipate mature symphonic form and lists 10 traits that contribute. Bibliography and thematic index.

Carl Ditters von Dittersdorf (1739-1799)[g,b]

175. Badura-Skoda, Eva, ed. *Carl Ditters von Dittersdorf: Six Symphonies* in *Symphony*, series B, vol. I, pp. xi-lxviii, 1-178.

Extensive biography (14 pages) prefaces symphonic materials (lacks style analysis) and detailed analysis of edited symphonies (includes one program symphony with each movement in a different national style). Grave (see entry 176) supplied thematic index of 118 authentic and 84 spurious works. Bibliography.

176. Grave, Margaret. "First-Movement Form as a Measure of Dittersdorf's Symphonic Development." 2 vols. Ph.D. dissertation, New York Univ., 1977. 344, 219p

Sought to establish greater level of authenticity in symphonies and to set chronology through style analysis. Findings: increased complexity of form as style matures and awareness of evolution of Viennese classical style, both supported by complex formal analysis. Lists 206 symphonies (100+ authentic, 36 questionable, doubtful and 26 "unauthentic"). Impressive results.

177. Krebs, Carl. *Dittersdorfiana*. New York: Da Capo, 1972. 182p. ISBN 0-306-70259-2 ML410 D6K8 1972

Thematic index of 127 symphonies and overtures on pp.
56-86. Is reprint of 1900 edition.

Anton Eberl (1765-1807)[g,b]

178. Coeyman, Barbara, and Stephen C. Fisher, editors.
     Anton Eberl: One Symphony, Op. 33 in *Symphony*, series
     B, vol. IX, pp. xxx-xliii, xlvii, 243-317.

     Introduction presents an extended biography and dis-
     cussion of the five symphonies, two of which can be
     considered mature. Notes influence of Beethoven's
     Eroica on latter. Thematic index from Duane White's
     dissertation on Eberl's piano music (Wisconsin, 1971).

Johann Ernst Eberlin (1702-1762)[g,b]

179. Schneider-Cuvay, Maria- Michaela. *Johann Ernst Eber-
     lin: Three Symphonies* in *Symphony*, series B, vol.
     VIII (Salzburg, Part 2), pp. xiii-xxxi, 1-55.

     Introduction, translated by Bruce C. MacIntyre, has
     lengthy biography and fairly detailed symphonic style
     coverage. Analyzes three edited works, all from pre-
     classic generation (primarily noted in melodic style).
     Thematic index lists 26 extant and 10 lost symphonies.

Joseph Leopold Eybler (1765-1846)[g,b]

180. Hermann-Schneider, Hildegard, ed. *Joseph Leopold
     Eybler: One Symphony* in *Symphony*, series B, vol. V,
     pp. xxvii-xxxv, 123-223.

     Remembered as composer Mozart's widow asked to finish
     Requiem, Eybler wrote primarily church music, comple-
     ting his two symphonies before 1799. One, in five
     movements, is related to the divertimento. Thematic
     index. Short bibliography.

Johann Baptist Gänsbacher (1778-1844)[g,b]

181. Hermann-Schneider, Hildegard, ed. *Johann Baptist Gäns-
     bacher: One Symphony* in *Symphony*, series B, vol. V,
     pp. xxxvii-xlv, 225-78.

Gänsbacher's lone symphony was promoted by Weber in a performance in Mannheim in 1810. Editor writes on composer's life and analyzes form of symphony. Thematic index. Brief bibliography.

Florian Gassmann (1729-1774)[g,b]

182. Hill, George Robert. "The Concert Symphonies of Florian Gassmann." Ph.D. dissertation, New York Univ., 1975. 418p.

Has well-documented biography, exhaustive examination of sources (with appendix of watermarks) and "stylistic profile" built from analysis of 45 symphonies. Covers Gassmann's change of style, avoidance of "normal" sonata form, adoption of four-movement scheme, and systematic approach to composition. Includes thematic index of orchestral works, index of themes, form charts (themes, harmonic rhythm, tonal changes, phrase structure) for all concert symphonies analyzed in thesis.

183. Hill, George Robert, ed. *Florian Leopold Gassmann: Seven Symphonies* in *Symphony*, series B, vol. X, pp. xi-xxxviii, 1-274.

Discusses life, works and symphonic style. Earlier works influenced by *ritornello* principle in first movements; later examples move closer to mature sonata form with some recapitulations starting in either subdominant or submediant keys ("bifocal recapitulation"). Thematic index has 32 concert symphonies, 26 opera overtures, 5 questionable and 8 spurious works, and 12 that survive only as incipits. Bibliography.

184. Hill, George Robert. *A Thematic Catalog of the Instrumental Music of Florian Gassmann.* Hackensack (N.J): Boonin, 1976. 171p. ISBN 0-913574-12-0 ML113 M8x No. 12

Symphonies listed on pages 1-23.

Adalbert Gyrowetz (1763-1850)[g,b]

185. Rice, John A., ed. *Adalbert Gyrowetz: Four Symphonies* in *Symphony*, series B, vol. XI, pp. xi-xxxi, 1-177.

Excellent biography precedes symphony discussion on
genealogy and style, both quite detailed. Symphonies
were extremely popular in their day since they did not
make "intellectual demands on listeners." Analyzes
four works briefly. Bibliography. Thematic index is
in *Symphony* collection's reference volume (pp. 284-90).

186. Doernberg, E. "Adalbert Gyrowetz." *ML* 44 (1963): 21-
      30.

Examines composer's biography (published in 1848),
noting that Mozart included one of Gyrowetz' symphonies
in a Vienna concert, that Gyrowetz served as Haydn's
mentor during the Salomon concerts and other facts
associated with symphonic activity.

Franz Joseph Haydn (1731-1809)[g,b]

187. Adler, Guido. "Haydn and the Viennese Classical
      School." *MQ* 18 (1932): 191-207.

Contains description of Haydn style with many references to symphonies. Description of sonata form has
strong 19th century roots (I: Joy in work, II: Sin-
cerity - Artlessness, III: Naive - Everyday activity -
Dance of Life, IV: Concluding apostrophe - "All's well
that ends well" - round of existence).

188. Alston, Charlotte Lenora. "Recapitulation Procedures
      in the Mature Symphonies of Haydn and Mozart." Ph.D.
      dissertation, Univ. of Iowa, 1972. 220p.

Based on study of 17 Haydn symphonies (82-87, 93-104)
and 8 Mozart symphonies (319, 338, 385, 425, 504, 543,
550 and 551). Summarizes 18th and 19th century writings
on sonata form. Includes chapter on retransition to
recapitulation. Findings: lack of uniformity disputes
concept that restatement is repetition of first section.
Claims Haydn is formally more imaginative while Mozart
strives for tonal and harmonic expansion. Appendix has
translation of Reicha's "Principes pour la grande Coup
(ou dimension) binaire" (from *Traité de Mélodie*) in which
use of form is discussed.

189. Andrews, Harold L. "The Submediant in Haydn's Development Sections" in *Haydn Studies*, pp. 465-71.

    Studies quartets, symphonies and keyboard trios and sonatas. Finds expansion of development's tonal plan often results from avoiding resolution of dominant tonal area by evasion to submediant. Many examples.

190. Bartha, Denés. "Volkstanz-Stilisierung in Joseph Haydns Finale-Themen" in *Festschrift Wiora*, pp. 375-84.

    Shows relationship between contradance style and style of some Haydn rondo finales in symphonies.

191. Bawel, Frederick Henry. "A Study of Developmental Techniques in Selected Haydn Symphonies." Ph.D. dissertation, Ohio State Univ., 1972. 258p.

    Studies seven symphonies, one from each Landon period (2, 23, 26, 56, 77, 88, 100). Early works use either verbatim statement of exposition materials or unrelated materials. Later developments are longer, limit sources of development and avoid insignificant materials. Evolves definition of Viennese classic style. Much of bibliography relates to matters about form.

192. Beenk, Eugene Lester. "*Ländler* Elements in the Symphonic Minuets of Haydn." Ph.D. dissertation, Univ. of Iowa, 1969. 209p.

    Shows that 35 symphony minuets show traces of *Ländler* style while 6 (symphonies 9, 50, 85, 86, 96, 97) could actually be considered *Ländlers*.

193. Brook, Barry S. "Musical and Historical Context: The Commissioning of the Symphonies" in *Haydn Studies*, pp. 244-45.

    Panel discussion covers Haydn's Paris symphonies. Brook feels that size of commission made Haydn write group of new works rather than repackage earlier works.

194. Brown, A. Peter, and James T. Berkenstock with Carol Vanderbilt. *Joseph Haydn in Literature: A Bibliography*. *H-St* 3 (July 1974): 173-356 (entire issue).

Covers writings in all languages through 1972, including books, periodicals, theses, dissertations and
some newspaper articles. Dictionary and encyclopedia
coverage limited to early accounts and, more recently,
to those written by known Haydn scholars. Indices (3):
topics, proper names and places, works. Some annotation. Valuable.

195. Brown, Peter J. "New Light on Haydn's 'London' Sym-
      phonies." *MT* 100 (1959): 260-61.

      Reveals supposedly more stylistically accurate data
      on symphonies and their performances, based in part on
      1810 edition by Robert Birchall (thought to be editions
      prepared by Salomon). Latter now in British Museum.

196. Bryan, Paul Robey. "Haydn's Alto Horns: Their Effect
      and the Question of Authenticity" in *Haydn Studies*,
      pp. 190-92.

      Makes strong case for evolutionary approach to
      Haydn's use of both alto and *basso* horns. Indicates
      that Haydn may have used alto horns earlier than
      thought, that Haydn rarely mixed *clarini* with alto
      horns, and that the B-flat horn was probably *basso* in
      range at that time. Well-documented.

197. _____. "Haydn's Hornists." *H-St* 3 (1973-74): 52-58.

      Is detailed account of Haydn's 17 Esterhazy hornists
      (1769-1790), with biographical data on most. Coordi-
      nates tenure with Haydn's output. Had six hornists in
      1769-72 and five at four other periods. Multiple list-
      ings perhaps caused by strings doubling in brass.

198. Burkat, Leonard. "Haydn's Symphonies: A Collation."
      Notes 15 (Dec. 1942): 39-55.

      Provides check list of the symphonies with corre-
      sponding numbers from 22 sources (Mandyczewski; edi-
      tions by Banck, Bote & Bock, Breitkopf, Leduc, Peters;
      catalogs by Fuchs, Deldevez, Haydn, Wotquenne, Zuleh-
      ner, Breitkopf, Pohl biography, Pohl manuscript; series
      at London and Paris; and Haydn autograph scores. Care-
      fully identifies and evaluates each source.

199. Busch, Ulrich. "Ein brandneues Menuett: Das Menuett beim späten Haydn in Symphonie und Quartett." *Musica* 36 (1982): 148-51.

Shows gradual change from recreational dance to variety of styles in late Haydn symphonies and quartets, noting development sections in some menuets and trios. Analyzes minuets in symphonies 2, 85, 92, 95, 101 and 103 and in four quartets.

200. Butcher, Norma Perkins. "A Comparative-Analytical Study of Sonata-Allegro Form in the First Movements of the London Symphonies of Franz Joseph Haydn." Ph.D. dissertation, Univ. of Southern California, 1971. 172p.

Findings: expositions have greatest rigidity and consistency in design; motives are driving forces in each movement; recapitulations all continue development; folk music is important in Haydn symphonic style. Substantial by-product: Haydn's folk style (pp. 20-27) and its roots in actual folk music.

201. Churgin, Bathia. "The Italian Symphonic Background to Haydn's Early Symphonies and Opera Overtures" in *Haydn Studies*, pp. 329-36.

Supporting argument: wide popularity and dissemination of Italian symphony, Italian birthplace of symphony, basic style of Italian overture, Haydn's use of latter form, influx of Italian style into pre-1750 Vienna, orchestral scoring and Haydn's adoption of many Italian devices in early symphonies. Bibliography. Later discussion by Grout, Rosen, Webster, Churgin, Croll and Helm. LaRue joins from audience.

202. Cole, Malcolm S. "Haydn's Symphonic Rondo Finales: Their Structural and Stylistic Evolution." *HYb* 13 (1982): 113-42.

Includes all symphonies and defines rondos as minuet-trio (two types), two-couplet, multi-couplet and sonata rondo. Tables locate each category in finales. Groups works: early years, Esterhazy, 1775-84, Haydn-Mozart exchange (1785-90), and London symphonies. Summary of literature on form included.

203.   _____. "Momigny's Analysis of Haydn's Symphony 103."
        MR 30 (1969): 261-84.

        Includes Momigny's essay on symphony (first movement
        in particular), his suggested program for work and his
        recognition of Haydn's compositional techniques. Not
        literal translation but more explanation of concepts.

204.   _____. "The Rondo-Finale: Evidence for the Mozart-
        Haydn Exchange." *MozJb* (1968-70): 242-56.

        Through study of Haydn's *Symphony No. 85* and Mozart's
        piano concerto (K 595) postulates influences: Mozart
        gave Haydn idea of sonata-rondo and ABA reprise concept
        in rondos; Haydn gave Mozart abbreviated returns of
        refrain, development in place of central couplet (C
        theme) and development as concluding section. Includes
        analysis of earlier writings. Extensive bibliography.

205.   Cushman, David Stephen, "Joseph Haydn's Melodic Mate-
        rials: An Exploratory Introduction to the Primary and
        Secondary Sources together with an Analytical Catalog
        and Tables of Proposed Melodic Correspondence and/or
        Variance." 2 vols. Ph.D. dissertation, Boston
        Univ., 1973. 400, 387p.

        Traces 225 melodies (80 from symphonies) to sources,
        some unverifiable (47 tunes). Measures degree of in-
        fluence. Has 115 pages of primary and secondary
        sources and extensive bibliography.

206.   E., F.G. "Haydn in England: The 'Surprise' Symphony
        and a Surprise." *MT* 50 (May 1, 1909): 297-300.

        Relates events surrounding Haydn's London visits.
        Provides data on surprise chord and its absence from
        first score. Liberal quotations from London press.

207.   Einstein, Alfred. "Haydns Sinfonie." *ZfM* 91 (April
        1924): 169-74. Reprint: Einstein, *Von Schütz bis
        Hindemith*, pp. 63-71. Zurich & Stuttgart: Pan-
        Verlag, 1957.

        Details influences of other styles on early Haydn
        symphony style. Used as preface to Eulenberg edition
        of early symphonies.

208. Feder, Georg. "Die beiden Pole im Instrumentalschaffen des jungen Haydn" in *Kongress Graz/1970*, pp. 192-201.

Two poles (Baroque-Rococo, Learned-Galant, etc.) appear to operate simultaneously rather than successively in early works, depending on genre and type of movement being written. Refutes earlier theory that style posture consistent in all genres within same time frame.

209. _____. "Bemerkunden über die Ausbildung der klassischen Tonsprache in der Instrumentalmusik Haydns" in *Kongress New York/1961*, pp. 305-13.

Early instrumental style derives from Austro-Italian divertimento style (Wagenseil), enriched (or updated) with elements from Italian *cantilena*, *siciliana*, and Haydn's own native folk music. Baroque influences fugal usages (especially quartet finales and early symphonies). Expressive focus came from C.P.E. Bach. Evolving style also traced in works of Haydn's contemporaries. Style stability noted by 1775. Defines pre-classic (p. 305) and classic (p. 306) styles.

210. _____. "Drei Publikationen zur Haydn-Forschung." *Mf* 17 (1964): 62-66.

Discusses *Haydn Yearbook I* (1962), Landon's supplement to *The Symphonies of Joseph Haydn* and Gotwals' *Joseph Haydn: Eighteenth Century Gentleman and Genius*.

211. _____. "Haydns Paukenschlag und andere Überraschungen." *ÖMz* 21 (1966): 5-8.

Treats frequent surprise events, detailing absence of *Symphony No. 94* drum beat in original score and listing other surprises in symphonies 31, 45, 60, 98, 100, 103 and other non-symphonic works. Thinks surprise principle was a fundamental Haydn style feature.

212. _____. "Similarities in the Works of Haydn" in *Festschrift Geiringer/70th*, pp. 186-97.

Sees similarities between symphonies 61 and 100; 45 and 85; 45 and 60; 31 and 48; and 74, 80 and 101.

213. Fellerer, Karl Gustav. "Zum Joseph-Haydn-Bild im
      frühen 19. Jahrhunderts" in *Festschrift Hoboken/75th*,
      pp. 73-86.

      Quotes comments on symphonies (and other works). Ex-
      plains Haydn's image in early 19th century.

214. Fisher, Stephen Carey. "A Group of Haydn Copies for
      the Court of Spain: Fresh Sources, Rediscovered
      Works, and New Riddles." *H-St* 4 (1978): 65-84.

      Discusses connections between Haydn and court as
      seen in Library Congress holdings (from court library).
      Analyzes symphonies Hob. Ia:6, Ia:1 pasticcio and I:63.
      Lists works in Library of Congress and Madrid library
      written in same hand. Gives call numbers for both
      sources and shows need for more research.

215. _____. "Haydn's Overtures and Their Use as Concert
      Orchestral Works." Ph.D. dissertation, Univ. of
      Pennsylvania, 1985.

      Has description of 18th-century overture and its var-
      ious forms (reprise, three-movement, two-movement, one-
      movement). Evaluates Haydn's handling of genre as part
      of his symphonic development. Continues study of copy-
      ists' hands, as done earlier by Wolf and others. Note-
      worthy documentation and bibliography.

216. _____. "Sonata Procedures in Haydn's Symphonic Rondo
      Finales of the 1780s" in *Haydn Studies*, pp. 481-87.

      Minimizes cross-influences between Haydn and Mozart
      in use of sonata-rondo. Asserts that Haydn's type is
      more continuous while Mozart's is strophic, with latter
      becoming more continuous later. Thinks both arrived at
      form independently at about same time.

217. Flothius, Marius. "Die Instrumentation der 'Londoner'
      Sinfonien" in *Kongress Vienna/1982*, pp. 183-88.

      Studies orchestration with regard to composer's en-
      vironment and relationship between creative activity
      and musical practice. Statistical tables reflect use
      of flutes, strings and timpani.

218. Foster, Jonathan. "The Tempora Mutantur Symphony of
      Joseph Haydn." *HYb* 9 (1975): 328-9.

      Proposes that sub-title of *Symphony No. 44* relates to
      John Owen's (ca. 1565-1612, Wales) epigram, *Tempora mu-
      tantur*. Fits words of English translation under theme
      of finale to show relationship.

219. Gal, Hans. "A Re-discovered Haydn Symphony." *MMR* 69
      (1939): 12-4.

      Pertains to Hoboken I:B2. Marion Scott's reply to
      discovery noted in his article, "Mi-Jo Haydn." See
      also entry 298.

220. Geiringer, Karl. "Eigenhändige Bemerkungen Haydns in
      seinen Musikhandschriften" in *Festschrift Hoboken/-
      75th*, pp. 87-92.

      Explains some of Haydn's score annotations, some of
      which apply to performance of symphonies.

221. _____, editor. *Franz Joseph Haydn: Symphony No. 103
      in E-flat major ("Drum Roll")*. New York: Norton,
      1974. ISBN 0-393-09349-2 M1001 H4

      Score edited by Unverricht (from new Haydn edition).
      Contains analyses and commentaries by Greisinger (his-
      torical background), Tovey, Kretzschmar, Landon, Hadow,
      Rosemary Hughes, Hadow, Marion Scott, Burney, Lang,
      Geiringer, Rosen and one anonymous writer (*Journal des
      Luxus und der Moden*, Weimar, 1794). Most speak to sym-
      phonic style. Hadow quotes two Croatian folk songs in
      tracing roots of work. Scott comments on intervallic
      unity (carrying forward Carpani's comments from his
      1812 biography).

222. _____, with Irene Geiringer. *Haydn, a Creative Life*.
      3rd ed. Berkeley: Univ. of California Press, 1982.
      xii, 403p. ISBN 0-520-04316-2 ML410 H4 G4

      Known as one of definitive Haydn biographies with
      half of book on works. Covers sources and four periods:
      youth, romantic crisis, maturity and consummate mas-
      tery. In each period works studied by genre with sym-
      phonic evolution clearly defined, reflecting recent
      symphony research. Thorough indices and bibliography.

223. _____. "Haydn and His Viennese Background." in *Haydn Studies*, pp. 2-13.

Dissects background: Italian music, music patronage system, music in daily life, opera, drama, style *galant*, Wagenseil and Monn, Mozart, Artaria publishing house and others. Explains its influence on his style.

224. Gerlach, Sonja. "Die chronologische Ordnung von Haydns Sinfonien zwischen 1774 und 1782." *H-St* 2 (1969): 34-66.

Studies chronological problems in dating symphonies in subject period. Analyzes earlier works and presents persuasive argument supporting dates.

225. _____. "Eine Fund zu Haydns verschollener Sinfonie." *H-St* 3 (1973): 44-45.

Establishes Hoboken I: 106 as overture (*Le Pescatrici*) dating from 1769-70.

226. _____. "Haydns Orchestermusiker von 1761 bis 1774." *H-St* 4 (1976): 35-48.

Identifies musicians in Haydn's orchestra and their years of service. Relates this to composer's instrumental output at Esterhazy. Table (p. 47) shows doubling, especially strings who doubled on winds.

227. _____. "Haydns Orchesterpartituren: Fragen der Realisierung des Textes." *H-St* 5 (1982-1985): 169-83.

Studies resources in three periods: ca. 1757-1774, ca. 1775-1790 and 1792-1795, defining orchestral style from several aspects, stressing certain instruments (winds, bassoon as *obbligato* voice, *basso continuo* and harpsichord in London symphonies, viola, horn and others). Shows (in table) a period's normal resources, noting relatively small size of late 18th century ensemble (14-23 players with increase to 40 in London).

228. _____. "A Chronological Correlation of Haydn's Scoring and the Esterhazy Musicians" in *Haydn Studies*, pp. 93-94.

Reveals how knowledge of orchestral resources helps date many of Haydn's works.

229. _____, and Wolfgang Stockmeier. "Vorwort" to *Joseph Haydn: Sinfonien um 1775-76*. *JHW-HI*, series I, vol. 8, pp. vi-vii.

Places symphonies 61, 67, 68 and 69 in period and comments briefly on style (especially 67).

230. Gotwals, Vernon, ed. *Joseph Haydn: Eighteenth-Century Gentleman and Genius*. Madison: Univ. of Wisconsin Press, 1963. 275p,

Translates Griesinger (*Biographische Notizen über Joseph Haydn*, 1809) and Dies (*Biographische Nachrichten von Joseph Haydn*, 1810), with editor's introduction and notes. Dies' original had Haydn's own catalog of works (ages 18 to 73) and catalog of London works taken from Haydn's notebooks. See paperback issue by same publisher: *Joseph Haydn: Two Contemporary Portraits*, 1968. See also 1954 edition (Vienna: Paul Kaltschmid) with annotations by Franz Grasberger.

231. Gray, Cecil. "Joseph Haydn (1732-1804)" in *The Symphony*, edited by Ralph Hill, pp. 22-54. Hammondsworth: Penguin, 1949. ISBN 0-403-01578-2 ML1255 H498

Supports Haydn as greatest innovator in symphonic history. Analyzes symphonies 85, 92, 94, 100, 101, 103 and 104. Quotes 25 excerpts. Insightful argument on Haydn's role as innovator.

232. Gresham, Carolyn D. "Stylistic Features of Haydn's Symphonies from 1768 to 1772" in *Haydn Studies*, pp. 431-34.

Expansive period's (*Sturm und Drang*) main features: greater use of minor, longer and more continuously-unfolding phrases, abrupt dynamic changes, sudden changes of harmony and emphasized dissonance.

233. Grim, William E. "Form, Process and Morphology in the *Sturm und Drang* Symphonies of Franz Joseph Haydn." Ph.D. dissertation. Kent State Univ., 1985. 337p.

Procedure employs both traditional analysis and Leonard Meyer's morphological approach. Studies theories of *Sturm und Drang* (pp. 7-54); charts form and compositional processes of 44 works involved. Findings: variables (form, process and morphology) don't differentiate *Sturm und Drang* symphonies from others; style reaches maturity in early works and endures throughout output. Added benefit: depth of *Sturm und Drang* study.

234. Harich, János. "Das Haydn-Orchester im Jahr 1780." *HYb* 8 (1971): 5-52.

Details biographical data on 25 members of Esterhazy group (1780), each discussed in great detail. English summary by Eugene Hartzell, pp. 53-69.

235. Hastings, Baird. "Concertante Elements in the Symphonies of Joseph Haydn." M.A. thesis, Queens College of City Univ. of New York, 1966. 99p.

Findings: 74 Haydn symphonies have *concertante* features while 48 of 100 symphonies by other composers (incl. entire Mozart) contain *concertante* passages.

236. Hauschild, Peter. "Liedthema und Entwicklung in den Expositionen von Haydns 'Londoner' Sinfonien" in *Kongress Vienna/1982*, pp. 175-83.

Studies *Lied* themes in last movements of 93, 99, 100, 103 and 104 and this melodic type's relation to development in exposition sections.

237. Hinrichsen, Max. "The Rediscovery of a Haydn Autograph (Hoboken No. 97)." *HMYb* 7 (1952): 457-59.

Covers *Symphony No. 97* and offers table of numberings of London symphonies.

238. Hoboken, Anthony van. *Joseph Haydn: thematisch-bibliographisches Werkverzeichnis.* Vol. I: Instrumentalwerke. Mainz: B. Schott's Söhne, 1957. 848p. ML134 H27 H6

See reviews: Geiringer (*Notes* 14 [1957], 565-66); Deutsch (*MR* 18 [1957]; lists omissions) and item 840 in Brown and Berkenstock (entry 194) for other reviews.

239. Hodgson, Anthony. *The Music of Joseph Haydn - The
      Symphonies*. London: Tantivity Press, 1976. 208p.
      ISBN 0-8386-1684-4 ML410 H4 H56

      Layman's approach lacks documentation, usually treat-
      ing each symphony with brief paragraph which may or may
      not deal definitively with symphonic form or style.
      Has 40-page discography, attractive illustrations (some
      in color) but sparse reading list.

240. Hughes, Rosemary S.M. *Haydn*. The Master Musician
      Series. 2d ed., rev. London: Dent; New York:
      Pellegrini and Cudahy, 1970. 244p. ML410 H4 H8

      Symphony coverage (pp. 173-93) brief but probing.
      Has bibliography, list of works, list of personalia
      (with explanations) and calendar equating Haydn's dates
      with other events.

241. Johns, Donald C. "In Defence of Haydn: the Surprise
      Symphony Revisited." *MR* 24 (1963): 305-12.

      Detailed analysis of second and third movements. La-
      Rue responds in his "In Defence of Haydn," *MR* 25
      (1964), p. 159.

242. Jones, David Wyn. "Haydn's Music in London in the
      Period 1760-1790." *HYb* 14 (1983): 144-72.

      Recalls London performance and publication of Haydn's
      music, relating these to those of Abel, J.C. Bach,
      Richter and J. Stamitz. Gives perspective on London
      concert life. Lists Haydn's London publications during
      period, noting symphonies' publication in 1773.

243. Kassler, Michael. "On the Name of Haydn's 'Surprise'
      Symphony." *ML* 52 (1971): 106.

      Reveals existence of program notes (Bodelian library
      shelf-mark 17405D.6) originally owned by flutist Andrew
      Ashe (member of Salomon orchestra in 1792). Ashe's
      marginal notes (in his own hand): "I christened it the
      'Surprise' when I announced it for my benefit concert
      ..the year it was composed..and..Haydn thanked me for
      giving it such an appropriate name."

244. Kinsky, Georg. "Haydns Kunst der Orchesterbehandlung."
      DM-Z 33 (1932): 42-44.

      Shows Haydn's orchestral procedure similar to that of
      Mannheim composers. No musical examples.

245. Kolb, Doris C. "Haydn's London Symphonies: a Study of
      Texture." M.A. thesis, Univ. of Texas, 1946. 134p.

      Illustrates balance between homophony and polyphony
      in development sections in particular, with less empha-
      sis on counterpoint in other sections. Sees Haydn's
      great talent in blend of counterpoint and homophony.

246. Kretzschmar, Hermann. "Die Jugendsinfonien Joseph
      Haydns." *JaP* 15 (1908): 69-90.

      Studies recently (1907-8) issued collected edition
      and shows variety of influences on emerging style.
      Landon later brings more insight into matter.

247. Krienitz, Willy. "78 neue Haydn-Symphonien." *AMz(Bln)*
      60 (1933): 153.

      Speaks to Sandberger's disclosure that Mandyczewski
      omitted at least 78 works from his Haydn symphony list
      and had labeled authentic symphonies as spurious while
      overlooking many authentic works. For over ten years
      controversy swirled around Sandberger and Larsen, who
      was supportive of Mandyczewski's research. Eventually
      Sandberger's claims were refuted.

248. Landon, H.C. Robbins, ed. *Joseph Haydn: Critical Edi-
      tion of the Complete Symphonies*. 12 vols. Vienna:
      Universal Edition, 1965-68.

      Each volume (in miniature score format) contains: I
      (1-12, plus A and B)), II (13-27), III (28-40), IV (41-
      49), V (50-57), VI (58-65), VII (66-73), VIII (74-81),
      IX (82-87), X (88-92 plus *Sinfonia concertante*), XI
      (93-98), XII (99-104). Each has foreword explaining
      sources, early performances, musical style, and other
      details about the edition. Notes editorial changes
      made. New data derived after publication of editor's
      book on symphonies (1955) included (e.g., Fürnberg
      parts found in Budapest Royal Museum). Text in German
      and English.

249. _____. *Haydn: Chronicle and Works*. Vol. I (The Early Years, 1732-1765). Bloomington: Indiana Univ. Press, 1980. 655p. ISBN 0-253-37005-1 ML410 H4 L26 Vol. 1

Encompasses early symphonies (pp. 103-13, 280-96, 552-74). Gives definition of Viennese symphony, its origins and antecedents, early Viennese composers, its evolving style and its relationship to emerging Haydn symphonies. Works described historically and analytically. New materials update author's 1955 book, enhancing value of this first volume. Feels symphony "school" springs from Haydn's works (pp. 296-303). Bibliography in vol. V.

250. _____. *Haydn: Chronicle and Works*. Vol. II (Haydn at Esterhazy, 1766-1790). Bloomington: Indiana Univ. Press, 1978. 709p. ISBN 0-253-37002-7 ML410 H4 L26 Vol. 2

Symphonies discussed in three eras: 1766-1775 (pp. 284-315), 1776-1784 (560-66) and 1785-1790 (606-14, 629-34). Each work (48 symphonies) afforded historical and musical treatment with excellent stylistic insight. Significantly augmented coverage of 1955 effort. See vol. V for bibliography.

251. _____. *Haydn: Chronicle and Works*. Vol. III (Haydn in England, 1791-1795). Bloomington: Indiana Univ. Press, 1976. 640p. ISBN 0-253-37003-5 ML410 H4 L26 Vol. 5

In addition to documents and printed material relative to London symphonies, has sections on symphonies (pp. 490-618) with facts on publication and 18th century sources, works' position in history and detailed analytical comments on each work, especially valuable as update of earlier book. Vol. V has bibliography.

252. _____. *Haydn Symphonies*. Seattle: Univ. of Washington Press, 1969. 64p. Reprint of 1966 BBC guide.

Synopsis of earlier and more detailed *The Symphonies of Joseph Haydn* (1955). Reviewed by Sadie (*MT* 108 [1966], 1060-61).

253. _____. "The Newly Discovered Authentic Scores of Haydn's `London' Symphonies from the Library of

Johann Peter Salomon" in *Kongress Vienna/1982*, pp. 549-50.

Comments on A. Hyatt King's discovery of remaining autograph scores (93, 94, 97, 99, 100, 101, 102, 103, 104), all with corrections in Salomon's hand.

254. _____. "Notes" in booklets for *The Complete Symphonies of Haydn*. 10 vols. London ffrr Stereo Treasury Series sound recordings (LP). Vol. 1 (65-72) STS 15135-8; 2 (57-64) STS 15131-4; 3 (49-56) STS 15127-30; 4 (78-81) STS 15182-5; 5 (82-92) STS 15229-34; 6 (36-48) 15249-54; 7 (20-35) STS 15257-62; 8 (1-19) STS 15310-15; 9 (93-104) STS 15319-14; Appendix (A, B, optional endings, alternate versions 22, 53, 63, 103) sts 15316-17. London: Decca Record Co., Ltd., 1970-74.

Each volume has elaborate notes with interesting and valuable illustrations, concise style commentaries, updated historical data and analyses of each symphony. Approximates materials in *Chronicle* (see entries 249-251). Recorded by Antal Dorati and the Philharmonia Hungarica using Landon's edition of symphonies.

255. _____. "The Original Versions of Haydn's First 'Salomon' Symphonies." *MR* 15 (1954): 1-32.

Covers early copies and printed editions of 94-98 and *Sinfonia Concertante*. Details inaccuracies in printed parts. Exhaustive treatment.

256. _____. *The Symphonies of Joseph Haydn*. London: Universal Edition and Rockliff, 1955. 863p, 23p (examples). Supplement, 1961, 64p. ML410 H4 L28

Broad scope and scholarship characterize effort with emphasis on authenticity, sources, chronology, textual and performance problems. Divides symphonies into seven groups, each period characterized. Reviewed by many scholars (e.g., Lang, *MQ* 43 [1957], 411-15). Supplement added information and corrections. Considered seminal work in field.

257. _____. "The Symphonies of Joseph Haydn: Addenda and Corrigenda." *MR* 19 (1958): 311-19, 20 (1959): 56-70.

Details corrections of 1955 book, describes holdings in Fürstenburg library at Donaueschingen not available to Landon earlier, notably the Haydn-corrected copies (made by Johann Elssler) of Salomon symphonies. Second report comments further on Croatian folk song influence and gives more information on sources (see appendix).

258. _____. "Die Verwendung gregorianischer Melodien in Haydns Frühsymphonien." *OMz* 9 (1954): 119-26,

Reveals Gregorian sources for two early symphony tunes: one in *Symphony No. 26*, first and second movements, and later in trios of symphonies 45 and 80; another in *Symphony No. 30*, first movement. Shows conformance of source tunes with symphony themes.

259. Larsen, Jens Peter. "The Challenge of Joseph Haydn" in Larsen: *Handel, Haydn, and the Viennese Classical Style*. Translated by Ulrich Krämer, pp. 95-108. Ann Arbor: UMI Research Press, 1988. ISBN 0-8356-1851-4 ML195 L13 1988

Three areas of concern: Haydn and Viennese classicism, Haydn's personal and artistic character and old or new prejudices, Haydn's music as viable concert repertoire today. Includes comments on symphonies and their chronology. Isolates factors influencing Haydn's development: his duties at each job, kind of creative demands made on him, his place in music history (accident of birth with style determined by his generation), crucial nature of 1765-72 period, the duality of style and others. Originally published in *Proceedings of the International Joseph Haydn Congress, Vienna, Sept. 5-12, 1982 (Munich, 1986)*, pp. 9-20.

260. _____."Probleme der chronologischen Ordnung von Haydns Sinfonien" in *Festschrift Deutsch/80th*, pp. 90-104.

Table (pp. 101-4) compares dates of symphonies as listed in Mandyczewski, *Sohlmans Musiklexicon*, Haydn Society, Grove fifth edition, Landon, *Musik in Geschichte und Gegenwart* and Hoboken.

261. _____. "Zu Professor Adolph Sandberger Haydn-Forschung." *ActaM* 8 (1936): 149-54. Also *ZfM* 103 (1936): 1325-34.

Restates position on Vaňhal symphony felt Sandberger wrongly attributed to Haydn. Comments on 78 "unknown" Haydn symphonies Sandberger said were omitted from collected edition and supports now-established view the 78 were spurious.

262. _____. "Haydn's Early Symphonies: the Problem in Dating" in *Festschrift Brook*, pp. 117-32. Also in Larsen: *Handel, Haydn, and the Viennese Classical Style*, pp. 159-70 (Ann Arbor: UMI Research Press, 1988).

Updates Deutsch festschrift article (entry 260). Covers most efforts: Mandyczewski (1907-8 collected edition), Breitkopf catalogs (1762-87), Gottweig catalog (1830), Rywosch study (1934), Larsen dissertation (1928), Haydn's Entwurf catalog (1765), Haydn Society edition (1950), Landon's book (1955), Landon's edition of symphonies (1965-68), *MGG* Haydn article (1956), Hoboken catalog (1957), Gerlach's article on 1774-82 symphonies (1969), Fürnberg discovery (ca. 1959), Landon's Haydn biography (1980), Feder's *NGDMM* essay, Larsen's study of three Haydn catalogs (1979), and another study by Gerlach (1973). Evaluates all efforts and concludes study of early symphony types would prove a more valuable project.

263. _____. "Zu Haydns künstlerischer Entwicklung" in *Festschrift Fischer*, pp. 123-29.

Establishes eight periods in style development: ca. 1750-ca. 1760, ca. 1760-ca. 1765, ca. 1765-1772, 1773-1777/8, 1779-1783/4, ca. 1784-1790, 1790-1795, 1795-1809. Modifies this in *New Grove Haydn* (p. 86). English translation in Larsen: *Handel, Haydn, and the Viennese Classical Style*, pp. 109-15 (Ann Arbor: UMI Research Press, 1988). See also entry 164.

264. _____. "The Haydn Tradition" in Larsen: *Handel, Haydn, and the Viennese Classical Style*. Translated by Ulrich Krämer, pp. 185-224. Ann Arbor: UMI Research Press, 1988. ISBN 0-8357-1851-4 ML195 L13 1988

Based in part on Larsen's dissertation (*Die Haydn-Überlieferung*, Copenhagen, 1934). Evaluates *Entwurf* catalog as major authenticity resource for works from

1765-1777 period. Focuses on symphonies. Claims style research in establishing authenticity valid only if other hard evidence exists in source. Says style study useful in examining two known bodies of literature.

265. _____, and Georg Feder. "Haydn, (Franz) Joseph" in *NGDMM*, vol. 8, pp. 328-407.

Includes symphonic style discussion (pp. 351-3, 355-6). Summary (pp. 359-60) probes into the nature of Haydn's talent and its relation to his music. Feder prepared bibliography and list of works.

266. _____, with Georg Feder. *The New Grove Haydn*. New York: Norton, 1983. 237p. ISBN 0-393-30085-4

Brief but accurate biography with Feder's excellent list of works (adds page references when work discussed elsewhere in book), documented and dated as per latest research. Extended bibliography grouped in categories but without publisher identity (a common practice in most reference books).

267. _____, Howard Serwer and James Webster, editors. *Haydn Studies: Proceedings of the International Conference Washington, D.C., 1975*. New York: Norton, 1981. xvii, 590p. ISBN 0-393-01454-1 ML36 I59593 1975

Involved participation of most Haydn and classical period scholars (Geiringer, Larsen, Feder, Lowens, Bartha, Croll, Mörner, Gerlach, LaRue, Rosen, Fellerer, Brook, Grout, Churgin, Ratner, and others). Numerous Haydn symphony papers. Lists all works cited as bibliography (pp. 531-57). General index and index of music discussed. Unexpected bonus: records faithfully discussions after papers and panels.

268. _____, and Newell Jenkins, Barry Brook, Ludwig Finscher, Charles Rosen, P.H. Lang, Irving Lowens, Boris Schwartz. "Specific Problems of Performance Style: Sonority - Symphonies" in *Haydn Studies*, pp. 284-87.

Panel discussion on small versus large orchestra for today's Haydn performances. Excellent reaction from panel with no one position dominant.

269. LaRue, Jan. "The Gniezno Symphony not by Haydn" in
      Festschrift Larsen/75th, pp. 255-60.

      Concerns spurious Haydn symphony discovered in Gniez-
      no (Poland) cathedral in 1964. Using phrase treatment
      analysis and comparing results with authentic Haydn
      symphony data from same period, establishes work by
      Christian Ernst Graf and not Haydn. Good example of
      LaRue's stylistic analysis procedures.

270. _____. "In Defense of Haydn." *MR* 25 (1964): 159.

      Replies to Johns' article on Haydn's *Surprise Sympho-
      ny*. See entry 241 this volume.

271. _____. "A New Figure in the Haydn Masquerade." *ML* 40
      (1959): 132-39.

      Identifies Baron Theodor von Schacht (1748-1823) as
      another composer whose works were attributed to Haydn,
      providing list of all known (in 1959) false Haydns.

272. Livingston, Ernest F. "Unifying Elements in Haydn's
      Symphony No. 104" in *Haydn Studies*, pp. 493-96.

      Thematic unity: basic ideas presented in introduc-
      tion. Structural unity (via basic ideas above): in
      development sections, introductions and codas, climax
      points and midpoints. Sees first movement's unifying
      motives applied in remaining movements.

273. Lorenz, Howard Roberts. "Development of Style and Form
      in the Symphonic Minuets and Trios of Franz Joseph
      Haydn." M.A. thesis, West Chester State College,
      1982. vi, 107p.

      Finds some consistency in use of rhythmic and melodic
      motives throughout life, decline of imitation in later
      minuets and a maturing use of tonality, tempo, coda,
      dynamics, silence, pauses, hemiola, and location of
      minuet in symphonic form.

274. Mahling, Christoph-Hellmut. "Orchesterpraxis und Or-
      chestermusiker zur Zeit des jungen Haydn (1740-1770)"
      in *Kongress Graz/1970*, pp. 98-113.

Examines orchestras in Vienna, München, Stuttgart, Kassel, Salzburg, and Esterhazy. Includes Haydn's experimental scoring in early symphonies (e.g., extended solo passages in concerto style) and contemporary comments on orchestras known to Haydn. Bibliography.

275. _____. "Size of Orchestra" in *Haydn Studies*, pp. 242-44.

Thinks that, except for London ensemble, Haydn's orchestra was small. Brook disagrees: Paris orchestra might be exception. Panel focuses on *Symphony No. 85*.

276. Marco. Guy A. "A Musical Task in the 'Surprise' Symphony." *JAMS* 11 (1958): 41-44.

Analyzes first movement, using Siegmund Levarie's "musical task" concept. Shows movement expanding a motive in exposition, interrupting the "accomplishment of the task of the motive" in various ways and finally completing task in recapitulation (latter becoming synthesis of exposition materials).

277. Matthäus, Wolfgang. "Die Frühdrucke der Londoner Sinfonien Joseph Haydns. Ein Versuch der Darstellung ihrer Zusammenhänge." *AfMw* 21 (1964): 243-52.

Establishes chronology of early editions by Andre, Sieber, Artaria, Imbault, Gombart, Pleyel, and Hummel. Also notes published arrangements of same works.

278. _____, and Hubert Unverricht. "Zur Abhängigkeit der Frühdrucke von Joseph Haydns Londoner Sinfonien." *AfMw* 24 (1967): 145-48.

Uses publishers' plate numbers to establish dates of publication.

279. Menk, Gail Ellsworth. "The Symphonic Introductions of Joseph Haydn." Ph.D. dissertation, Univ. of Iowa, 1960. 138p.

Studies tonality, harmony and phrase structure in all 29 slow introductions. Findings: no observable form, symmetrical and asymmetrical phrases, I-V tonal plan with further modulations after 93, unified by opening melodic or rhythmic motives, no dynamic patterns (ex-

cept the unexpected), and *tutti* orchestration. Offers
pre-Haydn history of introduction.

280. Moore, John Terence. "Haydn's Treatment of the Reca-
      pitulation in Sonata Form." M.A. thesis, Univ. of
      Illinois, 1941. 30p.

      Based on study of 51 movements from 37 of 77 string
      quartets. Found only 20% with complete restatements.

281. Mörner, C.G. Stellan. "Vorwort" to *Sinfonien 1767-
      1772* in *JHW-HI*, series 1, vol. 6, pp. vii-ix.

      Contains Hoboken I: 35, 49, 42, 45-47 and four in
      Sturm und Drang period (39, 44, 48, 52). Includes data
      on orchestration and events surrounding each work.
      Mentions Haydn's experimentation, key choices, surprise
      effects and form. Generous bibliography.

282. Nakano, Hiroshi. "Vorwort" to *Pariser Sinfonien, 1.
      Folge* in *JHW-HI*, series 1, vol. 12, pp. vi-vii.

      Covers events related to composition of Paris sym-
      phonies. Works: 83, 85 and 87. Lengthy bibliography.

283. Oldman, Cecil B. "Haydn's Quarrel with the `Profes-
      sionals' in 1788" in *Festschrift Vötterle/65th*, pp.
      459-65.

      Documents Haydn's unfortunate negotiations with Lon-
      don Professional Concerts in 1780s for six new sym-
      phonies. Sent three "Paris" symphonies as first in-
      stallment, forgetting he had previously issued them for
      publication in Vienna, Paris and London. London pub-
      lished versions emerged month before their Professional
      premiere there, this vexing his London sponsors.

284. Palm, Albert. "Unbekannte Haydn-Analysen." *HYb* 4
      (1968): 169-94.

      Covers analyses by Jérôme-Joseph de Momigny (1762-
      1838) of symphonies 103 and 104, and keyboard trios
      Hob. XV: 14 and 27. Momigny's theories of phrasing
      were basis for studies by Lussy, Westphal and Riemann.

285. Paul, Steven E. "Comedy, Wit, and Humor in Haydn's
      Instrumental Music" in *Haydn Studies*, pp. 450-56.

Wit in general related to element of surprise with
many examples from symphonies. Well-documented.

286. Riehm, Diethard. "Die ersten Sätze von Joseph Haydns
Londoner Sinfonien." Ph.D. dissertation, Wilhelm
Univ. (Münster), 1971. 144p.

Analyzes first movements with considerable reference
to other writings and analyses on symphonies, including
those from 19th century. Reduced offset copy available
at Catholic Univ.

287. _____. "Zur Anlage der Exposition in Joseph Haydns
Sinfonien." *ÖMz* 21 (1966): 255-60.

Contrasts expositions of first movements of 102 and
104, showing differences in construction of themes and
motives, use of counterpoint, instrumentation and other
basic compositional elements. Suggests works represent
two different aspects of Haydn's symphonic style.

288. Riemann, Hugo. "Josef Haydn Werke. Serie I. Symphonien." *MbM* 1 (1908): 60-64.

Riemann, discover of Mannheim School, shows similarities between Mannheim style and that of Haydn.

289. Roosa, Walter Laidlaw. "Haydn's treatment of the Recapitulation in Sonata Form - the Early Symphonies."
M.A. thesis, Univ. of Illinois, 1946. 71p.

Based on first 46 symphonies. Notes ways sections
vary. Tables summarize usages: regular or modified
recapitulations, modified first and second subjects,
shortened or extended second subjects, transitions,
independent or derived second subjects. See entry 838.

290. Rywosch, Bernard. *Beiträge zur Entwicklung in Joseph
Haydns Symphonik.* Turbenthal: (none provided), 1934.
134p.

Divides works into four periods: 1759-1771 (Rational-
ism and Rococo), 1771-1774 (*Sturm und Drang*), 1774-1781
(process of organization), and 1781-1795 (Classic) and
describes style of each. Includes short analysis of
each symphony, adding table of tonalities in develop-

ment sections of sonata-allegro movements. Author's
dissertation at Zurich University.

291. Sandberger, Adolph. "Schlussreplik." *ActaM* 9 (1937):
      39-41.

      Sandberger's last word on conflict between himself
      and Larsen on Vaňhal symphony Sandberger attributed
      to Haydn. Sandberger's position proved faulty.

292. Schroeder, David. "Melodic Source Material and Haydn's
      Creative Process." *MQ* 68 (1982): 496-515.

      Chronicles 19th century attempts to locate Haydn's
      melodic sources for symphonies. Likely roots: plain-
      chant, hymns, folk songs and folk dances. Examples
      show relationship between symphony *allegro* themes and
      folk dance tunes.

293. Schwartz, Judith Leah. "Thematic Asymmetry in First
      Movements of Haydn's Early Symphonies" in *Haydn
      Studies*, pp. 501-9.

      Haydn's asymmetrical themes are reflection of general
      tendency noted in other composers of period. Contains
      excellent examples of several types of asymmetry.

294. Schwarz, Boris. "Some Specific Problems in the First
      Movement (of *Symphony No. 85*)" in *Haydn Studies*, pp.
      245-52.

      Relates to rhythm and tempo (dotted or double-dot-
      ted and others). Discussion by Woldike, Jenkins, Mah-
      ling, Zaslaw, Bryan, Dorati, LaRue, and Brook broadens
      into instruments,

295. Scott, Marion M. "Haydn: Fresh Facts and Old Fancies."
      PRMA 68 (1941-42): 87-105.

      Symphony No. 103 included in works discussed.

296. _____. "Haydn in England. *MQ* 18 (1932): 260-73.

      Relates to London symphonies. Biographical.

297. _____. "Haydn: Relics and Reminiscences in England."
      ML 13 (1932): 126-36.

Concerns manuscripts of London symphonies in various English libraries, early editions, portraits, musical instruments, and letters written during Haydn's stay.

298. _____. "Mi-Jo Haydn." *MMR* 69 (1939): 67-73.

Studies spurious symphony in B-flat (Hob. I: B2). Feels Michael Haydn wrote first three movements with finale possibly by Joseph Haydn. Hans Gal found 18th century edition of work by Bremner in Edinburg library.

299. Searle, Arthur. "The Royale Philharmonic Society Scores of Haydn's 'London' Symphonies." *HYb* 14 (1983): 173-86.

Relates history and discovery of Salomon scores. Of twelve, two are in Haydn's hand. Others done by two distinct copyists with editing marks either by Haydn or Salomon, Searle favoring latter.

300. Sisman, Elaine R. "Haydn's Variations." Ph.D. dissertation, Princeton, 1978. 357p.

In symphonies, half of variations are strophic (up to 1772). After 1772, favors melodic outline variations (adds tonal variation in minor, expands length of variation, and attaches coda). Thinks Haydn was working toward a more unified movement.

301. _____. "Haydn's Hybrid Variations" in *Haydn Studies*, pp. 509-22.

Hybrid implies combining strophic variation with rondo or ternary forms or constructing an "alternating variation" type. Finds hybrid examples in symphonies 42, 51, 53, 55, 63, 70, 74, 76, 78, 82, 88, 89, 90, 92, 101, 103, and 104. Summarizes 18th century literature.

302. _____. "Small and Expanded Forms: Koch's Model and Haydn's Music." *MQ* 68 (1982): 444-75.

Applies Koch's concepts to Haydn's works (esp. symphonies). Illustrates how 18th century composers understood sonata-allegro form. Ref: Heinrich Christoph Koch: *Versuch Anleitung zur Komposition*. 3 vols. Leipzig, 1782-93. Facsimile edit., Hildesheim, 1969.

303. Somfai, László. "The London Revision of Haydn's Instru-
      mental Style." *PRMA* 100 (1974): 159-74.

      Finds Haydn courted London audiences, studied variables
      differentiating London from Viennese patrons and used his
      popularity as license to "experiment with startling
      effects." Covers symphonies, sonatas and quartets.
      Notes lasting effects of changes in quartets. Numerous
      musical examples.

304. Stacey, William B. "Style and Register as Correlated
      Factors in the Horn Parts of Selected Symphonies of
      Joseph Haydn." M.A. thesis, Univ. of North Carolina,
      1969. 82p.

      Found use of horns was "consistently inconsistent,"
      not innovative and high register usage increasing with
      output. Employed IBM 1130 for correlation study. Sum-
      marizes use of computer in musicological environs.
      Factors weighed: chronology, thematic or filler usage,
      note density, keel action (similar to pedal point),
      clarino style and four registers.

305. Stockmeier, Wolfgang. "Vorwort" to *Sinfonien 1773 und
      1774* in *JHW-HI*, series 1, vol. 7, p. vii.

      Includes symphonies 54-57, with commentary stressing
      orchestration. Seeks origin of 57's nickname, "School-
      master." Short bibliography.

306. Stockmeier, Wolfgang, and Sonja Gerlach. "Vorwort" to
      Sinfonien 1775-76 in *JHW-HI*, series 1, vol. 8, pp.
      vi-vii.

      Covers symphonies 61, 66-69. Highlights instrumental
      style and piano arrangement of 69. Bibliography.

307   Therstappen, Hans Joachim. *Joseph Haydns sinfonische
      Vermächtnis*. Wolfenbüttel/Berlin: Georg Kallmeyer,
      1941. 275p. ML410 H4 T44

      Studies London symphonies, grouped by movements.
      Notes four second-movement types. Charts form of
      finales, adding commentary. Defines rondo themes as
      geschlossenen Themen (complete or united themes) and
      sonata-allegro themes as *offnend-entwickelnde Themen*

(open-developing themes). Was author's study, sub-
mitted with his application to Kiel Univ. faculty.

308. Tovey, Donald Francis. *Essays in Musical Analysis.* 2
vols. London: Oxford Univ. Press, 1981. MT 140 T6
1981. (Is reduction of original 7-vol. edition.)

Contains analyses of symphonies 88, 92, 94-5, 98-104.

309. Unverricht, Hubert. "Vorwort" to *Londoner Sinfonien* in
JHW-HI, series 1, vol. 18, pp. vi-vii.

Contains scores of symphonies 102-104 plus original
ending of 103's finale. Comments on reports of first
London performances, genealogy of instrumentation and
first printed editions. Short bibliography.

310. _____. "Zur Fragen nach den Frühdrucken von Joseph
Haydns Londoner Sinfonien." *AfMw* 22 (1966): 61-70.

Responds to Matthäus on early editions. See entries
277 and 309 this volume.

311. Van der Meer, John Henry. "Die Verwendung der Blasinstrumente im Orchester bei Haydn und seiner Zeitgenossen" in *Kongress Graz/1970*, pp. 202-20.

Traces expansion of Haydn's orchestra from eight
parts to large London ensemble, relating use of added
instruments to practices of his contemporaries. Many
examples from Haydn's symphonies.

312. Walter, Horst. "Vorwort" to *Sinfonien 1764 und 1765* in
JHW-HI, series 1, vol. 4, pp. vi-vii.

Covers Hob. I: 21-4, 28-31;. two (21, 22) in church
sonata format, one in three movements (30) with remaining in four movements. Traces some melodies to other
works (earlier and later). Bibliography.

313. _____. "Vorwort" to *Londoner Sinfonien, 3. Folge* in
JHW-HI, series 1, vol.17, pp. vi-ix.

Encompasses symphonies 99-101 plus wind setting of
second movement of "Military." Discusses first performance data plus chronological details on origin of
works (Vienna or London?). Extensive bibliography.

314. Wappenschmitt, O. "Die Durchführung im I. Satz von
      Haydns 'Militär-Symphonie.'" *Die Musik* 8 (1908-
      1909): 243-50.

      Analyzes development section.

315   Webster, James. "Binary Variants of Sonata Form in
      Early Haydn Instrumental Music" in *Kongress Vienna/-
      1982*, pp. 127-34.

      Studies "double return" of tonality and principal
      theme at start of recapitulation in symphonies. Shows
      (table 1) nonsynchronous tonal and principal theme re-
      turns. Considers Haydn's incipient sonata-form binary
      movements normal for early works. Bibliography.

316. Wolf, Eugene K. "The Recapitulations in Haydn's London
      Symphonies." *MQ* 52 (1966): 71-89.

      Develops two rationales: continuing development and
      increased overall stability. Notes Haydn's large ad-
      justments (simplification of form via large-scale omis-
      sions, compression of transitions and expansions of
      latter portion of recapitulation) and small adjustments
      (small formal, harmonic, orchestration, melodic and
      rhythmic changes). Many examples. See entry 838.

Johann Michael Haydn (1737-1806)[g,b]

317. Halm, Hans. "Eine unbekannte Handschrift der 'Kinder-
      Symphonie'" in *Festschrift Hoboken/75th*, pp. 101-2.

      Discusses manuscript of work attributed to M. Haydn.

318. Sherman, Charles H., ed. *Johann Michael Haydn: Five
      Symphonies* in *Symphony*, series B, vol. VIII
      (Salzburg, Part 2), pp. li-lxxii, 177-355.

      While his main interest was church music, Haydn wrote
      large body of instrumental music, including 41 sympho-
      nies (some assembled from earlier works). Introduc-
      tion's coverage of life, works and symphonies is
      thorough. Latter are in either 3 or 4 movements. In-
      cludes thematic index, current discography and biblio-
      graphy. Editor has published at least 10 scores, in
      addition to 5 in volume.

Franz Anton Hoffmeister (1754-1812)[g,b]

319. Hickman, Roger, ed. *Franz Anton Hoffmeister: Two Symphonies* in *Symphony*, series B. vol. V, pp. xi-xxv, 1-121.

Covers biography, symphonic style and analysis of works. Thematic index lists 47 works: 31 extant, 13 lost, 2 *symphonies concertantes* and 1 lost concerted work. Claims popularity of works due to tunefulness and colorful orchestration. Composer attempted (1791) complete edition of symphonies. Only six printed.

Leopold Hofmann (1738-1793)[g,b]

320. Kimball, G. Cook, ed. *Leopold Hofmann: Four Symphonies* in *Symphony*, series B, vol. VII, pp. xxiii-xlviii, 65-148.

Contains concise and well-documented biography and style discussion. Thinks Hofmann anticipated Haydn's mature form (slow introduction, etc.). (Was one of Vienna's most popular composers in 1760s and 1770s.) Thematic index lists 67 authentic, 3 undecided and 24 spurious works. Bibliography of 18 entries.

321. _____. "The Symphonies of Leopold Hofmann (1738-1793)." Ph.D. dissertation, Columbia Univ., 1985. 521p.

Relates Hofmann's symphonic style to 18th century writings on style, assuming a more philosophical and speculative stance. Valuable delineation of Hofmann's Viennese stature. Based on study of 23 of the 67 authentic scores. Compares Hofmann's style with those of Giuseppe Bonno, Wagenseil, Gassmann, J.A. Hasse, Gluck and Joseph Haydn, with Hofmann better than first three but considerably inferior to the last. Thematic index is of greater detail than that of entry 320 above, with *incipits* for all movements of each symphony. Bibliography is germane to study, omitting irrelevant works.

322. Kreiner, Viktor. "Leopold Hofmann als Sinfoniker." Ph.D. dissertation, Univ. of Vienna, 1958.

According to Kimball, "Dr. Kreiner has given a bar-by-bar description of all the movements of the 36 works

he had available.." Contains thematic catalog. Not
examined. See entry 321 above.

Johann Christoph Mann (ca.1726-1782)[g]

323.   Rudolf, Kenneth E., ed. *Johann Christoph Mann: Sym-
        phony in C Major* in *Symphony*, series B, vol. I, pp.
        lxxi-xcii, 235-45.

        Introduction combines discussion of works of Georg
        Matthias Monn and brother, Johann Christoph Mann, de-
        fining their stylistic differences. Monn favors scor-
        ing for strings only while Mann writes for strings and
        winds with strings *a 4* versus Monn's *a 3*. Notes con-
        trasting thematic organization: Monn favors correlation
        between new material and new phrases. Mann uses less
        sequence and counterpoint. Thematic index shows Mann's
        9 known symphonies.

Georg Matthias Monn (1717-1750)[g,b]

324.   Fischer, Wilhelm. "Wiener Instrumentalmusik vor und um
        1750." Introduction to *DToe*, vol. 39, pp. vii-xxiv,
        235-48.

        Includes five symphonies and two concertos by Monn
        plus discussion of symphonic style (especially melody).
        Overshadowed by more recent studies. See entries 323,
        325 and 326.

325.   Rudolf, Kenneth E. *Georg Matthias Monn: Five Symphon-
        ies* in *Symphony*, series B, vol. I, pp. lxxi-xcii,
        179-234.

        Edits 5 symphonies and adds thematic index that in-
        cludes 16 Monn works. See entry 323.

326.   _____. "The Symphonies of Georg Matthias Monn (1717-
        1750)." Ph.D. dissertation, Univ. of Washington, 1982.
        309p.

        Contains best and most extended current biography in
        English. Studies 16 symphonies, extracting style sum-
        mary supporting Monn's transitional but conservative
        position in Viennese symphony. Works are mostly in
        three movements and for strings only (except famed four-
        movement example with minuet as third movement).

Bonus: study of sources, including tables for European manuscript holdings, library location (with holdings) and individual works with identifying factors (including library location).

Leopold Mozart (1719-1787)[g,b]

327. Eisen, Leopold. "The Symphonies of Leopold Mozart and Their Relationship to the Early Symphonies of Wolfgang Amadeus Mozart." Ph.D. dissertation, Cornell, 1986. 366p.

Emphasizes authentication and style delineation, with major effort to identify and then establish chronology of Leopold's works with exhaustive data on copyists, paper and watermarks. Describes in great detail Salzburg orchestral music, listing composers and works written prior to 1780. Establishes link between Wolfgang and Leopold in orchestration, overall form and foreign influences. Lists the Mozarts' 32 copyists and the 29 watermarks (illustrated) associated with era and with Leopold. Superb bibliography and 172-page thematic catalog. Adviser: Zaslaw.

328. _____. *Leopold Mozart: Three Symphonies* in *Symphony*, series B, vol. VII (Salzburg, Part 1), pp. lxix-lxxx, 269-315.

Reflects rigorous authentication and chronology efforts of dissertation (entry 327) and supports emerging view of Leopold's quality talents. Suggests Leopold, contrary to accepted history, continued symphony composition after 1760, implying some early Wolfgang works may be Leopold's. Brief analysis of edited works. See entry 327 for thematic index. Extended bibliography.

329. Theiss, Ernst Ludwig. "Die Instrumentalwerke Johann Georg Leopold Mozarts." *ZhVfS* 62/63 (1962): 397-468.

Contains list of works, including 28 symphonies (36 in Eisen, entry 327 above). Studies both symphonies and orchestral program music (pp. 406-57) with thorough style coverage (overall form, tonality, instrumentation and form of each movement. Article is summary of author's 1942 thesis (Giessen).

Wolfgang Amadeus Mozart (1756-1791)[g,b]

330. Abert, Anna Marie. "Stilistischer Befund und Quellen-
      lage zu Mozarts Lambacher Sinfonie" in *Festschrift
      Engel/70th*, pp. 43-56.

      Feels older style of KV 45a implies Leopold Mozart as
      composer while more modern style of Leopold's G16 indi-
      cates Wolfgang's hand, noting that monastery copyist
      often interchanged Wolfgang and Leopold names. Later
      research disagrees, restoring each to rightful owners.

331. Abert, Hermann. ("Mozart: Symphony in G Minor - an
      Analysis") in *Mozart: Symphony in G Minor, KV 550*,
      edited by Nathan Broder, pp. 69-83. Norton Critical
      Scores. New York: Norton, 1967. ISBN 0-393-02064-9
      M1001 M93 K550 B75

      Analysis sometimes borders on the affective. Broder's
      commentary moderates Abert's perspective, adding more
      recent approaches. Taken from Abert's 1956 biography
      (vol. II, pp. 479-90); translated by Broder.

332. Addams, Eugene Bayne. "Source and Treatment of Thematic
      Material in the Developments of Sonata-Allegro Move-
      ments in the Symphonies of Wolfgang Amadeus Mozart."
      Ph.D. dissertation, Eastman School of Music of Univ. of
      Rochester, 1962. 484p.

      Evaluates section using 12 variables: source of mate-
      rial developed, techniques used to modify materials,
      tonality, modulation, harmony, counterpoint, sequence,
      transposition, repetition, restatement in original key,
      rhythm, and "sectioning" within development. Symphonies
      show "enormous growth" overall in developmental tech-
      niques, with progress made "in an irregular way."

333. Allroggen, Gerhard. "Mozarts erste Sinfonien" in *Fest-
      schrift Becker/60th*, pp. 392-404.

      Concerns supportive data for authenticating KV 45a,
      KV 19a and KV 16. Notes Leopold's hand in corrections
      in some manuscripts. Music examples and bibliography.

334. _____. "Vorwort" to *NMA-K*, series IV (Orchesterwerke),
      group 11 (Sinfonien), vol. I, pp. viii-xiii.

Includes KV 16, 19, Anh. 223, KV 22, 76, 43, 45, Anh. 221, Anh. 214, KV 48 and 73. Discussed authenticity. Excellent bibliography through 1984.

335. _____. "Vorwort" to *NMA-K*, series IV (Orchesterwerke), group 11 (Sinfonien), vol. II, pp. viii-xvi.

Discusses authenticity of some early symphonies. Contents: scores of KV 75, 81, 84, 95, 96, 110 (with finale), 111, 112, 114, 120, and 124. Bibliography up to 1985.

336. _____. "Zur Frage der Echtheit der Sinfonie KV Anh. 216 = 74g." In *Colloquium 'Mozart und Italien', Rome 1974*, edited by Friedrich Lippmann, pp. 237-45. Cologne: Arno Volk, 1978.

Considered by author to be one of Leopold's works as per current thought that he continued his own composition (after 1760) while promoting his son's career.

337. Anderson, John. "Brass Scoring Techniques in the Symphonies of Mozart, Beethoven and Brahms." Ph.D. dissertation, George Peabody for Teachers of Vanderbilt Univ., 1960. 385p.

Findings: composers "lag behind" mechanical developments on instruments. One of 51 tables shows limits of Mozart's scoring of harmony for brass section.

338. Angermüller, Rudolph, and Otto Schneider, editors. *Mozart-Bibliographie (bis 1970), (1971-1975), (1976-1980), (1981-1985)*. Kassel: Bärenreiter, 1976, 1978, 1982, 1987. 364p, 68p, 175p, 121p. ISBN 3-7618-0516-0, 0603-5, 0678-7, 0808-9 ML5 M61

Index includes: *Stil, Sinfonien, Instrumentalmusik, Instrumentation, Ouverture* and other related entries. Stresses broad coverage and currentness. Valuable.

339. Beck, Hermann. "Zur Entstehungsgeschichte von Mozarts D-Dur Sinfonie, KV 297: Probleme der Kompositionstechnik und Formentwicklung in Mozarts Instrumentalmusik." *MozJb* 1955: 95-112.

Examines historical data related to genesis of "Paris" symphony and painstakingly analyzes work (form, texture,

dynamics and other features of style). Ample musical
quotations.

340. Benary, Peter. "Metrum bei Mozart: zur metrischen Ana-
      lyse einer letzten drei Sinfonien." *SMZuS* 114 (1974):
      201-5.

      Presents metric analysis of works, saying meter is as
      important as form in understanding style. Author's
      text on rhythm and meter issued in 1967.

341. Biancolli, Louis, ed. *The Mozart Handbook*. New York:
      Grosset & Dunlap, 1962. 629p. ML410 M9 B38

      Uneven collection of essays by various authors (some
      esteemed) with ten symphonies discussed (KV 183, 201,
      297, 338, 385, 425, 504, 543, 550 and 551) by one or
      more writers (Philip Hale, Eric Blom, Saint-Foix, Bian-
      colli, Einstein, William Foster Apthorp, Donald Ferguson
      and Felix Borowski). Homer Ulrich and Noel Strauss
      provide history of Köchel thematic catalog and its edi-
      tions. Adds chronology that correlates Mozart's life
      with world events (from Lingg biography, 1946). Inclu-
      sion of several program annotators tends to minimize
      scholarly impact.

342. Blom, Eric. *Mozart*, rev. ed. Musician Series. Lon-
      don: J.M. Dent & Sons, 1952. 387p. ML410 M9 B6

      Symphonies on pp. 189-209. Covers symphonic style
      evolution and several symphonies (KV 183, 184. 200,
      *201, 202, 318, 319, 338, *385, *425, *504, *543, *550,
      and *551 [* denotes extended discussion]).

343. _____. "Wolfgang Amadeus Mozart" in *Sym/Hill*, pp. 55-
      91.

      Stresses importance of contrapuntal skills in
      Mozart's symphonic genius. Includes brief analysis of
      nine works (29, 31, 34, 35, 464, 38, 29, 40 and 41).
      Adds 56 examples (themes and important sections).

344. Blume, Friedrich. "Mozart's Style and Influence."
      Translated by H.C. Stevens. In *Moz/Comp*, pp. 10-31.

While pleading difficulty of establishing consistent style definition, Blume succeeds admirably, especially in melodic style. Feels Mozart's impact was greater in 19th century.

345. Broder, Nathan, ed. *Mozart: Symphony in G minor, KV 550.* Norton Critical Scores. New York: Norton, 1967. 114p. ISBN 0-393-02064-9 M1001 M93 K.550 B75

Contains valuable commentaries and analyses by other historians and writers: Landon on editorial changes; Abert's analysis from his revision of Jahn biography; Heuss on the minor second generating interval; Jalowetz on 12-tone writing in work; Schoenberg's analysis of first movement's transition; Fetis' review of concert (1828); Oulibicheff's discussion of work from his 1843 Mozart biography; Hanslick on beauty of KV 550; Grove's refutation of grief meaning of first movement; Tovey's assertion that form was not barrier to expression in work; Adler on Mozart and romanticism; and Einstein's expressive commentary ("...plunges into the abyss of the soul...," etc.). Short annotated bibliography.

346. _____. "The Wind Instruments in Mozart's Symphonies." *MQ* 19 (1933): 238-57.

Establishes three symphonic schools (orchestration): Italian opera overture (winds double or reinforce strings), Mannheim (greater independence of winds) and North German (C.P.E. Bach, but too late to influence Mozart until his final Viennese period). Examines gradual maturing of Mozart's orchestral style.

347. Brown, Maurice J.E. "Mozart's Recapitulations: A Point of Style." *ML* 30 (1949): 109-17.

Studies section immediately following restatement of principal theme. Many examples from symphonies.

348. Bryan, Paul Robey. "The Horn in the Works of Mozart and Haydn: Some Observations and Comparisons." *HYb* 9 (1975): 189-265.

Identifies hornists known to composers and studies how each may have influenced works. Factors included: range, stopping, orchestral usages and Haydn's *alto* and

basso scorings. Notes contrast in orchestral styles of
composers, mentioning Haydn's "clear and somewhat dry
brilliance" and Mozart's "warm and romantic orchestral
sound to which horns..contribute tellingly." Assesses
Mozart as "true father of the symphonic orchestra."
Summary in German. Many musical examples and numerous
(118) footnotes. Bibliography.

349.   Bushler, David. "Harmonic Structure in Mozart's
       Sonata-form Developments." *MozYb* 1984-85: 15-24.

       Includes tonal analysis of KV 550, last movement.
       Denotes favorite progressions: roots up or down fifths.
       Studies tonality more than harmony.

350.   Dankwardt, Marianne. *Die langsame Einleitung: ihre
       Herkunst und ihr Bau bei Haydn und Mozart.* 2 vols.
       Tutzing: Schneider, 1977.   372, 99p.   ISBN 3-7952-
       0196-9   ML5 M74 v.25 pt.1 (pt.2) 1977

       Relates mostly to slow introduction in symphonies.
       Covers genre before 1750 and its appearance in other
       works before 1780 (France, Mannheim, South and North
       Germany, Salzburg, etc.).   Traces origins, relating
       this to 18th century writings.   Sums up history of
       genre after Mozart and Haydn.   Excellent music exam-
       ples, documentation and bibliography.   Was author's
       1975 dissertation (Ludwig-Maxmilian, Munich).   Impres-
       sive; worthy of translation.

351.   David, Hans T. "Mozart's Modulations." In *The Creative
       World of Mozart*, edited by P.H. Lang, pp. 56-75.
       New York: Norton, 1963.   ISBN 0-393-000218-7

       Focuses on tonality in sonata-allegro, including di-
       verse examples (some from symphonies).

352.   David, Johann Nepomuk. *Die Jupiter-Sinfonie: eine
       Studie über die thematisch-melodischen Zusammenhänge.*
       Göttingen: Verlag Deuerlich, 1953.   39p.   Also Göt-
       tingen: Vandenhoek & Ruprecht, 1956, 1960.

       Claims work rests on cantus (c-d-f-e-a-g-f-e-d-c) and
       shows its connection to symphony's themes.

353.   Davis, Shelley. "Harmonic Rhythm in Mozart's Sonata
       Form." *MR* 27 (1966): 25-42.

Database covers 65 movements, including 9 symphonies (KV 297, 319, 338, 385, 425, 504, 542, 550, 551). Examines harmonic-rhythmic organization underlying tonal framework. Findings: exposition has increasing rate of harmonic change.

354. _____. "Structural Functions of Harmonic Rhythm in Mozart's Sonata-Allegro Form." M.A. thesis, New York Univ., 1960.

Patterns of harmonic progression and rhythm seem to be idiomatic to particular sections of sonata-allegro form. Adviser: LaRue. See entry 353.

355. Dearling, Robert. *The Music of Wolfgang Amadeus Mozart: The Symphonies*. Rutherford, Madison, Teaneck (N.J.): Fairleigh Dickinson Univ. Press, 1982. 224p. ISBN 0-8386-2335-2 MT130 M8 D33

Focuses on non-technical approach, with nominal analysis. Groups works (1-14, 15-34, 35-38 and 39-41) in extracting conclusions. Offers chronological listing of Mozart's symphonies coordinated with those of Haydn. J.C. Bach and others.

356. De Lerma, Dominique-René. "Wolfgang Amadeus Mozart; The Works and Influences of his First Ten Years." Ph.D. dissertation, Indiana Univ., 1958. 315p.

Covers symphonies (pp. 191-206, 238-54) and influences of Abel, J.C. Bach and others less dominant. Bonus: studies of Nannerl and Nameday notebooks and London sketchbook. Biographical calendar (1759-1766) noteworthy. Adviser: Paul Nettl.

357. Della Croce, Luigi. *Le 75 Sinfonie di Mozart. Guide e Analisi Critica*. Turin: Eda, 1977. 316p. MT130 M8 D35

Analyzes all (authentic, questionable and spurious) works, including symphonies for strings, symphonies *concertante* and dramatic symphony (*Thamos re d'Egitto* intermezzo). Provides *incipits* for each movement and discussion of evolution of Mozart's symphonic style with chronological chart of style changes (pp. 41-55).

358.   Deutsch, Otto. *Mozart: a Documentary Biography*.
       Translated by Eric Blom, Jeremy Noble and Peter
       Branscombe. Stanford (CA): Stanford Univ. Press,
       1966. 680p. ISBN 0-8047-0233-0   ML410 M9 D4782 1966

       Valuable collection of documents, with detailed index
       of names and topics and catalog of works. Symphonies
       on p. 624 with comments on about half.

359.   Dickinson, A.E.F. *A Study of Mozart's Last Three Sym-
       phonies*. St. Clair Shores (Mich.): Scholarly Press,
       1978. 58p. ISBN 0-403-0154-3. Repr. of 1927 edition.

       Presents complete and lucid analysis with outlines of
       movements and examples of themes. Glossary of terms.

360.   Dumesnil, René. "Mozart symphoniste." *RM* 14 (1933):
       54-65.

       Takes some exception to Saint-Foix chronology, gives
       more background information on some works but generally
       supports Saint-Foix's efforts.

361.   Engel, Hans. "Haydn, Mozart und die Klassik." *MozJb*
       1959: 46-79.

       Develops definition of classicism from supporting
       literature and relates Haydn and Mozart's symphonies to
       18th century concepts of symphonic form. Bibliography.

362.   _____. "Mozart's Instrumentation." *MozJb* 1956: 51-
       74.

       Studies influence of Baroque style and concentrates
       on individual instrument usage. Shows doubling and
       grouping schemes. Establishes five basic orchestral
       treatments. Examples from all symphonies.

363.   _____. "Die Orchesterwerk." In *W.A. Mozart*, edited
       by Paul Nettl, pp. 106-21. Frankfurt am Main: Fischer,
       1955.

       Covers symphonic style (form mainly) and analyzes
       KV 16, 114, 130, 184, 183, 297, 319, 338, 385, 425,
       504, 504, 543, 550, and 551. Examples (mostly themes).

364. _____. "The Smaller Orchestral Works." In *Moz/Comp*,
      pp. 138-55.

      Shows insight into phrase structure of dance move-
      ments, this relating to dance movements in symphonies.

365. _____. "Über Mozarts Jugendsinfonien." *MozJb* 1951:
      22-33.

      Stresses Haydn's influence on Mozart in symphonies 1-
      29. Divides influences by geographical-composer groups:
      London (J.C. Bach and south German style), Italy (*sin-
      fonia*), Salzburg (Italian influence, Michael Haydn,
      Viennese composers other than Haydn), Paris (Mannheim)
      and final Viennese period where these styles were
      blended.

366. Estes, David John. "Scoring for Wind Instruments in
      the Symphonies of Johann Chrisostimus Wolfgang Ama-
      deus Mozart." M.A. thesis, San Diego State Univ.,
      1973. 293p.

      Traces evolution of wind idiom, noting influences
      (J.C. Bach, Mannheim, etc.) and ending with descrip-
      tion of mature orchestral wind style "unmatched by any
      of his contemporaries." Chronicles life in relation to
      symphonic output.

367. Fellerer, Karl Gustav. "Mozart et l'école de Mann-
      heim." In *Mozart Influences*, pp. 85-90.

      Identifies Mannheim style features materializing in
      Mozart's music, with references to symphonies and to
      use of winds in orchestral works.

368. Fischer, Wilhelm. "W.A. Mozart, der Symphoniker."
      ZhVfS 62/63 (1962): 491-96.

      Brief overview of Mozart's symphonic evolution and
      influences and his place in symphony history.

369. _____. "Eine wiedergefundene Jugendsymphonie
      Mozarts." *MozJb* 1923: 35-68.

Discusses author's discovery of Mozart symphony (Anh.
221/45a) in Lambach monastery and style of work.

370. Floros, Constantin. *Mozart Studien I: Zu Mozarts Sin-
fonik, Opern und Kirchenmusik*. Wiesbaden: Breitkopf
& Härtel, 1979. 172p. ISBN 3-7651-0167-2 ML410 M9
F715 v.1

Includes study of last three symphonies (pp. 7-20)
and opera overtures (pp. 29-72).

371. Gerstenberg, Walter. "Über den langsamen Einleitungs-
satz in Mozarts Instrumentalmusik." In *Festschrift
Fischer/70th*, pp. 25-32.

Speaks primarily to philosophical-stylistic rationale
for slow introduction. Gives chronological work list
(chamber and symphonic) and discusses style of several.

372. Glastras, Thomas. "Thirty-five First Movements of Mozart
Symphonies: Their Structural Development, Distribution
of Instruments and Parts, and Character." M.M. thesis,
Indiana Univ., 1954. 65p.

Studies first 38 symphonies (through KV 202). Defines
four sonata-allegro types and four thematic types.

373. Grove, George. "Mozart's Symphony in G minor." *MT* 48
(1907): 25-28.

Astute analysis. Quotes themes from all movements.

374. Hess, Ernst. "Remarques sur l'authenticité de l'ouverture KV 311a = Anh 8." In *Mozart Influences*,
pp. 227-35. See entry 442.

Identifies specific passages and style mannerisms
that suggest work not written by Mozart.

375. Heuss, Alfred. "Die kleine Sekunde in Mozarts g-moll
Symphonie." *JaP* 40 (1934): 54-60.

Shows unifying of work by an interval that projects
grieving affection into symphony. Analysis (*Hermeneu-
tics*) was in vogue in early 20th century Germany. See
entry 345 for English translation.

376. King, A. Hyatt. *Mozart: a Biography, with a Survey of Books, Editions and Recordings*. Hamden (Conn.): Shoe String Press, 1970. 114p. ML410 M9 K54

     Devotes only 45 pages to life and remainder to references in English (source books and letters, biography, criticism, church works, opera, piano concertos, symphonies, chamber music and miscellaneous).

377. _____. *Mozart in Retrospect: Studies in Criticism and Bibliography*, revised edition. London: Oxford Univ. Press, 1976. ML410 M9 K5

     Appendix 2 lists other appearances of "Jupiter" finale principal theme in Mozart's works and in works by other composers. Appendix 3 covers theme's origins.

378. _____. "Mozart's Counterpoint: Its Growth and Significance." *ML* 26 (1945): 12-20.

     Senses that Mozart's contrapuntal skills in part express his genius. Frequent reference to symphonies.

379. _____. "A Survey of Recent Mozart Literature." *MR* 3 (1942): 248-58.

     Mentions Saint-Foix (entry 410) and Dickinson article (entry 359) on last three symphonies.

380. Kingdon-Ward, Martha. "Mozart and the Bassoon." *ML* 30 (1949): 8-25.

     Covers style and orchestration. Symphonies: pp. 8-9.

381. _____. "Mozart and the Clarinet." *ML* 28 (1947): 126-53.

     Traces history of Mozart's clarinet usage with section on symphonies (pp. 142-44). Lists works with clarinet(s).

382. _____. "Mozart and the Flute." *ML* 35 (1954): 294-312.

     Discusses orchestral style (symphonies, pp. 300-302).

383. _____. "Mozart and the Horn." *ML* 31 (1950): 318-23.

Symphonies stressed on pp. 318-19. Emphasizes technical requirements for horn expected by Mozart.

384. Komorzynski, Egon. "Mozarts Sinfonien als persönliche Bekenntnisse." *Die Musik* 33 (1940-41), pp. 84-87.

Studies last symphonies (425, 504, 543, 550, 551), indicating works point to mature style of Beethoven.

385. Landon, H.C. Robbins. "La crise romantique dans le musique autrichienne vers 1770. Quelques précurseurs inconnus de la symphonie en sol mineur (KV 183) de Mozart." In *Mozart Influences*, pp. 27-47.

Attributes sudden shift by Mozart to more serious style in KV 183 to Viennese "reform" ensuing about 1770, especially in output of Vaňhal and Haydn. Both wrote more somber works in minor keys at that time.

386. _____. "Die Symphonien; ihr geistiger und musikalischer Ursprung und ihre Entwicklung." In *Mozart Aspekte*, edited by Paul Schaller and Hans Kühner, pp. 39-62. Olten & Freiburg: Otto Walter, 1956.

As one of best available descriptions of Mozart's symphonic evolution, stresses early influences and shows similarities between Mozart's themes and those of J.C. Bach and Abel.

387. _____. "Two Orchestral Works Wrongly Attributed to Mozart." *MR* 17 (1956): 29-34.

Asserts that *Musikalische Schlittenfahrt* (Musical Sleigh Ride) is *Sinfonie in F* by Johann Wassmuth and that *Symphony in C Major* (edited by Nino Negrotti and published by Carisch in Milan in 1944) is by Anton Eberl. For confirmation on Eberl, see entry 178.

388. _____, and William Mitchell, editors. *The Mozart Companion*. New York: Norton, 1981. 397p. ISBN 0-393-00499-6 ML410 M9 M63 1981

Articles related to symphony: Blume (Mozart's Style and Influence), Larsen (The Symphonies), Engel (The

Smaller Orchestral Works), Blume (The Concertos: Their Sources), Landon (The Concertos: Their Musical Origin and Development). See those entries. Index. Earlier printings by Rockliff (1956) and Norton (1969).

389. Lang, Paul Henry, ed. *The Creative World of Mozart: Studies by Eminent Scholars in Mozart's Style, Technique, Life, and Works.* New York: Norton, 1963. 149p. ISBN 0-393-00218-7

Originally published in *Musical Quarterly*, symphony-related essays include Hertzmann (Mozart's Creative Process), Lowinsky (On Mozart's Rhythm), David (Mozartean Modulations) and Schmid (Mozart and Haydn). See those entries in this volume.

390. Larsen, Jens Peter. "The Symphonies." In *Moz/Comp*, pp. 156-97.

Concise and cogent coverage of Mozart's evolving symphonic style with some musical examples. Possibly best such discussion available. Bibliography by editors. Index.

391. LaRue, Jan. "Mozart or Dittersdorf - KV 84/73q." *MozJb* 1971/72: 40-49.

Using stylistic analysis (with numerical values for harmonic activity and melodic style), concludes work closer to Mozart than to Dittersdorf. Responses by Anna Amalie Abert and Hermann Beck included.

392. Leeson, Daniel, and Robert D. Levin. "On the Authenticity of K. Anh. C14.01 (297b), a Symphonia Concertante for Four Winds and Orchestra." *MozJb* 1976-77: 90-76.

Using a statistical-structural study of work's form, determines it is probably not by Mozart. Charts compare specifications with other Mozart concertos.

393. Lesure, François. "L'Oeuvre de Mozart en Paris de 1793 à 1810." In *Kongress Vienna/1956*, pp. 344-47.

Mentions performance of symphonies (especially by Conservatory orchestra), quoting contemporary critics.

394. Lowinsky, Edward E. "On Mozart's Rhythm." *MQ* 42
     (1956): 162-86. See also entry 389.

     Findings based on studied irregularity of phrase
     length, metrical stress, diversity of rhythmic motion,
     continuous increase in motion ("increasing animation of
     motion"), strict symmetry, and gradual changes of
     rhythmic motion. Compares Mozart's rhythmic style with
     those of Haydn. J.C. Bach, and Dittersdorf. Supported by
     musical examples, including KV 550 finale.

395. Mahling, Christoph-Hellmut. "Mozart und die Orchester-
     praxis seiner Zeit." *MozJb* 1967: 229-43.

     Concerns size of orchestras and Mozart's scoring for
     each ensemble. Many comments on symphonies. Review of
     literature. Extensive documentation.

396. Münster, Robert. "Authentische Tempi zu den sechs
     letzten Sinfonien W.A. Mozarts?" *MozJb* 1962/63: 185-
     199.

     Provides Hummel's metronome markings for 385, 435,
     504, 543, 550 and 551. Compares these tempi with those
     used by 20th century conductors.

397. _____. "Mozart bearbeitet Cannabich." In *Festschrift
     Senn/70th*, pp. 142-57.

     Describes Mozart's relationship with Cannabich. Fo-
     cuses on early editions of Cannabich's music, especially
     that issued by Gotz (Mannheim).

398. _____. "Neue Funde zu Mozarts symphonischen Jugend-
     werk." *Mitteilungen der internationalen Stiftung
     Mozarteum* 30 (1982): 2-11. Also in *Acta Mo* 28
     (1981).

     Further authentication of KV 45a ("Lambach") symphony
     by music librarian at Munich State Library (discovered
     parts that verified Wolfgang as composer). Thirteen
     symphonies analyzed stylistically in this project were
     on list compiled by Leopold.

399. _____. "Wer ist der Komponist der 'Kindersinfonie'?"
     ActaMo 16 (1969): 76-82.

Reviews data on work, proposing several possible composers. Extensive review of various manuscript sources for work. Lengthy bibliography.

400. _____. "Wiederauffindung und einer verschollenen Jugendsinfonien Wolfgang Amadeus Mozarts durch die Bayerische Staatsbibliothek." *Forum Musikbibliothek* 1981: 32-36.

Discusses KV Anh. 223/19a symphony.

401. Newman, Ernest. "Mozart and Two Symphonies: Changing Points of View." In *More Essays from the World of Music*, pp. 89-93. London: Calder, 1958. ML60 N49

Contrasts writings of Jahn with those of Abert on the aesthetic of symphonies 39 and 40.

402. Newman, Sidney. "Mozart's G minor Quintet (K. 516) and Its Relationship to the G minor Symphony (K. 550)." *MR* 17 (1956): 287-96.

Maintains symphony adopts and adapts main premise of idea discarded for the finale of quintet.

403. Nys, Abbé Carl de. "Mozart et les fils de Jean-Sebastien Bach." In *Mozart Influences*, pp. 91-115.

Stresses influence of Wilhelm Friedmann Bach, in addition to those of J.C. and C.P.E. Bach. Some mention of symphonies.

404. Plath, Wolfgang. "Ein 'geistlicher' Sinfoniesatz Mozarts." *Mf* 27 (1974): 93-95.

Features KV 130 (F major) and KV 132 (E-flat major).

405. Racek, Jan. "Zur Frage des 'Mozarts-Stil' in der tschechischen vorklassischen Musik." In *Kongress Vienna/1956*, pp. 493-524.

Relates Mannheim style to Mozart's style. Profuse illustrations.

406. Rehberg, Karl. "Mozart and die Sinfonie." *Die Musik*
      31 (1938): 104-7.

      Short essay (with some analysis) on final trilogy.

407. Sadie, Stanley. *The New Grove Mozart*. New York: Norton,
      1983. 247p. ISBN 0-393-30084-6

      Updated version of author's Grove article (1980).
      List of works serves as index to all references to works
      in book. Symphonies (listed on pp. 193-97) are discussed
      in sections of book (early symphonies [1-21], pp. 22-26;
      middle [26-28], 40-41; symphonies 32-34, 66-67). Biblio-
      graphy in categories (orchestral on pp. 236-39). Index
      of proper names.

408. Saint-Foix, Georges de. "Une fausse symphonie de
      Mozart." *Le Menestrel* 73 (1907): 228-29.

      Early comment on Michael Haydn work (KV 444/425a) for
      which Mozart wrote first movement's slow introduction.
      Quotes *incipits* for each of the three movements.

409. _____. "Publication d'une symphonie inédite de
      Mozart." *RM1* 28 (1946): 61-4.

      Comments on recently discovered (1943, by Italian
      conductor Nino Negrotti in Cremona library archives of
      Pia Instituzione Musicale) three-movement work. Suggests
      Mozart wrote work during his second Cremona visit in
      1773. Provides *incipits* for three movements. See entry
      387 for final attribution.

410. _____. *The Symphonies of Mozart*. Translated by
      Leslie Orrey. New York: Dover, 1968. 222p.

      Represents republication of original English version
      of 1947 (London: Dennis Dobson) with original French
      volume issued in 1932. Discusses symphonic style evo-
      lution, relating travels and influences to genre's
      maturation. Index has movements' *tempi*. Larsen (entry
      390) and Zaslaw (entry 434) supersede.

411. Schmid, Ernst Fritz. "Mozart and Haydn." In *The Crea-
      tive World of Mozart*, edited by Paul Henry Lang, pp.
      86-102. New York: Norton, 1963. ISBN 0-393-00218-7

Traces differences in breeding, appearance, training and influences and details influences of each composer on the other. First published in *MQ* 47 (1956), 145-61.

412. Schmid, Ernst Fritz. "Zur Entstehungszeit von Mozarts italienischen Sinfonien." *MozJb* 1958: 71-77.

Concerns KV 81 (73-1), 97 (73-n), 84 (73-q) and 74. Provides evidence to authenticate dates.

413. Schneider, Otto, and Anton Algatzy. *Mozart-Handbuch; Chronik - Werk - Bibliographie.* Vienna: Verlag Brüder Hollinek, 1962. 508p. ML410 M9 S365

Chronicle proceeds year-by-year, briefly detailing events and production of works and reinforcing with bibliographical references. Information on symphonies starts on page 157. Comments on each work also supported by references. Bibliography has 3,871 entries with its own index (pp. 457-73). Extremely valuable for all aspects of Mozart research.

414. Senn, Walter. "Zu den Sinfonien KV Anh. C 11.10, 11.11 und 11.12." *MozJb* 1968/70: 391-97.

Discusses genealogy of symphonies attributed to Holzmann (11.12), Pleyel (11.10) and Gyrowetz (11.11).

415. Sievers, Gerd. "Analyse des Finale aus Mozarts Jupiter-Symphonie." *Mf* 7 (1954): 318-31.

Analyzes movement with references to previous efforts and reviews origin of principal theme.

416. Souper, F.O. "Mozart's Haffner Symphony." *MMR* 63 (1933): 123-24.

Relates events surrounding composition of work, with quotes from Mozart's letters. Analyzes first movement as "sonata-fugue hybrid." Shows finale's use of Osmin's theme from *Abduction*.

417. _____. "The Prague Symphony. Mozart K. 504." *MMR* 57 (1927): 230-31.

Provides insight into events related to work and into thematic similarities between it and *Don Giovanni* and *Figaro*.

418. Steger, B. Werner. "Rhythmischen Kernformeln in Mozarts letzten Sinfonien." *Mf* 23 (1970): 41-50.

Proposes that each of last three symphonies has an underlying rhythmic motive that unifies work.

419. Subotnik, Rose Rosengard. "Evidence of a Critical World View in Mozart's Last Three Symphonies." In *Festschrift Lang*, pp. 29-43.

Offers that "the three last symphonies give musical articulation to an incipient shift in philosophical outlook; this shift showed itself in a number of ways in number of late 18th-century works of genius, took on concrete implications with the success of the French Revolution, and marked a decisive turn in Western cultural beliefs toward..a modern world view."

420. Tenschert, Roland. "Die Ouvertüren Mozarts." *MozJb* 2 (1924): 109-81.

Presents analysis of 22 overtures, emphasizing types of sonata-allegro, tonality, rhythm and connection to each opera. Stresses formal detail.

421. Tovey, Donald Francis. *Essays in Musical Analysis.* London: Oxford Univ. Press, 1981. 561p. ISBN 0-19-315146-4 MT90 T6 1981

Mozart symphonies included: 297, 330, 425, 543, 550 and 551. Is one-volume version of two-volume 1935 edition.

422. Tyson, Allan. "The Slow Movements of Mozart's Paris Symphony, K 297." *MT* 122 (1981): 17-20.

Establishes to some extent that 3/4 *Andante* movement was first version while the 6/8 *Andantino* was second.

423. Valentin, Erich. "Mozart und die Sinfonie." *ÖMz* 11 (1956): 18-20.

Proposes that Mozart was far more important in development of symphony than is usually recognized, especially in the expressive dimension.

424. Verchaly, André, ed. *Étrangères dans l'oeuvre de W.A. Mozart.* Paris: Éditions du Centre National de la Recherche Scientifique, 1958? ML410 M9

Mounts superior effort to show concretely how Mozart was influenced by multitude of styles. Four papers related to symphonies: Fellerer (entry 367), Landon (385), Nys (403) and Wirth (428). In French.

425. Warren, Raymond. "Introduction and Allegro: A Mozartian Study." *MMR* 88 (1958): 164-69.

Studies unity between introduction and subsequent *Allegro* in instrumental works, including Linz and Prague symphonies.

426. Westrup, Jack A. "Cherubino and the g minor Symphony." In *Fanfare for Ernest Newman*, pp. 181-91. London: Arthur Barker, 1955.

Theorizes that symphony's first movement is related to Cherubino's aria, "Non so piu cosa son," in the aria's restless nature and in the style of its orchestral accompaniment. Stimulating.

427. Whitwell, David Elbert. "The First Nine Symphonies of Mozart: An Examination of Style." Ph.D. dissertation, Catholic Univ., 1964. 176p.

Establishes influence of J.C. Bach, Abel and Viennese composers of period and isolates unique Mozart style features (chromaticism, etc.) which begin to appear in early works.

428. Wirth, Helmut. "Mozart et Haydn." In *Mozart Influences*, pp. 49-57.

Traces Haydn's influence on Mozart, citing specific works, including symphonies.

429. Wollenberg, Susan. "The Jupiter Theme: New Light on its Creation." *MT* 116 (1975): 781-83.

Tracks origin back to Fux and *stylus antiquus* tradition in Vienna.

430. Zaslaw, Neal. "The 'Lambach' symphonies of Wolfgang and Leopold Mozart." In *Festschrift Lang*, pp. 15-20.

Presents careful historical analysis of two symphonies discovered in Lambach (Austria) monastery in 1923. One was assigned to Wolfgang (Anh. 221/45a), the other to Leopold (G16). Abert (entry 330) later supported a reverse parentage. Zaslaw backs original assignments.

431. _____. "Leopold Mozart's list of his son's works." In *Festschrift Brook*, pp. 323-58.

Coverage includes changes in the identity of some of 13 symphonies listed by Leopold.

432. _____. "Mozart, Haydn, and the *Sinfonia da chiesa*." *JM* 1 (1982): 95-124.

First, proves existence of church symphonies by study of 18th century writings, noting lack of details on exact nature of church symphonic style. Second, observes that composers either wrote in a specific church style or used concert symphonies for same purpose. Questions Landon's assumptions on slow first movement in church symphonies and on instrumental music restrictions in Holy Week masses. Excellent documentation.

433. _____. "Mozart's Paris Symphonies." *MT* 119 (1978): 753-57.

Covers events related to Mozart's Paris stay, trying to identify other symphony presented. Suggests Mozart possibly never wrote KV 311a/Anh. 8. (See also Hess, entry 374.) Extra benefit: Mozart's definition of Parisian taste in symphonic music around 1778.

434. _____. *Mozart's Symphonies: Context, Performance Practice, Reception*. London: Oxford Univ. Press, 1990 (projected). 800p.

Studies the almost 100 symphonies associated with Mozart, each work's place in his symphonic evolution, the performance traditions associated with 18th century orchestral music, and the cultural ambience affecting his symphonies. Information provided by publisher in advance of publication. Not examined.

435. Zaslaw, Neal, and Cliff Eisen. "Signor Mozart's Symphony in A Minor, K. Anhang 220 = 16a." *JM* 4 (1985-86): 191-206.

Work found in Odense (Denmark) in 1982 and later recorded on Unicorn-Kanchana DKP-9039. In spite of Larsen's authentication, questions whether either Wolfgang or Leopold wrote it. Good documentation.

Carlo d'Ordonez (1738-1786)[g,b]

436. Brown, A. Peter. *Carlo d'Ordonez (1734-86): A Thematic Catalog*. Detroit: Information Coordinators, 1978. 234p. ISBN 0-911772-89-8 ML113 D48 No. 39

Group I (symphonies) has bibliographical entries for some symphonies, specimens of watermarks and selected copyists' hands. High quality printing.

437. _____. "An Introduction to the Life and Works of Carlo d'Ordonez." In *Festschrift Kaufmann*, pp. 243-60.

Written sightly later than 1979 Garland volume (entry 438), covers overall output while dwelling on symphonic style (pp. 248-53). Excellent documentation.

438. _____. *Carlo d'Ordonez: Seven Symphonies* in *Symphony*, series B, vol. IV. xxxi, 255p.

Summarizes latest research on rarely-known composer, supplies brief bibliography and provides data on his 73 symphonies. Adds careful analysis of seven edited works and thematic index of symphonies. See also Landon's review in *HYb XIII* (1982), 244-49.

439. _____."The Symphonies of Carlo d'Ordonez: A Contribution to the History of Viennese Instrumental Music during the Second Half of the Eighteenth Century." *HYb XII* (1981): 5-121.

Studies 73 surviving authentic symphonies in three style periods, analyzes form (overall and movements),

tonality, orchestration, function (church, chamber or
theater) and gradual evolution of composer's mature
style. Also emphasizes authenticity, copyists and
printings. Only available detailed study of works.
Discusses plagiaristic practices of various copyists.
See David Young's comments and Brown's response in *HYb*
XVI (1985), 248-58 ("Correspondence").

Marian Carl Paradeiser (1747-1775)[g,b]

440. Freeman, Robert N., ed. *Marian Carl Paradeiser:*
      Symphonies 2, 3, 4 in *Symphony*. series B, vol. VI
      (Austrian Cloister Symphonists), pp. xxxv-xliv, lv-
      lvii, 279-335.

      Although a progressive Austrian cloister symphonist,
      wrote only three symphonies and one overture. Editor's
      discussion of works and their analysis is thorough.
      Bibliography. See Landon's review in *HYb XV* (1984),
      pp. 233-39. See thematic index in reference volume, p.
      411.

Wenzel Pichl (1741-1805)[g,b]

441. Zakin, Anita, and Richard J. Agee, editors. *Wenzel*
      Pichl: Three Symphonies in *Symphony*, series B, vol.
      VII, pp. xlix-lxviii, 149-267.

      Agee's biographical sketch quotes Dlabac's *Allgemeines*
      historisches Kunstler-Lexicon (1815) to establish basic
      dates and facts. Zakin's thematic index lists 36 authen-
      tic, 3 questionable and 9 spurious works, in contrast to
      Slonimsky's (*Baker* fifth edition) attribution of 89
      symphonies, 66 of which Pichl published. Thematic index
      is in series' reference volume (1986), pp. 416-23.

Antonio Salieri (1750-1825)[g,b]

442. Hettrick, Jan Schatkin, and Gordana Lazarevich, edi-
      tors. *Antonio Salieri: Three Symphonies, One Over-*
      ture in *Symphony*, series B, vol. II (Italians in
      Vienna), pp. xlix-lxxii, 159-368.

      Begins with five-page biography. followed by short
      discussion of symphonies (mostly drawn from operas) and
      extensive notes on each edited work. Salieri usually
      "assembled" a single concert symphony from several

opera overtures. Editor identifies these sources in edited scores and feels that Salieri's 40 operas may have spawned additional symphonies. Thematic index lists only five.

Franz Schneider (1737-1812)[g,b]

443. Robert N. Freeman, ed. *Franz Schneider: Symphony Q: C1* in *Symphony*, series B, vol. VI (Austrian Cloister Symphonists), pp. xxxiii-xxxv, 253-78.

Contains both brief biography and analysis of edited work. Thematic index lists only two symphonies, both questionable. See Landon's review in *HYb XV* (1984), pp. 233-39.

Franz Xaver Süssmayr (1766-1803)[g,b]

444. Inwood, Mary B.B., ed. *Franz Xaver Süssmayr: One Symphony* in *Symphony*, series B, vol. XIV, pp. lxiii-lxvii, 211-65.

Known primarily for his completion of Mozart's *Requiem*, Süssmayr composed two symphonies, including *Sinfonia turchesca* (Turkish Symphony) edited for this volume. Introduction emphasizes Süssmayr's life and popularity of Turkish music in 18th century. Examines carefully archaic Turkish instruments used in score but neglects symphonic style and analysis of edited work. No thematic included. Short bibliography.

Jan Krtitel Vaňhal (Johann Baptist Vaňhal) (1739-1813)[g,b]

445. Bryan, Paul Robey, Jr. "The Symphonies of Vaňhal." 2 vols. Ph.D. dissertation, Univ. of Michigan, 1955. 338, 168p.

While an early American study of preclassical symphony, effort is scholarly, authentic and insightful into emerging classic style. Years later Bryan would edit additional works for *Symphony* series. This study covers entire symphonic output and examines 17 early works by studying style through analysis of melodic style of first movement themes. Very effective study with thematic index and restored scores of six works.

446. _____, ed. *Jan Krtitel Vaňhal: Five Symphonies* in
     Symphony, series B, vol. X, pp. xli-lxxvi, 275-482.

     Contains translation of Dlabacz' biography (1815) and
     careful study of symphonic style. Concludes, in part,
     that most symphonies were in four movements, were seri-
     ous in style (little divertimento taint). Used sonata-
     allegro in first, second and fourth movements, and
     avoided contrapuntal textures. Analyzes edited works
     and adds thematic index of 76 symphonies (46 either
     possibly authentic, questionable or highly questionable
     works) plus 1 overture and 5 cassations.

Georg Christoph Wagenseil (1715-1777)[g,b]

447. Horwitz, Karl. "Georg Christoph Wagenseil als Symphon-
     iker." Ph.D. dissertation, Univ. of Vienna, 1906.

     Horwitz, a student of Guido Adler, followed his men-
     tor's lead in challenging Riemann's claim that Mannheim
     was primary precursor of symphonic classical style and
     link to Haydn style. Shows that Wagenseil's motivic
     developmental style was similar to that of Haydn, that
     he used *crescendo* before Stamitz and that his style was
     equal to those of Mannheim composers in forecasting
     Haydn's style.

448. Kucaba, John, ed. *Georg Christoph Wagenseil: Fifteen
     Symphonies* in *Symphony*, series B, vol. III, 382p.

     Biography shows high level of scholarship and sophis-
     tication and precedes historically and analytically ri-
     gorous commentary on scores edited. Thematic index has
     63 authentic, 20 questionable, 7 spurious and 4 incor-
     rectly identified (3 chamber, 1 concerto) works. Asserts
     that Wagenseil was master of early Viennese concert sym-
     phony who "convincingly transferred *galant* style to the
     symphonic medium (and) stabilized the form...at mid-
     century." Bonus: thematic index of Breitkopf's *Raccolta
     delle megliore Sinfonie* (1761-1762) and photocopy of one
     of three Wagenseil works arranged for keyboard in this
     collection. See review by Landon in *HYb XV* (1984), 233-
     39. See entry 116.

449. _____. "The Symphonies of Georg Christoph Wagenseil."
     2 vols. Ph.D. dissertation, Boston Univ., 1967.
     196, 336p.

Considered a transitional composer by Kucaba, Wagenseil was greatest Viennese symphonist in late 1750s and
early 1760s, this borne out by thorough analysis of 41
sinfonias from period. Discusses Wagenseil's printers
(Huberty, Venier, Boyer, Walsh and others) and offers
description of pre-1740 Viennese sinfonia. Concludes
with thematic index and two edited symphonies (No. 37,
E; No. 48, G). See also entry 448.

450. Roeder, Michael Thomas. "The Preclassical Symphony
with an Analysis of Representative Works by Georg
Christoph Wagenseil." 2 vols. M.A. thesis, Univ. of
New Mexico, 1968. 81, 62p.

Somewhat limited coverage of genre has been supple-
mented by later studies. Includes two scorings: Kucaba
36 (Garland E3) and Kucaba 25 (Garland D10). Former
also included in Garland series (entry 448).

451. Scholz-Michelitsch, Helga. *Das Orchester- und Kammer-
musikwerk von Georg Christoph Wagenseil: Thematischer
Katalog.* Vienna: H. Böhlaus, 1972. ISBN 3-205-
03175-X ML134 W27 S43

While published later than Kucaba thesis (entry 449),
to some extent is superceded by Kucaba's later index in
Garland series (entry 448). Symphonies and overtures
located on pp. 95-160. Thematic index has *incipits*
for all movements and adds bibliographical references
for many works, both attributes missing from Kucaba
index. Latter is more specific on authentication.

Paul Wranitzky (1756-1808)[g,b]

452. LaRue, Jan. "A 'Hail and Farewell' Quodlibet Symphony."
ML 37 (1956): 250-59.

Work begins with slow introduction with players gradually entering stage. Five movements quote two Austrian folk songs, a Paisiello tune, Mozart's "Non piu
andrai" (*Nozze*) and *Zauberflöte* overture (altered), a
Lowenherz march, a Salieri quartet, a Weigl opera aria,
a Mayr tune, and others. Wrote 61 symphonies and even
more (100+) chamber works.

Johann Georg Zechner (1716-1778)[g,b]

453. Freeman, Robert N., ed. *Johann Georg Zechner: Sym-
      phonies* in *Symphony*, series B, vol. VI (Austrian
      Cloister Symphonists), pp. xiii-xx, xlv-xlvi, 1-31.

      Introduction delineates role of monastery in growth
      of Austrian symphony and breadth of symphonic activity
      in each community. Briefly covers Zechner's life and
      symphonies, with analysis of two edited works. Thematic
      index has eight questionable symphonies. See Landon
      review in *HYb XV* (1984), pp. 233-39.

Bohemia

General

454. Dlabacž, Gottfried Johann. *Allgemeines historisches
      Künstler-Lexicon für Böhmen und zum Theil auch für
      Mähren und Schlesien.* 3 vols. Prague: Haase, 1815.
      Reprint by Hildesheim (Olms), 1973.

      Bohemia's first encyclopedia of its cultural history,
      covering music, literature and the arts. Draws upon
      author's direct contact with writers, composers and
      artists. Includes many of 18th century Czech composers
      and musicians important in growth of symphony.

455. Garrett, Edith Vogl. "The Influence of 18th Century
      Czech Composers on the Development of Classical Music."
      In *The Czechoslovak Contribution to World Culture*.
      Edited by Misolav Rechcigl, Jr., pp. 134-40. The
      Hague/London/Paris: Mouton, 1964.

      Infers influence of Stamitz, Benda and other Czech
      composers on Mozart, Beethoven and others. Valuable in
      its disclosure of specific Czech style traits. Covers
      Stamitz' symphonic style thoroughly. Thesis may be
      overstated but tends to explain leadership of early
      Czech composers.

456. Jirák, Karel B. "Music in Czechoslovakia." In *The
      Czechoslovak Contribution to World Culture*. Edited
      by Miloslav Rechcigl, Jr., pp. 119-33. The
      Hague/London/Paris: Mouton, 1964.

Brief history of Czech music with bibliography; limited but useful because of Czech sources quoted.

457. Nettl, Paul. "The Czechs in Eighteenth-Century Music." *ML* 21 (1949): 362-70.

Stresses importance of church music, literary brotherhoods and choirs, private choirs, emigration of Czech musicians, Mannheim school, and influence of folk music on Stamitz (in particular, the minuet themes in symphonies).

458. Racek, Jan. "Die tschechische Musik des 18. Jahrhunderts und ihre Stellung in der europäischen Musikkultur." In *Festschrift Schmidt-Görg/70th*, pp. 296-308.

Identifies four streams of Czech composers: western Europe (Stamitz), southern Europe (Myslivecek), Vienna (Tuma, Gassmann, Vaňhal) and east (Poland and Russia). Stresses that Czech composers were part of primary source connecting preclassic with high classic.

Bohemian Composers

Josef Bárta (ca. 1746-1787)[g,b]

459. Rutová, Milada, ed. *Josef Bárta: Two Symphonies* in *Symphony*, series B, vol. XIII, pp. xxxiii-xxxix, 191-248.

Very brief discussion of life and symphonies prefaces thematic index of 13 authentic works. See 1975 dissertation (Charles Univ. of Prague) by Jaromír Havlík on symphonies of Bartá and Laube (not examined).

František Xaver Brixi (1731-1771)[g,b]

460. Novák, Vladimír, ed. *František Xaver Brixi: (Two Symphonies)* in *Symphony*, series B, vol. XII (The Symphony in Bohemia), pp. xxix-xxxii, xlii, 183-232.

Novák's introduction (translated by Mark Germer), drawn from his *NGDMM* article, covers biography, symphonic style and discussion of two edited works. Thematic index lists three symphonies. Notes editor's ownership of unpublished thematic catalog of Brixi's works.

Georg Druschetzky (1745-1819)[g,b]

461. Powley, Harrison, ed. *Georg Druschetzky: Two Sympho-
     nies* in *Symphony*, series B, vol. XIV, pp. xxxv-liv,
     71-157.

     Extensive introduction features detailed biography
     and discussion of symphonic style, careful analysis of
     two edited works, bibliography and thematic index of
     25 extant and 2 lost symphonies.

František Xaver Dušek (1760-1812)[g,b]

462. Altner, Vladimír, ed. *Frantisek Xaver Dusek: (Four
     Symphonies)* in *Symphony*, series B, vol. XII (The Sym-
     phony in Bohemia), pp. xxi-xxviii, xxxvii-xli, 69-
     181.

     Introduction includes biography, short discussion of
     sources of edited works and brief coverage of style and
     limited analysis of four symphonies. Thematic index
     shows 38 authentic, 1 questionable and 2 spurious sym-
     phonies; 16 are in four movements.

Jan Ladislav Dussek (1760-1812)[g,b]

463. Craw, Howard Allen. "A biography and thematic catalog
     of the works of J.L. Dussek (1760-1812)." Ph.D. dis-
     sertation, Univ. of Southern California, 1964. 489p.

     Dussek wrote only one symphonic work, a *concertante*
     for two pianos and orchestra, known to some as the
     first romantic two-piano concerto. Thesis is basis for
     editor's *New Grove* article. Thematic index is chrono-
     logical with indices for opus numbers and for titles.

464. _____, ed. *Jan Ladislav Dussek: One Symphonie concer-
     tante* in *Symphony*, series B, vol. XI, pp. xxxiii-
     xlii, 179-260.

     Includes a markedly shortened version of author's
     earlier biography and a brief description of the *con-
     certante*. Score is photocopy of copyist's score in
     Berlin Staatsbibliothek preussischer Kulturbesitz.

Antonín Kammel (1730-ca. 1787)[g,b]

465. Pilková, Zdenka, ed. *Antonín Kammel: Two Symphonies* in *Symphony*, series B, vol. XIII, pp. xvii-xxii, 25-87.

Offers a useful symphonic style description (prefers three movements, homophony and "advanced" sonata from in later works), a short biography and an analysis of the two works. Can be noted as skillful orchestrator. No thematic index included.

Antonín Laube (1718-1784)[g,b]

466. Rutová, Milada, ed. *Antonín Laube: One Symphony* in *Symphony*, series B, vol. XIII, pp. xi-xvi, 1-23.

Composed 16 authentic symphonies (see thematic index), using four-movement form in only three. Style description is minimal but notes emphasis on homophonic textures. See dissertation mentioned in entry 459.

Vincenc Mašek (1755-1831)[g,b]

467. Pesková, Jitřenka, ed. *Vincenc Mašek: One Symphony* in *Symphony*, series B, vol. XIII, pp. xli-xlvi, 249-95.

Known for his music for wind ensembles, Masek's symphonies were probably written between 1780 and 1800. His compositional skills are described as "more characteristic of the 1760's." No thematic index.

Josef Mysliveček (1717-1781)[g,b]

468. Pilková, Zdeňka, ed. *Josef Mysliveček: Three Symphonies* in *Symphony*, series B, vol. XIII, pp. xxv-xxxi, 89-189.

Mysliveček's operas established him as a major composer. His style often was confused with that of Mozart. Exact symphonic output is unknown but probably is in excess of 25 (with opera *sinfonias*), most in three movements. The use of themes with strong Czech folk roots is noted in some symphonies. Editor's symphonic style summary and analyses of works supports these generalizations. No thematic index is available.

Franz Christoph Neubauer (ca. 1760-1795)^{g,b}

469. Sjoerdsma, Robert David. "The Instrumental Works of
      Franz Christoph Neubauer." Ph.D. dissertation, Ohio
      State Univ., 1970. 585p.

      Wrote 11 symphonies including *La Bataille*, a program
      symphony. Favors three-movement form. Development
      sections more adventuresome with third relation modula-
      tions and changes of mode. Generally wrote, however, in
      a style typical of period.

470. Wright, Elizabeth, ed. *Franz Christoph Neubauer: One
      Symphony* in *Symphony*, series B, vol. XIV, pp. lv-lxi,
      159-210.

      Contains well-developed biography and analysis of
      program symphony edited for series. Work memorializes
      battle in which Russians and Austrians defeat Turks at
      Martinestie on Sept. 22, 1784. Has seven movements,
      each with subtitle and depicting stage of battle.
      Lacks thematic index for 18 symphonies (11 extant).

Antoine Reicha (1770-1836)^{g,b}

471. Fisher, Stephen C., ed. *Antoine Reicha: Two Symphonies*
      in *Symphony*, series B, vol. IX, pp. xi-xiv, xxi-xxx,
      141-242.

      Opens with lengthy biography and discussion of sym-
      phonies, noting four-movement form favored and degree
      of conformity of first movement form with Reicha's
      description (*la grande coupe binaire*) in his 1832
      treatises. Summarizes Reicha's definition and compares
      dimensions of Reicha's movements with those of the
      treatise. Valuable approach. Both scores are facsimile
      autograph scores with marginal legibility.

472. Šotolová, Olga. *Antonín Rejcha*. Prague: Supraphon,
      1977.

      Contains thematic catalog of entire output, including
      symphonies. Not examined.

Antonín Vranický (Wranitzky) (1761-1820)g,b

473. Hennigová-Dubová, Eva, ed. *Antonín Vranický: Symphony
      in C minor* in *Symphony*, series B, vol. XII (The Sym-
      phony in Bohemia), pp. xxxii-xxxv, xlv-xlvii, 233-
      329.

      Introduction (translated by Mark Germer) based on
      author's dissertation on Vranický's symphonies (Charles
      Univ. in Prague, 1968; not examined) and offers concise
      style discussion (some preference for program works,
      use of mature Viennese classic four-movement form with
      strong influence by Haydn, and some expansion of or-
      chestration). Thematic index lists 13 extant works.

Croatia

General

474. Županović, Lovro. *Centuries of Croatian Music.* Trans-
      lated by Vladimir Ivir, vol. 1. Zagreb: Music Infor-
      mation Center, Zagreb Concert Management, 1984.
      206p. ISBN 0-919660-52-1

      Covers medieval, renaissance, baroque and classic.
      Discussion of 18th century symphony starts on p. 118.
      Matters of style reinforced by several full score exam-
      ples. Originally published in 1980 as part of one-vol-
      ume history. Later up-dated and issued in English as
      three volumes, this entry being edition's first volume.

Croatian Composers

Julije Bajamonti (1744-1800)g

475. Saula, Dorde. "Oktriće Bajamontijevih simfonija" (Dis-
      covery of Bajamonti's symphonies). *Vjesnik*, July 24,
      1975.

      "Djodrle Saula's article is a newspaper review on the
      concert of July 19, 1975 in Split. There were played 5
      symphonies on the concert. It was supposed that their
      author was Bajamonti, but Ivan Bošković, the musicolo-
      gist from Split and author of the assumption, has not
      still (*sic*) proved it." (From letter to author from Dr.
      Lovro Županović, dated June 23, 1987.)

476. Županović, Lovro, ed. *Julije Bajamonti: One Symphony*
      in *Symphony*, series F, vol. VIII (The Symphony in
      Croatia), pp. xix-xxii, xxv, 31-53.

      Excellent discussion of Croatian music history pre-
      faces short introduction to Bajamonti's life and works.
      An Italian by birth, was physician by profession who
      wrote mostly church music. In 1975 nine unsigned sym-
      phonies were found in Split cathedral archives and at-
      tributed to Bajamonti by musicologist Ivan Bošković.
      Bojan Bujić, in his *NGDMM* article, lists all ten
      symphonies. Županović discounts attribution as lacking
      any credible documentation. Places style of edited
      work close to that of Viennese composers of period.
      Thematic index of single symphony and bibliography.

Amandus Ivančić (Ivanschiz) (fl. mid-18th century)[g,b]

477. Pokorn, Danilo, ed. *Amandus Ivančič: Two Symphonies* in
      Symphony, series B, vol. XIV, pp. xiii-xxiv, 1-44.

      Contains brief biography but extended study of sym-
      phonies (early classic, half in 4 movements, transi-
      tional developments in "Italian" style, modest orches-
      tration) with thematic index of 21 authentic and 1
      questionable work. Short bibliography indicates fair
      amount of earlier research.

478. Županović, Lovro. "Amando Ivančič i njegove simfonije"
      (Amando Ivančič and his symphonies) in *Spomenici
      hrvatske glazbene prolosti* (Monuments of the Croatian
      Musical Past), VI, VII, pp. 3-27. Zagreb: Music In-
      formation Center, Zagreb Concert Mgt., 1975, 1976.

      Introductory essay on Ivančič's symphonies, later
      issued in English (entry 474). Worked primarily in
      Pauline monastery in Graz (1755-58) and in other such
      communities surrounding Croatia.

Luka Sorkočevič (1734-1789)[g,b]

479. Kos, Koraljka. "Luka Sorkočevič i njegov doprinos
      pretklasičnoj instrumentalnoj muzici: Bilješke o
      kompozicijskom slogu i prilog stilskoj analizi nje-
      gova djela" (Luka Sorkočevič and his contribution to
      the preclassical instrumental style; remarks on the

compositional texture and a contribution to the stylistic analysis of his works). *Arti musices* 5 (1974): 67-93.

Summarized in English by author. Composer was minor figure who, most importantly, studied with Rinaldo di Capua in Rome in 1757. Stresses effect of this study on both composer's Italian style and his place in pre-classicism. Many musical examples.

480. _____, ed. *Luka Sorkočević: Two Symphonies* in *Symphony*, series F, vol. VIII (The Symphony in Croatia), pp. xv-xviii, xxiii-xxiv, 1-29.

Stresses early Italianate preclassic style of symphonies (3 movements, immature Rococo form of fast movements, uneven phrase lengths, homophonic texture) and lists 10 symphonies and 2 overtures in thematic index, all written between 1754 and 1770.

Denmark

General

481. Hatting, Carsten E., Niels Krabbe and Nanna Schiødt, editors. *The Symphony in Denmark* in *Symphony*, series F, vol. VI. xlvi, 377p.

Encompasses short history of music life in Copenhagen (1720-1840), review of Danish symphonies during that period and biographical sketches and analyses of select symphonies of Croubelis, Gerson, Johann Ernst Hartmann, Johan Peter Emilius Hartmann, Shall and Weyse.

482. Schousboe, Torben. "Danske Symfonier. En Kronologi" (Danish Symphonies. A Chronology). Mimeograph. Copenhagen: Musicological Institute of Copenhagen University, 1968. 14p.

Lists 292 symphonies by 96 composers written in Denmark, 1747-1965. Extracted from list are several summaries: each composer's output, output by years, etc. Available from Copenhagen University or from main library, California State University, Fullerton, Calif., 92634.

483. Winkel, Erling. "Danske Symfonier i det 18. Aarhundrede" (Danish symphonies in the 18th century). *DaM* 15 (1940): 172-76, 201-4; 16 (1941): 7-13.

Represents checklist of symphonies written in Denmark by Danish or foreign composers before 1800. Only four printed works from the period seem to exist, but list contains titles and information on about 60 ms. symphonies in Danish libraries. Adds introduction with short description of uses of symphonies in Denmark in second half of 18th century and organizes repertoire in four groups: early sinfonia or concerto; Italian symphonies; north German symphonies; and classical (*Wienerklassiske*) symphonies. Abridged from description supplied by Carsten E. Hatting.

Danish Composers

Simoni dall Croubelis (ca. 1727-ca. 1790)

484. Hatting, Carsten E., Niels Krabbe and Nanna Schiødt, editors. *Simoni dall Croubelis: (Two Symphonies)* in *Symphony*, series F, vol. VI (The Symphony in Denmark), pp. xvii-xix, xxxv-xxxvi, 1-54.

Called a *Kleinmeister* by editors, Croubelis was virtually unknown until recent research unearthed some of his works in Royal Library (Copenhagen). Thematic index reveals 12 symphonies, 1 overture and 1 *symphonie concertante*. Seven are in three movements; two finales are fugues. Four are entitled *symphonies concertantes*, but only one fits that definition. Latter is one of edited scores; contains solo group of flute, 2 clarinets and 2 horns.

485. Krabbe, Niels. "Simoni dall Croubelis - Compositeur ved Musiquen - København 1787" (Simoni dall Croubelis - composer and musician - Copenhagen 1787). *MF(Da)* 3 (1977): 11-25.

Discusses large manuscript collection in Royal Library of Copenhagen, comprising about 80 almost exclusively instrumental works from last half of 18th century. All appear in same hand, were probably written in Copenhagen and are either anonymous or attributed to "Simon" or "Croubelis," both probably same person. Relationship between composer and C.W.H.R.R. Giedde (known as patron,

collector, musical amateur) discussed since composer's
manuscripts were part of this Giedde collection (one of
most important holdings of 18th century music in that
library). Abridged from description provided by Niels
Krabbe.

Johann Ernst Hartmann (1726-1793)[g,b]

486. Hatting, Carsten E., Niels Krabbe and Nanna Schiødt,
      editors. *Johann Ernst Hartmann: (One Symphony)* in
      Symphony, series F, vol. VI (The Symphony in Den-
      mark), pp. xx-xxii, xxxvii, 55-82.

      As one of founding fathers of modern Danish music,
      was patriarch of family of musicians important in Den-
      mark since 1760, founder of Danish *singspiel* and an
      early composer of Danish romance. Little mention of
      his symphonies or their style; notes existence of 12,
      most now lost. Edited work (4 movements) has optional
      minuet from Lund University library. Thematic index.

Claus Nielsen Schall (1757-1835)[g,b]

487. Hatting, Carsten E., Niels Krabbe and Nanna Schiødt,
      editors. *Clauss Nielsen Schall: (One Symphony)* in
      Symphony, series F, vol. VI (The Symphony in Denmark),
      pp. xxii-xxiii, xxxix, 83-142.

      Known primarily as skillful conductor, produced only
      3 symphonies, including 2 *symphonies concertantes* (all
      dating around 1780/1790). No analysis of edited sym-
      phony nor style commentary included. Includes flutes,
      oboes, clarinets, bassoon, horns and strings. Movements
      are lengthy but still compatible with period styles.
      Thematic index.

Christoph Ernst Friedrich Weyse (1774-1842)[g,b]

488. Hatting, Carsten E., Niels Krabbe and Nanna Schiødt,
      editors. *Christoph Ernst Friedrich Weyse: (One Sym-
      phony)* in *Symphony*, series F, vol. VI, pp. xxiii-xxv,
      xli-xlii, 143-92.

      Original versions of symphonies completed prior to
      1800, with 5 of 7 revised between 1797 and 1838; added
      clarinets, trombones and timpani to *Symphony 4* in 1817.
      All revisions were remedy to flagging public support.

Editors omit both analysis of edited work (autograph of
Symphony 7) and overall style discussion. Thematic
index.

489. Lunn, Sven. "Schall og Weyse." *DaM* 11 (1936): 36-38.

Introduction to a Copenhagen public performance of
Schall's bassoon concerto (ca. 1790) and Weyse's *Symphony
No. 6 in C minor* (1798). Explains town's musical culture
ca. 1800 and position of two composers. Abridged from
materials supplied by Carsten E. Hatting.

England and British Isles

General

490. (Anon.) "An Eighteenth-Century Directory of London
      Musicians." *GaSJ* 2 (1949): 27-31.

Reproduction, in part, of Mortimer's *London Universal
Directory* (1763) of "Masters and Professors of Music and
Musical Instrument Makers, including Organ-Builders;"
e.g., "Abel,____, composer of Music and Teacher on the
Harpsichord. At Mr. Herve's, Watch-maker, in Greek-
street, Soho." See also Lyndesay G. Langwill's article
on London directories (entry 503).

491. Busby, Thomas. *Concert Room and Orchestra Anecdotes of
      Music and Musicians*. 3 vols. London: Clement,
      Knight & Lacey, 1825.

Encompasses composers and musicians who appeared in
England in the late 18th and early 19th centuries, including Arne, Boyce, Haydn and others.

492. Cudworth, Charles L. "The English Symphonists of the
      Eighteenth Century." *PRMA* 78 (1952): 31-51.

By far the most precise portrayal in its time, concise
and accurate, drawing upon materials in the British
Museum. Added thematic index in 1953 (entry 495) of 158
works studied. Both article and index were republished
as Kraus reprint in 1969 (Nendein/Lichtenstein). In 1983
LaRue further expanded index with additional composers,
music and documentation data (entry 497).

493. _____. "An Essay by John Marsh." *ML* 36 (1955): 155-64.

Comments on comparison between Baroque and Classic styles in 18th century London periodical, *The Monthly Musical Magazine* 2 (1796). Symphonic style is an important focus of article.

494. _____. "Symphonie" (England), in *MGG*, vol. 12, 1826-28.

Studies genre from time of Purcell to 1800 and includes most native English composers (Arne, Boyce, Erskine, Collett, Norris, Rush, Bates, Hook, Dibdin, Smethergell, Fisher, Arnold, Marsh, Storace and Wesley) and some *émigrés* (Abel, J.C. Bach and a few others).

495. _____. "Thematic Index of English Eighteenth Century Overtures and Symphonies." *PRMA* 78 (1953, appendix): iii-xxxv.

Supplements entry 492. Two divisions: list A, an alphabetical arrangement of composers, their works and sources for works; list B, the actual thematic index with *incipits* for first movements only. Updated in 1983 by LaRue (entry 497). See also entry 504.

496. _____. "The Vauxhall 'Lists'." *GaSJ* 20 (1967): 24-42.

Manuscript program book, *Lists of the Songs and Instrumental Music perform'd at Vaux-Hall, 1790-1791*, covering offerings at Vauxhall Gardens. Haydn entries on pp. 27-28, 35-36 and 40-41. Repertory summaries for each season show Haydn the most favored composer, well in advance of Salomon series. Others listed include Pleyel, J.C. Bach, Stamitz, Abel, Richter and Gossec.

497. _____, and Jan LaRue. "Thematic Index of English Symphonists." In *Festschrift Cudworth*, pp. 219-44.

LaRue's update of Cudworth's original listing (entry 513). Composers included: Michael and Thomas Arne, Samuel Arnold, William Bates, Boyce, Richard Clarke, John Collett, Crotch, Dibdin, John Abraham Fisher, Maurice Greene, Thomas Haigh, Hook, Samuel Howard, William Jackson (of Exeter), the Earl of Kelly, Linley (both),

John Marsh, Joseph Mazzinghi, Henry Moze, Thomas Norris, James Oswald, William Reeve, George Rush, Thomas Shaw, Shield, Smethergell, John Christopher Smith, John Valentine, Wesley and William Yates. Provides nature and location of sources and identifies printers. Type setting and music engraving are of highest order.

498. Elkin, Robert. *The Old Concert Rooms of London*. London: Edward Arnold, 1955. 167p. ML286.8 L5 E44

Includes Hickford's Rooms (where young Mozart performed his "overtures"), the Great Rooms at Spring Gardens (Abel's early appearances), Carlisle House (Bach-Abel or "Soho Square Concerts"), Hanover Square Rooms (Bach-Abel, Haydn-Salomon and others) and halls more related to 19th century concerts (Argyll Rooms, Exeter Hall, St. James Hall and others). Mentions composers and works associated with each hall. Shows facsimile programs with illustrations of halls.

499. Farmer, Henry George. "Concerts in 18th Century Scotland." *PRPSG1* 69 (1944-1945): 99-112.

Details how concerts in Edinburgh, Glascow and Aberdeen featured orchestras of size and merit, playing symphonies and overtures by major composers of period. Edinburgh Musical Society catalogs provided extensive data on its presentations from 1765 to 1835.

500. Fiske, Roger. *English Theatre Music in the Eighteenth Century*. New York: Oxford Univ. Press, 1986. 684p. ISBN 0-19-316409-4 ML1731.3 F58 1986

Offers data on dramatic works' overtures played in early orchestra concerts: Appendix B, Theatre Overtures and Ayres Published in Parts, 1698-1708; Appendix C, Theatre Overtures Published in Parts, 1740-1800. Reveals Arne's opera *Love in a Village* used Abel overture, as was custom. Appendix E (Borrowings, 1760-1800) traces practice in 11 popular operas. Provides information on orchestras (pp. 279-85), orchestral decoration (285-87) and the overture (287-93). May overstate Mannheim role in formation of *galante* style.

501. Hogwood, Christopher, and Richard Luckett, editors. *Music in the Eighteenth-Century; Essays in Memory of*

       Charles Cudworth. Cambridge: Cambridge Univ. Press, 1983. 265p. ISBN 0-521-23525-1 ML286

       At time of his death in 1977 was leading scholar on 18th century English music. Contains 14 essays (5 used in this volume). Index.

502. Jones, David Wyn. "Robert Bremner and the Periodical Overture." *Soundings* 7 (1979): 62-84.

       Contains brief history of offering and thematic index of 60 works involved. Composers: Abel, Arne, J.C. Bach, Boccherini, Cannabich, Crispi, Dittersdorf, Filtz, Fränzi, Gluck, Gossec, Guglielmi, J. Haydn, M. Haydn, Herschel, Holzbauer, Jommelli, Earl of Kelly, Piccini, Pugnani, Ricci, Richter, Sacchini, Schmitt, Schobert, Schwindl, J. Stamitz and Vañhal. Coordinates entries with *RISM* and provides source for each work.

503. Langwill, Lyndesay G. "Two Rare Eighteenth-Century London Directories." *ML* 30 (1949): 37-43.

       Includes J. Doane's *Musical Directory* (1794) that lists composers (Abel to Wesley), wind instrumentalists by type (very detailed), music sellers and instrument makers. Intended to issue new versions periodically but only published 1794 example.

504. LaRue, Jan. "The English Symphony: Some Additions and Annotations to Charles Cudworth's Published Studies." In *Festschrift Cudworth*, pp. 213-17.

       Stresses continental influences on 18th century British symphony (J.C. Bach, Abel and Mannheim) and two social channels in which symphony flourished (concert hall or drawing room symphony versus music hall or theatre symphony/overture. Underlines latter's importance in genre's growth. Notes borrowed tunes (often popular songs) in English symphonies. Contrasts key choices with those of "continental" symphonists.

505. Milligan, Thomas B. *The Concerto and London's Musical Culture in the Late Eighteenth Century*. Ann Arbor: UMI Research Press, 1983. 386p. ISBN 8357-1441-1 ML1263 M53 1983

Early chapter gives insight into London concert activity and relationships between concerts, economics and society. Chronicles (in appendix) diversity and richness of London concert life, 1790-1800.

506.   Parke, William Thomas. *Musical Memoirs*. 2 vols. London: Colburn and Bentley, 1830.

Anecdotal memoires cover much of London's musical life in late 18th and early 19th centuries. Documents performances, including symphonies, overtures and concertos in various locations in London. Parke was active as a composer. He and his brother John, however, primarily were excellent oboists.

507.   Platt, Richard, Susan Kirakowska, David Johnson and Thomas McIntosh, editors. *The Symphony and Overture in Great Britain - Twenty Works in Symphony*, series E, vol. I. 399p.

Studies composers and works in growth of English symphony, including Croft, Pepusch, Greene, Barsanti, Rush, Thomas Alexander Erskine (Earl of Kelly), Collett, John Abraham Fisher, Boyce, Arne, Barthélémon, Marsh and Haigh. Adds thematic indices for all except Croft, Pepusch, Greene, Rush and Marsh. Bibliography lists 43 sources. See entries for each composer.

508.   Sadie, Stanley John.. "Concert Life in Eighteenth Century England." *PRMA* 85 (1958-1959): 17-30.

Shows very active concert life outside London (Winchester, Norwich, Oxford, Cambridge, Birmingham, Manchester, Leeds, Newcastle, Bath, Ipswich, Swaffham and other small towns throughout England), implying rapid growth of public and subscription concerts in all areas. Notes existence of several sets of 18th century notebooks that chronicle these events.

509.   Sickbert, Murl Julius, Jr. "The Symphony in England: a Contribution to Eighteenth Century Music Scholarship." 2 vols. Ph.D. dissertation, Univ. of Colorado, 1979. 202, 277p.

Studies *galant* symphony based on examination of orchestral parts of 149 symphonies from Henry F. Walton Library of Manchester, England, available on microfilm at Univ.

of Colorado. Isolated 15 for study: native Englishmen
(Arne, Collett, Marsh, Smethergell), Germans and/or
Italians in London for some time (Abel, J.C. Bach,
Borghi, Giardini, Guglielmi, Sacchini) and short-stay
visitors who published in England (Alberti, Galuppi,
Nicolay, Porpora, Ricci). Prepared one score by each.
Excellent review of literature. Approaches style
thoroughly, developing excellent perspective. Shows
native symphonists as at times highly original and often
resistant to European models. To date is best available
source.

510. Temperley, Nicholas. "Mozart's influence on English
     music." *ML* 42 (1961): 307-18.

     Shows some evidence of influence in symphonies of
     Crotch, Bennett and Wesley.

511. Tilmouth, Michael. "The Beginnings of Provincial
     Concert Life in England." In *Festschrift Cudworth*,
     pp. 1-18.

     Spread of concerts noted especially in summer months
     with performances of concertos, overtures and sinfonias
     by small ensembles that anticipated larger orchestras
     in pleasure gardens in mid-18th century. Covers late
     17th and early 18th centuries. Helps explain growing
     public affection for orchestra music which peaked in late
     18th century in England.

English Composers

Carl Friedrich Abel (1723-1787)[g,b]

512. Beechy, Gwilym. "Carl Friedrich Abel's Six Symphonies,
     Op. 14." *ML* 51 (1970): 279-90.

     Focuses on isolated parts of several movements with
     good musical examples but little information on style.

513. Helm, Sanford Marion. "Carl Friedrich Abel, Symphonist;
     A Biographical, Stylistic, and Bibliographical Study."
     Ph.D. dissertation, Univ.of Michigan, 1953. 378p.

     Is one of earliest (in U.S.) preclassical projects.

Contains excellent biography, thorough discussion of
symphonic style, thematic index of instrumental music
and synoptical index of thesis. Adviser: Hans David.

514. Knape, Walter. *Bibliographische-thematische Verzeichnis
      der Kompositionen Karl Friedrich Abel*. Cuxhaven:
      Verlag des Herausgebers, 1971

      Organized by genres, with symphonies in first section.
      Coordinates numbers of symphonies with Abel's opus
      numbers (e.g., *Symphony No. 1* is also opus 1, no. 1).
      Inserts table of tonalities (p. 72) and listing of cata-
      logs consulted (pp. 285-88). Identifies modern catalogs
      helpful to research. Lists sources, locations of
      archives and other similar data.

515. _____. "Karl Friedrich Abel - ein zu Unrecht verges-
      sener Zeitgenosse Mozarts; zur geplanten Neuausgabe
      einiger seiner Sinfonien." *MuGes* 7 (1957): 144-46.

      Establishes rationale for issuing complete edition of
      Abel's works.

516. _____. *Karl Friedrich Abel: Leben und Werk eines
      frühklassischen Komponisten*. Bremen: Schünemann
      Universitätsverlag, 1973. ISBN 3-7961-3036-4

      Second portion studies works through style rather than
      genre (mostly wrote instrumental music). Proposes Abel
      as Germany's most important pre-classicist, defining that
      style at outset (pp. 108-19). Focuses on form, melody,
      rhythm, harmony, orchestration and development technique.
      Many examples from symphonies. Appendix gives list of
      works and format of collected edition. Author is editor
      of critical edition, issuing thematic index in 1971
      (Cuxhaven: Ad Portnam).

517. Zimmerman, Franklin B., ed. *Carl Friedrich Abel: Six
      Symphonies* in *Symphony*, series E, vol. II, pp. xi-xix,
      1-80.

      Includes biography and narrative on development of
      symphonic style. Analysis of edited works (from Opus
      1) stresses works' place in Abel's growth as symphonist.
      Listing of Helm dissertation (entry 513) is incorrect.
      Since does not refer to Helm's findings, may not have had
      access to it.

Thomas Augustine Arne (1710-1778)[g,b]

518. Cudworth, Charles L. "Boyce and Arne: 'The Generation
      of 1710'." *ML* 41 (1960): 136-45.

      Overtures discussed on pp. 142-44. Stresses biogra-
      phical data, especially contrasts in personalities.

519. Platt, Richard, ed. *Thomas Augustine Arne: Overture in
      E-flat major* in *Symphony*, series E, vol. I, pp. lxiii-
      lxxii, 281-98.

      Describes symphonic style, indicating several Mannheim
      traits in Arne's works. Thematic index of 19 symphony-
      overtures omits Arne's French overtures, a form used
      extensively in his earlier works. Seemingly disregards
      fact that both French and Italian models were played as
      concert symphonies in England.

520. Stedman, William Preston. "The Pre-Classical Symphony
      in England: Thomas Augustine Arne and William Boyce."
      M.M. thesis, Texas Christian Univ., 1948. 148p.

      Establishes influence of concerto, sinfonia, French
      overture, trio sonata and suite in early symphonies of
      both Arne and Boyce. Arne's 1741 publication of eight
      symphonies contains examples of both Italian and French
      models. Opening chapter has extended coverage of mid-
      18th century London musical life. Has 18th century
      score of overture to Arne's *Artaxerxes*.

Johann Christian Bach (1735-1782)[g,b]

521. Blomstedt, Herbert T. "Till kännedomen om J.C. Bachs
      symfonier." *SvTMf* 33 (1951): 53-86.

      Observes that library of Stockholm Music Academy
      holds almost half of Bach's known symphonies and lists
      them. Analyzes symphonies 23-25 in detail, noting 23
      is in 3 movements with first and last in sonata-allegro
      without secondary theme in recapitulations, 25 is typical
      sinfonia concertante and 24 was written by Stamitz. Has
      German summary.

522. Krabbe, Niels. "J.C. Bach's Symphonies and the Breitkopf
      Thematic Catalogue." In *Festschrift Larsen/70th*, pp.
      233-54.

Studies catalogs and updates listings of Bach's symphonies with *incipits*, commentary and documentation.

523. Lang, Paul Henry. "Editorial." *MQ* 44 (1958): 221-27.

Discusses Bach's symphonies, comparing them with
symphonies of same period by Haydn and Mozart.

524. Meyer, Douglas Edward. "A Performing Edition of Johann
Christian Bach's Symphonies 37 and 48." D.M.A. thesis,
Univ. of Cincinnati, 1972.

Contains two edited scores: symphony 37 (Terry: Op. 8,
No. 2; Tutenberg: no. 37) and symphony 48 (Terry: Op. 8,
No. 4; Tutenberg: no. 48). Inserts commentary for each.
Limited style description.

525. Schökel, Heinrich Peter. *Johann Christian Bach und die
Instrumentalmusik seiner Zeit*. Wolfenbüttel: Kallmeyer, 1926. 204p.

Examines Bach's Italian debt by tracing history of
Italian instrumental style and that of Italian *sinfonia*.
Adds detailed and well-illustrated discussion of symphonies. Organizes thematic index by categories, documen-
ting both mss. and printed works. Tutenberg (entry 529)
a more detailed and valuable study.

526. Simon, Edwin J. "A Royal Manuscript: Ensemble Concertos of J.C. Bach." *JAMS* 12 (1959): 161-77.

Style study of 11 *symphonies concertantes*.

527. Terry, Charles Sanford. *John Christian Bach*. 6th rev.
ed. Edited by H.C. Robbins Landon. London: Oxford
Univ. Press, 1967. 373p. ML410 B12 T3

Discussion of orchestral works on pp. 172-87, with
added comments and corrections by editor. Facsimile
edition: Westport (Conn.): Greenwood Press, 1980.

528. Tutenberg, Fritz. "J.C. Bachs Sinfonik." *Die Musik* 20
(1927): 727-2.

Summarizes author's book (entry 529).

529. _____. *Die Sinfonik Johann Christian Bachs: ein Beitrag zur Entwicklungsgeschichte der Sinfonie von 1750-80.* Wolfenbüttel, Berlin: Kallmeyer, 1928. 387p.

Significant early study of 18th century style through analysis of broad spectrum of symphonies by C.P.E. and J.C. Bach, Haydn, Monn, Wagenseil, Jommelli and many Mannheim composers. Establishes theory of first-movement form in four types: suite, song, Mannheim *ritornello* and Vienna *ritornello*. Analyzes 41 symphonies and 6 concerted works. See entry 61 for discussion (in English) of Tutenberg's first-movement form types.

530. Warburton, Ernest, and C.R.F. Maunder, editors. *Johann Christian Bach: Six Symphonic Works* in *Symphony*, series E, vol. II, pp. xxi-lvii, 93-338.

Lengthy discussion of symphonies focuses more on genealogy than on music. Analyzes 6 edited works, emphasizing style . Thematic index lists 17 overtures, 29 published and 56 mss. symphonies, 3 published and 17 unpublished *symphonies concertantes*. Some aspects of editing tend toward practical (e.g., "adjusting" string passages deemed impossible to play).

531. White, Joseph Addison. "The Concerted Symphonies of John Christian Bach." 2 vols. Ph.D. dissertation, Univ. of Michigan, 1957. 310, 239p.

Based on study of first movements of 15 works. Sets definition of movement: 1st tutti, 1st solo, 2nd tutti, 2nd solo, 3rd tutti, 3rd solo and 4th tutti. Conclusions drawn from examination of same section in all works. Discerns that genre is blend of symphony and concerto styles. Edits three works with critical commentary. Thematic index.

François-Hippolyte Barthélémon (1741-1808)[g,b]

532. Kirakowska, Susan, ed. *François-Hippolyte Barthélémon: Overture in G major* in *Symphony*, series E, vol. I (The Symphony and Overture in Great Britain), pp. lxxxv-xciii, 315-36.

Was not primarily a symphonist, composing only 6 symphonies and 7 overtures, almost all in *sinfonia*

style with 3 movements. Thematic index by Dan George
Saceanu lists also 6 concertos and 6 quartets.

Francesco Barsanti (1690-1772)[g]

533. Kirakowska, Susan, and David Johnson, editors. *Francesco Barsanti: Three Overtures* in *Symphony*, series E, vol. I, pp. xxiii-xxx, 37-68.

More active in Scotland than London. Overtures (9, his total output) are in French style, 6 having minuet finales. English popular tunes used for subjects in 3 fugues, noted in analysis of edited works. All published in 1742, one of earliest printed sets in England. Thematic index.

William Boyce (1711-1779)[g,b]

534. Cudworth, Charles L. "Boyce and Arne: 'The Generation of 1710'." *ML* 41 (1960): 136-45.

See entry 518.

535. _____. "The Symphonies of Dr. William Boyce." *Music* 2 (1953): 27-29.

Emphasizes Handel's overpowering influence. Places symphonies midway between the Baroque and style *galant* and notes *sinfonia* influence on them.

536. Finzi, Gerald. "Preface" (Boyce overtures). *Musica Britannica* 13 (1957): xiii-xxvii.

Identifies sources for overtures: odes for His Majesty's birthday for 1769, 1770, 1771, 1772, 1775, 1755, 1758, 1768; odes for the New Year for 1770, 1771, 1772, 1777, 1779, 1758, 1760; overture to *Peleus and Thetis*; overture, part 2, St. Cecilia Ode (Lockman); overture, *Ode for St. Cecilia's Day* (Vidal); symphony, *The Souls of the Righteous*; *Ode for His Majesty's Birthday*, 1755; *Ode for the New Year*, 1779. Latter two are same work.

537. McIntosh, Thomas, ed. *William Boyce: Overture in E-flat major* in *Symphony*, series E, vol. I (The Symphony and Overture in Great Britain), pp. lxxiii-lxxxiv, 299-313.

Emphasizes symphonic style, noting more conservative
manner Boyce favored. Thematic index lists 37 symphony-
overtures but (as with Arne, entry 519) omits French
overtures from index, dubious since both Italian and
French types were performed as concert symphonies.

538. Stedman, William Preston. "The Pre-Classical Symphony
in England: Thomas Augustine Arne and William Boyce."
M.M. thesis, Texas Christian Univ., 1948. 148p.

See entry 520.

539. West, Franklin. "William Boyce, 1711-1779; Six Unpublished Symphonies." D.M.A. dissertation, Peabody Institute of Johns Hopkins Univ., 1978. 280p.

Assets: biography with 18th century commentaries;
ample section on orchestral style; chapter on harmony,
melody and rhythm. Form charts produced for six unpublished symphonies, with facsimiles of autograph manuscripts included (*Overture in g minor*, 1736; *Symphony
in D major*, 1761; *Symphony in F major*, 1767; *Symphony
in E-flat major*, 1776; *Symphony in D major*, 1778).

Muzio Clementi (1752-1832)[g,b]

540. Bennett, Clive. "Clementi as Symphonist," *MT* 120
(1979): 207-10.

Documents output of 19 or 20 symphonies (only 4 survive) and evolution as symphonist. See entry 544.

541. Casella, Alfredo. "Ancora sulle Sinfonie de Clementi."
Md'O 20 (1938): 43-45.

Further explanation of genealogy of surviving works.

542. _____. "Muzio Clementi et ses symphonies." *RM* 17
(1936): 161-70.

Locates works in major libraries, discusses mature
works (19th century) and places composer in symphonic
history (influenced by Haydn, Mozart and Beethoven).

543. _____. "Le sinfonie di Muzio Clementi." *Md'O* 17
      (1935): 414-19.

      Essentially same as entry 542.

544. Hill, John Walter, ed. *Muzio Clementi: One Symphony* in
      Symphony, series E, vol. IV/V, pp. xv-xxxiv,
      69-248.

      Describes Clementi's career as symphonist, sources for
      manuscripts, earlier editions (e.g., Casella's "recompo-
      sitions") and his symphonic development. Findings on
      early works: thematic connections between movements,
      first movements with many themes, limited development
      and overall *buffa* style (texture, phraseology, form,
      harmony). Later works more in 19th style. Thematic
      index: 6 extant symphonies (12+ lost), 1 minuet and 17
      fragments. Not studied: J.W. Hill, "The Symphonies of
      Muzio Clementi" (M.A. thesis, Harvard Univ., 1965).

John Collett (ca.1735-1775)

545. Platt, Richard, ed. *John Collett: Two Symphonies* in
      Symphony, series E, vol. I (The Symphony and Overture
      in Great Britain), pp. xlvii-lvi, 181-256.

      Summarizes career in England and Scotland, traces
      Mannheim influence through Earl of Kelly, defines sym-
      phonic style and analyzes briefly edited works, one of
      which is earliest British four-movement example. The-
      matic index lists 6 symphonies and 1 overture.

William Croft (1678-1727)[g,b]

546. Platt, Richard, ed. *William Croft: Overture in C major*
      in *Symphony,* series E, vol. I (The Symphony and Over-
      ture in Great Britain), pp. xvii-xix, 1-9.

      Introduction covers beginnings of English symphony
      and unique social, cultural and environmental conditions
      that helped establish its form and style. Limited com-
      ments on edited work: written in 1702, in three movements
      and influenced by trumpet sonata style.

William Crotch (1775-1847)[g,b]

547. Temperley, Nicholas, ed. *William Crotch: One Symphony*
     in *Symphony*, series E, vol. IV/V, pp. ix-xiii, 1-68.

     Wrote an early overture (1795) and concerto (1784)
     plus 6 others (overture, symphonies, concertos)in 19th
     century, with Mozart and Haydn being models. Edited
     symphony (1814) is autograph manuscript.

John Abraham Fisher (1744-1806)[g,b]

548. McIntosh, Thomas, ed. *John Abraham Fisher: Symphony in*
     D major in *Symphony*, series E, vol. I (The Symphony
     and Overture in Great Britain), pp. lvii-lxi, 257-80.

     Brief summary of biography and musical factors. Edited
     work in Mannheim style. Notes orchestral progress in
     score. Thematic index includes 6 symphonies, all in 3
     movements.

Maurice Greene (1696-1755)[g,b]

549. Platt, Richard, ed. *Maurice Greene: Symphony in D major*
     in *Symphony*, series E, vol. I (The Symphony and
     Overture in Great Britain), pp. xv-xvii, xx-xxii, 23-
     35.

     Introduction focuses on growth of early English sym-
     phony and remarks on Greene's life and symphonic style.
     Brief analysis. No thematic index.

Thomas Haigh (1769-ca. 1820)[g,b]

550. Platt, Richard, ed. *Thomas Haigh: Symphony in D major*
     in *Symphony*, series E, vol. I (The Symphony and Over-
     ture in Great Britain), pp. ci-cix, 373-99.

     Mentions study with Haydn during Salomon series. One
     surviving orchestral work (edited for series) shows Haydn
     influence. Thematic index.

William Herschel (1738-1822)[g,b]

551. Murray, Sterling E., ed. *William Herschel: Three Sym-*
     phonies in *Symphony*, series E, vol. III, pp. xiii-
     xxxv, 1-40.

Contains lengthy discussion of life (noted for discovery of planet Uranus) and works. Covers symphonies,
their sources, instrumentation, cyclic structure and
style (latter very detailed). Bibliography of 42 entries. Thematic index: 24 symphonies and 1 fragment.

552. Ronan, Colin A. "William Herschel and his Music." *Sky
      and Telescope*, 1981 (March): 195-96, 204.

      Famed German astronomer who lived most of life in
      England originally musician and composer (24 symphonies,
      completed before 1765 when career change made). One of
      earliest classical symphonists in England.

Thomas Alexander Erskine, Earl of Kelly (1732-1781)[g]

553. Johnson, David, ed. *Thomas Alexander Erskine, sixth
      earl of Kelly: Two Overtures* in *Symphony*, series E,
      vol. I (The Symphony and Overture in Great Britain),
      pp. xxxix-xlvi, 133-80.

      Most of life spent in Scotland, interrupted by his
      studies with Stamitz in Mannheim prior to 1756.
      Brought Mannheim style to Britain. Thematic index has
      6 overtures and 4 periodical overtures, all in 3 move-
      ments. Listing under "Kelly" in *NGDMM*.

John Marsh (1752-1828)[g,b]

554. Marsh, John. "An Essay by John Marsh; Introduced by
      C.L. Cudworth." *ML* 36 (1955): 155-66.

      Comparison between ancient (Baroque) and modern
      (Classic) styles in which the "merits and demerits of
      each are respectfully pointed out." Originally pub-
      lished 1796.

555. McIntosh, Thomas, ed. *John Marsh: Symphony No. 3 in D
      major* in *Symphony*, series E, vol. I (The Symphony and
      Overture in Great Britain), pp. xcv-c, 337-71.

      Marsh aware of conflicts between Baroque and Classic
      styles and wrote of this (see entry 554). Edited work
      shows influence of Stamitz. No thematic index.

John Christoph Pepusch (1667-1752)[g,b]

556. Platt, Richard, ed. *Johann Christoph Pepusch: Symphony in F major* in *Symphony*, series E, vol. I (The Symphony and Overture in Great Britain), pp. xvii-xx, 11-21.

   Originated as overture to Pepusch's masque *Venus and Adonis* (1715)and is written primarily in Italian style. Concerto influence noted in first movement. No thematic index.

George Rush (fl. 1760-1780)[g,b]

557. McIntosh, Thomas, ed. *Thomas Rush: Four Symphonic Works* in *Symphony*, series E, vol. I (The Symphony and Overture in Great Britain), pp. xxxi-xxxvii, 69-132.

   Contains minimal stylistic insight into either works or their place in history. Works edited are in *sinfonia* style. No thematic index.

William Smethergell (ca.1745-1825)[g]

558. Platt, Richard, ed. *William Smethergell: Four Overtures* in *Symphony*, series E, vol. III, pp. xxxvii-xlvi, 41-154.

   Notes influence of Mannheim's second generation and English nature of slow movements. Provides brief analysis of each work. Thematic index: 12 overtures, mostly in 3 movements.

Samuel Wesley (1756-1837)[g,b]

559. Divall, Richard, and John I. Schwarz, Jr., editors. *Samuel Wesley: Two Symphonic Works* in *Symphony*, series E, vol. III, pp. xlix-lviii, 155-273.

   Introduction (Schwarz, chiefly) includes long biography plus detailed account of symphonic works (style, sources, instrumentation). Complete analysis of each edited work (Divall). Thematic index: 5 symphonies and 1 *sinfonia obligato* (*concertante*, actually).

560. Schwarz, John Irvin, Jr. "The Orchestral Music of Samuel Wesley; A Style-Critical Analysis." 3 vols. Ph.D. dissertation, Univ. of Maryland, 1971. 1,194p.

Covers 8 violin and 3 organ concertos, 6 symphonies
and 3 overtures. Vols. 2 and 3 contain facsimiles of
autograph scores of these works. Wesley prepared keyboard accompaniments for works (see vol. 1). Valuable:
historical context of works and European influences on
English orchestral style. See pp. 127-206 for symphonies
and overtures.

Finland

General

561. Anderson, Otto. "The Introduction of Orchestral Music
into Finland." *SIMG* 13 (1911-1912): 454-57.

Recounts early concerts at Abo University in Abo, then
capital of Finland (semi-autonomous grand duchy under
Sweden's rule). Employed its first conductor in 1741.
Later Musical Society of Abo assumed sponsorship. Symphonies performed identified only by composer. Makes no
mention of native Finnish composers.

France

General

562. Brenet, Michel (Marie Bobillier). *Les concerts en France
sous l'ancien régime.* Paris: Librairie Fischbacher,
1900. 407p. Reprinted by Da Capo in 1970. ML270 B83
1970

Associates Stamitz's presence in Paris with growth of
French symphony. Comprehensive coverage of entire
spectrum of 18th century concert activities, starting
on p. 115.

563. _____. *Histoire de la symphonie à orchestre depuis
ses origines jusqu'à Beethoven inclusivement.* Paris:
Gauthier-Villars, 1882. 168p. ML1255 B66

Instructive particularly on early French symphony.
Notes importance of Sammartini. Analysis and documentation establishes esteem of this early work, particularly on France's role in early symphonic history.

564. Brook, Barry Shelley. "The symphonie concertante: an
interim report." *MQ* 47 (1961): 493-516.

Valuable discussion of Paris as cultural center of
late 18th century western Europe and of *sinfonia con-*
certante, a popular form in 18th century France. Noteworthy: list of 220 symphonic works by 46 composers active in France, organized by composer (with opus number,
solo instruments, movement and date of composition).
Addendum in *MQ* 48 (1962), p. 148, adds Guillemain's 1752
symphony and Papavoice's 1757 symphony.

565.   _____, ed. *The Symphonie concertante* in *Symphony*,
series D, vol. V. 456p.

Introduction (pp. xiii-xx) is most current history
of genre. Composers included in volume: Davaux, Cambini,
Barriere, Breval and Bertheaume. Eleven works edited in
full score. See entries below.

566.   _____. "The symphonie concertante: its musical and
sociological bases." *IRASM* 6 (1975): 9-28, 114-25.

Excellent summary of Brook's findings also offers
sociological rational for form's sudden growth and
popularity, all related to music's changing patronage
base and to expressive impact of *Sturm und Drang*. States
Paris was best social environ for rise of genre.

567.   _____. *La Symphonie française dans la seconde moitié*
du XVIIIe siècle. 3 vols. Paris: Institut de Musicologie de l'Université de Paris, 1962. 684, 726,
231p. ML1255 B87

Covers history of French symphony, 1740-1830, including
some 1,200 works by 156 composers. Establishes understanding of that history and presents extensive bibliographical ground work for subsequent study. Vol. 1,
history; vol. 2, thematic catalog and bibliography;
vol. 3, edited scores (François Martin, Filippo Ruge,
Gossec, Simon Le Duc, Rigel, Rague, Saint-Georges and
Bréval). Major contribution.

568. Brown, A. Peter, and Richard Griscom. *The French Music*
Guéra of Lyon: A Dated List. Detroit Studies in Music
Bibliography Number Fifty-Seven. Detroit: Information
Coordinators, 1987. 117p. ISBN 0-89990-033-X ML145
G9 B44 1987

Lists symphonies and/or *symphonies concertantes* by
Cauciello, Ordonez, Hoffmeister, Lochon, Haydn, Pichl,
Demachi, Vañhal, Hemberger and Foisses. Entries related
to existing thematic indices and RISM notations. Index
of locations of copies and general index.

569. Burton, Humphrey. "Les Académies de musique en France
      au XVIIIe siècle." *RMI* 37 (1955): 122-47.

      Reveals widespread concert activities sponsored by
      local "academies," including frequent performance of
      symphonies. Orchestral resources defined. Tables for
      performances in Marseille and Aix-en-Provence.

570. Charlton, David. "Orchestra and Chorus at the Comédie-
      Italienne (Opéra-Comique), 1755-99." In *Abraham
      Festschrift*, pp. 87-108.

      Illustrates growth of orchestra from strings
      3/3/(1)/3/0 in 1755 to strings 10/10/6/9/3 or 4 in 1796
      with addition of trombones and double or triple woodwinds
      in same time span. Excellent bibliography.

571. Charlton, David, ed. *The Overture in France, 1790-1810*
      in *Symphony*, series D, vol. VII, pp. xii-xxvii, 1-144.

      Includes study of the overtures of Mehul, Catel,
      Boieldieu and Kreutzer. See entries below. Introduc-
      tion explains changes in symphonic composition immedi-
      ately after French Revolution (1789), rise of one-move-
      ment wind symphony, continued popularity of *symphonies
      concertantes*, evolution of dramatic overture and rela-
      tionship of overture to symphony in France. Explains
      French composers' declining interest in symphony.

572. Cucuel, Georges. *Étude sur un orchestre au XVIIIe
      siècle. L'instrumentation chez symphonistes de la
      Pouplinière; oeuvres musicales de Gossec, Schencker
      et Gaspard Procksch.* Paris: Librairie Fischbacher,
      1913. 489p.

      Series of studies on orchestral music played in con-
      certs sponsored by French nobleman (La Pouplinière).
      Half of book on evolution of orchestration as related
      to above concerts (1745-1762), with sections on clari-
      net, horn, harp and trombone. Second half on Gossec's
      symphonies (with thematic index), with short essays on

symphonies of Schencker and Procksch (also with thematic indices).

573. _____. *La Pouplinière et la musique du chambre au XVIIIe siècle.* Paris: Librairie Fischbacher, 1913. 459p.

Alexandre-Jean-Joseph Le Riche de la Pouplinière (1693-1762), wealthy Parisian nobleman and statesman, was music patron of unequaled activity, sponsoring concerts in own theater. Gossec once was director. Stamitz introduced there to Paris. Covers symphony on pp. 306-10; orchestra leaders, 312-28; musicians, 329-55; concerts, 356-80; and music played, 381-93.

574. _____. "Quelques documents sur la librairie musicale au XVIIIe siècle." *SIMG* 13 (1911-1912): 385-92.

Inventory of certain manuscripts in Bibliotheque Nationale, 1726-1783, including symphonies by Tessarini, Stalder, Wagenseil, Holzbauer, Filtz, Touchemolin, Stamitz, Dun, Glasser, Graef, Schwindl, Davaux, Sauvel and Haydn and instrumental works by other composers.

575. Cudworth, Charles L. "Baptist's Vein - French Orchestral Music and its Influence, from 1650 to 1750." *PRMA* 83 (1956-1957): 29-47.

Defines Lully's orchestral style and performance practices (exaggerated rhythmic emphasis, etc.). Shows growth of orchestral music from *ouverture* through instrumental "symphonies" (not related to later preclassical genre) and works of Mouret and Rameau. Reveals linkages in England, Italy, Spain, Germany and Sweden.

576. Deane, Basil. "The French operatic overture from Gretry to Berlioz." *PRMA* 99 (1972-1973): 67-80.

Emphasizes dramatic connection between overture and its opera, changing form of overture and experimentation in harmony, form, instrumentation and rhythm.

577. Devriès, Anik. "Deux dynasties d'éditeurs et de musiciens: les Leduc." *RBM* 28-30 (1974-1976): 195-213.

Details show symphony publishing, publisher score
numbers correlated with dates and complex family tree.

578. _____, and François Lesure. *Dictionnaire des éditeurs
de musique française*. 2 vols. Archives de l'édition
musicale française, vol. IV. Geneva: Minkoff, 1979.
ISBN 2-8266-0460-0 ML112 D45

Summarizes history of French music printing, listing
music periodicals in 18th century France. Volume I
covers Parisian publishers, provincial publishers,
French music engravers (years of activity), index of
catalogs in volume II and index of publishers' signs or
marks (with years sign in use). Volume II includes 219
facsimiles of catalogs from publishers in vol. I and
dates each catalog, 1744 to 1828.

579. Dudley, Walter Sherwood, Jr. "Orchestration in the
Musique d'harmonie of the French Revolution." 2
vols. Ph.D. dissertation, Univ. of California
(Berkeley), 1968. 154, 121p.

Immediately after French Revolution, military band
(called *musique d'harmonie*) designated official artistic
resource, replacing elitist orchestra as residue of
dethroned aristocracy. Music periodically published
for band as volume of compositions, the first always a
symphony or overture. Lists contents of 12 existing
volumes and edits six overtures (Mehul, Catel, Blasius,
Kreutzer and Soler). These reflect form and style of
late 18th century symphony. Analyzes technical prowess
of each wind instrument. See entry 586.

580. Gaudefroys-Demombynes, Jean. *Les jugements allemand
sur la musique française au XVIIIe siècle*. Paris:
Librairie Orientale et Americaine, 1941. 457p.
ML270.3 G38

Evaluates symphonic music on pp. 295-300 with references on use of French overture by German composers.

581. Glasenapp, Franz von. "Eine Gruppe von Sinfonien und
Ouvertüren für Blasinstrumente." In *Festschrift
Schneider/80th*, pp. 197-207.

Studies works by Gossec, L.E. Jadin, Catel, Mehul, Devienne, Blasius, Soler, H. Jadin and Eler. Some emphasis on instrumentation. See entries 579 and 586.

582. Johansson, Cari. *French Music Publishers' Catalogues of the Second Half of the Eighteenth Century.* 2 vols. Uppsala: Almquist & Wiksell, 1955. 228, 146p.

Compiles 145 catalogs with commentary and index (names, titles, publishers). Includes facsimiles of each catalog in vol. 2.

583. _____. "Publishers' Addresses as a Guide to the Dating of French Printed Music in the Second Half of the Eighteenth Century." *Fontes* 1 (1954): 14-19.

Provides year and address changes for Bailleux, Bureau d'Abonnement de Musique, Huberty, Imbault, Le Duc and Sieber (père).

584. La Laurencie, Lionel de. *Inventaire critique du Fonds Blancheton de la Bibliothèque du Conservatoire de Paris.* Paris: Société française de musicologie, 1931.

Contains 27 volumes of about 300 works by 104 composers, collected sometime before 1750. Includes scores and parts of early symphonies (e.g., largest single collection of Sammartini symphonies). Describes each entry, attaching biographical data on each composer.

585. La Laurencie, Lionel de, and Georges de Saint-Foix. "Contribution à l'histoire de la symphonie française vers 1750." *AM* 1 (1911): 1-123.

Establishes existence of active symphonic culture in France when supposedly only opera being written and performed. Studies year-by-year offerings of *Concert spirituel* (1741-1764), adding musical examples and analysis of works. Lists French symphonists (chronologically) and their works, 1727-1764. Reprint by Minkoff (Geneva, 1972).

586. LaRue, Jan, and Howard Brofsky. "Parisian Brass Players, 1751-1793." *BQ* 3 (1959-1960): 133-40.

Based on *Almanach des spectacles*, published in Paris,
1751-1815. Shows brass complement of four Paris orchestras. Lists 83 active brass players.

587. Pierre, Constant. *Histoire du Concert spirituel, 1725-*
1790. Paris: Société française de musicologie, 1975.
ML270.3 P53

Covers history of administration, offerings and oper-
ation of concerts under each management (with statisti-
cal studies of repertoire) and content of each program
(listed chronologically from 1725 to 1790). Study was
completed in 1900 but was only discovered recently.
François Lesure provided preface.

588. _____. *Musique des fêtes et cérémonies de la révolu-*
tion française. Paris: Imprimerie Nationale, 1899.
583p.

Contains official music for post-Revolution holidays,
festivals, military victories and funerals, plus settings
of popular tunes. Inserts piano reductions of Gossec's
Symphonie militaire and *Symphonie en ut*, Jadin's *Sym-*
phonie pour instruments à vent and overtures (some for
winds) by Catel, Mehul, L. Jadin, Devienne, Blasius,
Soler, H. Jadin and Eler, all dated 1793-95.

589. Prod'homme, Jacques Gabriel. "Austro-German Musicians
in France in the Eighteenth Century." Translated by
Theodore Baker. *MQ* 15 (1929): 171-95.

Focuses on concerts. Symphony composition covered on
pp. 180-84 and *Concert spirituel* on 184-90. Shows nature
of 18th century German influence on French music.

590. _____. "A French Maecenas of the time of Louis XV:
M. de La Pouplinière." Translated by Theodore Baker.
MQ 10 (1924): 511-31.

Covers patron's relationship with orchestral music,
the growth of the symphony and orchestral musicians and
composers active in *Concerts spirituel*. Impressive.

591. _____. "La Musique à Paris, de 1753 à 1757, d'après
un manuscript de la Bibliothèque de Munich." *SIMG* 6
(1904-1905): 568-87.

Six-volume chronicle (sent to Mannheim library) of
Paris musical events. Includes *Concerts spirituel*,
opera and diary of events in each year. Notes performances of symphonies and other orchestral works.

592. Rice, John A., general ed. *The Symphony in France* in
      Symphony, series D, vol. I, pp. xiii-lxi, 1-275.

Introduction dwells on emerging symphonic style (early
dance symphony, beginnings of *sinfonia* style, overture-
symphonies, Italian style works, orchestra trios and
large-scale Parisian symphonies with influence of Stamitz
observed). Composers included: Rebel, Cupis, Aubert,
Martin, Talon, Guénin, Navoigille, Pelissier and Cardonne. See those entries below.

593. Schwarz, Boris. *French Instrumental Music between the
      Revolutions*, 1789-1830. New York: Da Capo, 1987.
      303p. ISBN 0-306-795435-0 ML497 S38 1987

Represents major revision of author's Ph.D. dissertation (Columbia Univ., 1950), with two divisions: Paris
musical life and French instrumental music. Latter
studies Mehul's opera overture and symphonies; Cherubini's overtures and single symphony; Herold's symphonies; overtures of Catel, Boieldieu, Leseur and Spontini;
early works of Berlioz; symphonies of Onslow and the
symphonie concertante. Provides analysis of most symphonies. Also covered: violin concerto, piano music and
chamber music. Bibliography updated to mid-1980s.

594. Stoltie, James M. "A symphonie concertante type: the
      concerto for mixed woodwind ensemble in the classic
      period." Ph.D. dissertation, Univ. of Iowa, 1962.
      384p.

Emphasizes sources and extant concerti while moder-
ating style matters. Includes critical edition of Devienne's *IIe Simphonie Concertante pour Hautbois ou
Clarinet et Basson Principal*. Partially annotated bibliography further enhances value of project.

595. Viano, Richard J., general ed. *Foreign Composers in
      France, 1750-1790* in Symphony, series D, vol. II, pp.
      xiii-xlvii, 1-229.

Explains Paris position of cultural leadership as primary factor for migration of foreign musicians to France. Notes blend of French, Italian and German styles into a distinctive French instrumental style in which French traits remain strong. Composers include: Miroglio, Ruge, Leemans, Schobert, Roeser, Rigel and Bambini. See entries below.

French Composers

Louis Aubert (1720-after 1783)[g,b]

596. Rice, John A., Dan George Saceanu and Alston E. Lambert, editors. *Louis Aubert: Symphony* in *Symphony*, series D, vol. I (The Symphony in France, 1730-1790), pp. xv-xx, xxix, 49-64.

Mentions conservative style (almost in style of Baroque suite) of composer's overture-symphonies. Genre at times is amalgam of French overture and Italian *sinfonia*. Thematic index.

Felix Bambini (ca. 1742-after 1794)

597. Stansell, John, and Richard J. Viano, editors. *Felix Bambini: One Symphonie périodique* in Symphony, series D, vol. II, pp. xxviii-xxix, xlvii-xlviii, 215-29.

Explains concept of "periodical" symphony and offers brief biography and discussion of symphonies. Of 25 symphonies, only 7 have survived, with only one in 4 movements. Thematic index.

Etienne-Bernard-Joseph Barrière (1748-1816 or 1818)[g,b]

598. Carlson, Paul B., ed. *Etienne-Bernard-Joseph Barrière: (One Symphonie concertante)* in *Symphony*, series D, vol. V, pp. lvii-lxi, 271-317.

Notes a more cosmopolitan style in works, a life of esteem and an admirable pedagogical career. Thematic index lists 3 symphonies and 2 *symphonies concertantes*, the former in *sinfonia* style.

Ignaz Franz Beck (1734-1809)[g,b]

599. Callen, Anneliese, and Donald H. Foster, editors.
Ignaz Franz Beck: Four Symphonies, Two Overtures in
Symphony, series D, vol. II (Foreign Composers in
France, 1750-1790), pp. xlix-lxxiv, 231-393.

Introduction (Callen) contains biography (native of
Mannheim, student of Stamitz), a style-oriented discussion of symphonies and analyses of four edited symphonies written under Mannheim influence. Wrote no symphonies after 1766 (had moved to Bordeaux). Overtures
are single-movement dramatic preludes, the second with
slow introduction (described by Foster). Years of research still accord Beck position of symphonic esteem.
Thematic index lists 28 published, 6 unpublished, 1 lost
and 1 questionable symphonies. Wrote at least 6 dramatic
overtures; much of dramatic music lost.

600. Foster, Donald H. "Franz Beck's compositions for the
theatre in Bordeaux." *CM*, no. 33 (1982): 7-35.

Analyzes several overtures, Beck's primary symphonic
genre in later life. Works show "more emphasis on an
independent writing for the winds." Lists dramatic
works with specifications for each.

601. Sondheimer, Robert. "Die Sinfonien Franz Becks." *ZfMw*
4 (1922): 323-51, 449-84.

Summarizes author's dissertation (Basel, 1919),
stressing Beck's early position as mature symphonist
(instrumentation, thematic contrast and dramatic impact
of use of dynamic, rhythmic and harmonic devices). As-
says Beck's skill at thematic development as reinforce-
ment of mature classic style. Was Stamitz pupil. Subsequent research does little to dispel author's original
evaluation.

Isidor Bertheaume (1752-1802)[g]

602. Vasseur, Jean Philippe, ed. *Isidor Bertheaume: (One
Symphonie concertante)* in *Symphony*, series D, vol. V,
pp. lxxix-lxxxvii, 391-456.

Primarily an excellent violinist, fled Paris after
Revolution and, in 1801, settled in Russia as leader of

imperial orchestra at St. Petersburg. Wrote sonatas, concerti, piano trios and *symphonies concertantes* in conservative style. Thematic index.

François-Adrien Boieldieu (1775-1834)[g,b]

603. Charlton, David, ed. *François-Adrien Boieldieu: Overture to Zoraïme et Zulnar* in *Symphony*. series D, vol. VII (The Overture in France, 1790-1810), pp. xi-xxviii, 79-126.

Notes French dramatic overture's continued popularity after Revolution and (banned) symphony's declining level of acceptance. Discusses composer's *opera comique* overtures and includes edited version (with musical connection with opera). No thematic index.

Jean-Baptiste Sébastien Bréval (1752-1823)[g,b]

604. Viano, Richard J., ed. *Jean-Baptiste Sébastien Bréval: (Two Symphonies concertantes)* in *Symphony*, series D, vol. V (The Symphonie concertante), pp. lxv-lxxviii, 319-89.

Includes full discussion of life and works, noting output of 170 works (mostly for strings, including 7 cello concerti and 10 *symphonies concertantes*). Adds lengthy analysis of edited works. Was cello soloist at Haydn's first Salomon concert. Thematic index.

Giuseppe Maria Cambini (ca. 1746-ca. 1825)[g,b]

605. Parcell, Amzie D., Jr., ed. *Giuseppe Maria Cambini: (Four Symphonies concertante and One Symphony)* in *Symphony*, series D, vol. V (The Symphonie concertante), pp. xxxv-lvi, 87-270.

Covers life, music (with excellent documentation) and symphonic works (sources, style and instrumentation). Analyzes four edited works. Notes both impressive success enjoyed by composer's works during his life and almost complete neglect accorded them after his death. Thematic index lists 82 *symphonies concertantes* (51 survive) and 9 symphonies (all in 3 movements).

606. _____. "The symphonies concertante of Giuseppe Maria Cambini." 2 vols. Ph.D. dissertation, Univ. of Cincinnati, 1974. 214, 276p.

Consists of lengthy biography and in-depth study of Cambini's genre style. Latter typified by virtuosic writing for soloists, standard two-movement form (both in fast tempo), orchestra in eight parts, little use of sonata principles, homophonic texture, simple harmony and a light expressive touch. Thematic of 82 works (51 extant). Includes editions of 7 in second volume.

Jean-Baptiste Cardonne (1730-after August 1792)[g,b]

607. Rice, John A., Dan George Saceanu and Jeanne Halley, editors: *Jean-Baptiste Cardonne: One Symphony* in *Symphony*, series D, vol. I (The Symphony in France, 1730-1790), pp. xxiv, xlv, 243-75.

Surintendant de la musique du roi when French revolution began, was skillful composer of modest output of operas, ballets, motets, sonatas, concertos and symphonies. Thematic index list three works, only one surviving (included in volume). Representative of more cosmopolitan style evolving after 1750.

Charles-Simon Catel (1773-1830)[g,b]

608. Charlton, David, ed. *Charles-Simon Catel: Overture to Sémiramis* in *Symphony*, series D, vol. VII (The Overture in France, 1790-1810), pp. xiii-xix, xxi-xxiii, 51-77.

Discusses opera overture in general before coverage of lives and works of 4 composers included. Catel's overture shows connections with opera proper and dates from around 1801. Lacking development section, may mirror Cherubini's manner. Dramatic overture was one of few post-Revolution orchestral forms "available" immediately after the Revolution. Most composers wrote wind overtures and wind symphonies in that period. See entry 579.

Louis François Chambray (1737-1807)[g]

609. Brook, Barry S. "Fakaerti: Incognito Symphonist, or Cutting Down the Anhang." *Fontes* 2 (1955): 166-70.

Chambray, an officer in army, used pseudonym "Fakaerti" for some works, including 5 symphonies.

Jean-Baptiste Cupis (1711-1788)[g]

610. Rice, John A., Dan George Saceanu and Anne Tapie, editors. *Jean-Baptiste Cupis: One Symphony* in *Symphony*, series D, vol. I (The Symphony in France, 1730-1790), pp. xvii-xviii, 29-48.

Comments on Cupis' adoption of Italian taste and style, noting publication between 1742 and 1745 of six *sinfonia*-style works . Thematic index lists set, noting *ciaconna* finale of two-movement *Symphony in D major* (last of six).

Jean-Baptiste Davaux (1742-1822)[g,b]

611. Foster, Donald H., ed. *Jean-Baptiste Davaux: Three Symphonic Works* in *Symphony*, series D, vol. V (The Symphonie concertante), pp. xxi-xxxiii, 1-86.

Describes large output of instrumental music, including 13 very traditional *symphonies concertantes*. Analyzes 2 edited for volume plus single symphony. Thematic index shows 12 extant *symphonies concertantes* and 4 symphonies.

Prosper-Didier Deshayes (ca. 1745-ca. 1815)[g,b]

612. Metz, John R., ed. *Prosper-Didier Deshayes: One Symphony* in *Symphony*, series D, vol. X, pp. xiii-xxi, 1-55.

Noted primarily as stage composer, his 5 symphonies discovered in 1965 Regensburg library by Brook. Comments on life (little known) and on each of symphonies (3 movements except for 4). Four have either slow first movements (no. 4) or slow introductions to first movements (nos. 2, 3, 5). Works probably date before 1790. Thematic index.

François Devienne (1759-1803)[g,b]

613. La France, Albert, Jesse Read and R. Allen Lott, editors. *François Devienne: Two Symphonies concertantes* in *Symphony*, series D, vol. X. pp. xxxv-lii, 159-289.

Recounts at length activities as bassoonist, flautist and composer. Extended discussion of symphonic works. Symphony (*La Bataille de Gemmapp*, commemorating victory over Austrians in 1792) may have first symphonic use of trombones. *Symphonies concertantes* feature two or more solo winds. Thematic index lists 7 *concertante* works and single symphony.

614. Montgomery, William L. "The life and works of François Devienne, 1759-1803." Ph.D. dissertation, Catholic Univ., 1975. 742p.

Includes study of 7 *symphonies concertantes* in which genre examined. Notes rich instrumental output of concertos (12 flute, 4 bassoon, 2 horn), 25 quartets (most include flute), 46 trios, 147 duos and 67 sonatas (winds chiefly). Wind contribution is significant.

Christoph Willibald Gluck (1714-1787)[g,b]

615. Gerber, Rudolph. "Unbekannte Instrumentalwerk von Christoph Willibald Gluck." *Mf* 4 (1951): 305-18.

Discusses previously unknown instrumental works, including several symphonies and overtures. Provides thematic index of works with location of each. *New Grove* lists 18 symphonies, some probably spurious.

François-Joseph Gossec (1734-1829)[g,b]

616. Brook, Barry S., gen. ed. *François-Joseph Gossec: Eight Symphonic Works* in *Symphony*, series D, vol. III. 344p.

Brook and Dan Saceanu provided concise biography, detailing events around Revolution leading to decline of French symphony. John A. Rice wrote on Gossec as symphonist and traces evolution carefully. Also provides analysis of edited works (scored by David Day, Glenn R. Williams, James D. Anderson, Charles T. Clauser and Garland staff). Thematic index (Brook-Saceanu) lists 49 symphonies, 5 *symphonies concertantes*, 5 overtures, and number of spurious or doubtful works. Index updates Brook's earlier listing (entry 567).

617. Clauser, Charles Theodore. "François-Joseph Gossec: an edition and stylistic study of three orchestral works

and three quartets." Ph.D. dissertation, Univ. of
Iowa, 1966. 458p.

Supports Gossec's reputation as skilled orchestrator
in careful analysis of works. Includes biography.
Symphonies edited: Brook 103, 62 and 91. Edition of 91
appears also in entry 616.

618. Dufrane, Louis. *Gossec, sa vie et ses oeuvres*. Paris:
      Librairie Fischbacher, 1927. 267p. ML410 G56 D9 1927

Contains short discussion of symphonies (pp. 221-34).
Proposes Gossec as equal of Haydn and Mannheim school
in growth of symphony. Catalog of works shows span of
symphonies, 1756-1809.

619. Macdonald, Robert Jones. "François-Joseph Gossec and
      French instrumental music in the second half of the
      eighteenth century. Ph.D. dissertation, Univ. of
      Michigan, 1968. 879p.

More historical than style study, focuses on slow
evolution of French symphony, Gossec's life, French
instrumentation and orchestration, Paris orchestras and
Gossec's entire output. Adds 39 pages of corrections
of Gossec citations and 30 pages of works not included
in Brook (entry 567). Symphonic style covered on pp.
513-55. Edits *Symphony in F* (Brook 44).

620. Gossec, François-Joseph. "Notes concernant l'introduc-
      tion des cors, des clarinettes et des trombones dans
      les orchestres français, extraité des manuscrits au-
      tographes de Gossec." *RM* 5 (1929): 217-23.

Shows importance of Italian composers in Paris in
introduction of horn, of Stamitz and the clarinet and
of others in expansion of orchestra.

Marie-Alexandre Guenin (1744-1835)[g,b]

621. Rice, John A.,and George Saceanu, editors. *Marie-
      Alexandre Guenin: Three Symphonic Works* in *Symphony*,
      series D, vol. I (The symphony in France, 1730-1790),
      pp. xxi-xxii, xxxv-xxxvii, 129-90.

Classified as "large-scale Parisian" symphonist.
Output included 12 symphonies, 3 orchestral trios, 3
string trios and an overture. Prefers sonata-allegro
in all movements. Used typical "Mannheim-Paris" style,
with concept fully explained by Rice. Thematic index.

Louis-Gabriel Guillemain (1705-1770)[g,b]

622. Castonguay, Gerald R., ed. *Louis-Gabriel Guillemain:
     Four Symphonies* in *Symphony*, series D, vol. I, pp.
     xlvii-lx, 277-323.

     Contains two-page biography and insightful discussion
     of style that shows preclassic devices in scores. Ex-
     plains transitional nature of style, identifying com-
     poser as earliest significant French symphonist. Relates
     string style (i.e., violin figurations) to the emerging
     French violin school. Thematic index lists 13 symphonies
     (written 1740-48) for 2 violins and bass.

623. _____. "The orchestral music of Louis-Gabriel Guille-
     main." 2 vols. Ph.D. dissertation, Rutgers, 1975.
     430, 61p.

     Concentrates on symphonies, all in 3-movement *sinfonia*
     style. Notes "comparatively advanced grasp" of first-
     movement form (i.e., dualism). Includes time-line graphs
     for all movements. Overall emphasis on style analysis,
     adding editions of two symphonies in second volume.
     Proposes Guillemain as France's best *galant* composer.
     Important in its reinforcement of history of France's
     early symphonic pioneering.

Rudolphe Kreutzer (1766-1831)[g,b]

624. Charlton, David, ed. *Rudolphe Kreutzer: Overture to
     Aristippe* in *Symphony*, series D, vol. VII (The Over-
     ture in France, 1790-1810, pp. xiii-xxviii, 127-44.

     Offers general introduction (Charlton) to genre and
     short biographies of composers. Notes violin pedagogue
     Kreutzer's tolerable success as opera composer. Includes
     analysis of edited work (sonata-allegro form, second
     theme from opera and contrapuntal development in coda).
     No thematic index.

Simon Le Duc (1741-1777)[g,b]

625. Brook, Barry S., and David Bain, editors. *Simon Le Duc: Five Symphonic Works* in *Symphony*, series D, vol. IV, pp. xi-xxxv, 1-194.

   Stresses style paradox of period (individual expression versus public taste) and how composers reacted. Notes Le Duc's independence from public pressures and style features that mirror his values. Describes Parisian environment, especially fusion of Italian, German and French styles. Extended study of Le Duc's symphonic style. Thematic index lists 7 symphonic works and 6 trio-divertimentos.

626. Brook, Barry S. "Simon Le Duc l'aîné, a French symphonist at the time of Mozart." *MQ* 48 (1962): 498-513.

   Wrote 3 orchestral trios, 3 symphonies (ca. 1774-1776) and 1 *symphonie concertante*. Feels his symphonies in 3 movements represent fusion of Italian, German and French mannerisms. Asserts that Duc's "bold use of chromaticism, sure sense of orchestral sonority, a creative approach to sonata structure, and the existence of a romantic crisis similar to the *Sturm und Drang* movement..." make his works worthy of a respected place in symphonic history.

Hébert Philippe Adrien Leemans (?-1771)[g,b]

627. Brook, Barry S. "Leemans of Bruges and Paris." *RBM* 15 (1961): 47-54.

   Most of works survive in Paris libraries, including 14 symphonies (all in Italo-Mannheim style, with 12 in 4 movements). Lists extant works, many self-published.

628. Viano, Richard J., ed. *Hébert Philippe Adrien Leemans: One Symphony* in *Symphony*, series D, vol. II (Foreign Composers in France, 1750-1790), pp. xxi-xxii, xxxv-xxxvi, 87-117.

   Flemish cellist and composer settled in Paris in 1750s, becoming music teacher to Parisian nobility. In symphonies placed primary emphasis on winds by giving them important thematic materials. Thematic index lists 14 symphonies, 1765-1771.

François Martin (1737-1757)[g,b]

629. Rice, John A., Dan George Saceanu, Douglas F. Hedwig,
Eric Milnes and Michael Bondi, editors. *François
Martin: Three Symphonies* in *Symphony*, series D, vol.
I (The Symphony in France, 1730-1790), pp. xx-xxi,
xxxi-xxxii, 65-114.

Wrote both French overture and Italian *sinfonia* style
symphonies, both forms included in editions. Explains
duality of style. Thematic index includes 6 symphonies
and overtures, written in 1751 or earlier.

Etienne-Nicolas Méhul (1763-1817)[g,b]

630. Charlton, David, ed. *Etienne-Nicolas Méhul: Overture
to Adrien* in *Symphony*, series D, vol. VII (The Overture in France, 1790-1810), pp. xi-xxvi, 1-50.

Stresses connection between overture and its opera
and its origin as overture to another Méhul opera,
Horatius Coclès, 1794. Thematic index of symphonies in
vol. VIII (series D), pp. xxv-xxvii.

631. _____, and Anthony Caston, editors. *Etienne-Nicolas
Méhul: Three Symphonies* in *Symphony*, series D, vol.
VIII, 443p.

Insightful account of failing fortunes of French
concert symphony in late 18th and early 19th centuries
and of Méhul's obscured reputation as France's great
symphonist of that period. Discusses style and chronology of works edited. Hidden asset: list of contemporary reviews and references. Thematic index.

632. Ringer, Alexander. "A French symphonist at the time of
Beethoven: Etienne-Nicolas Méhul." *MQ* 37 (1951):
543-65.

Shows influence of non-French (esp. Beethoven) on
Méhul's symphonic style. Reveals high quality of symphonies and how their international style doomed them
to failure with a prejudiced French public and academy.
Feels Mehul was greatest French symphonist of his time.

Jean-Baptiste Miroglio (ca. 1725-ca. 1785)[g,b]

633.   Viano, Richard J., ed.   *Jean-Baptiste Mirolgio: One
       Symphony* in *Symphony*, series D, vol. II (Foreign
       Composers in France, 1750-1790), pp. xiii-xix, xxxi-
       xxxii, 1-29.

       Discusses Miroglio's publishing venture (first Paris
       music-lending and subscription press) and nature of
       French music-printing as business operation. Contends
       that symphonies are "fusion of French, Italian and
       Mannheim styles." Thematic index: 12 symphonies, 1751-
       1764.

Guillaume Navoigille (ca. 1745-1811)[g,b]

634.   Rice, John A., and George Saceanu, editors.   *Guillaume
       Navoigille: One Symphony* in *Symphony*, series D, vol.
       I (The Symphony in France, 1730-1790), pp. xxii-xxix,
       xxxix-xli, 191-216.

       Wrote 9 symphonies, 3 trios and 3 orchestral trios in
       "large-scale Parisian" (i.e., international) style, 1765-
       1776. Thematic index.

Étienne Ozi (1754-1813)[g,b]

635.   Griswold, Harold Eugene.   "Étienne Ozi (1754-1813),
       Bassoonist, Teacher and Composer." D.M.A. thesis,
       Peabody Institute of Johns Hopkins Univ., 1979.
       243p.

       Analyzes *symphonies concertantes* in part III. Stresses
       Ozi's teaching career. Notes widespread success of his
       bassoon *Méthodes* throughout Europe.

636.   _____.   *Étienne Ozi: Two Symphonies concertantes* in
       Symphony, series D, vol. X, pp. xxiii-xxxiii, 57-158

       Contains well-documented and detailed coverage of life
       and works, discussion of style (sources, performances and
       instrumentation) and analysis of edited works. Reveals
       Ozi's use of solo clarinet and solo bassoon in 3 works
       and 2 solo bassoons in another. Thematic index of 4
       symphonies concertantes.

(Victor?) Pelissier (ca. 1740s–ca. 1820?)[g]

637. Rice, John A., and Dan George Saceanu, editors. *Pelissier: One Symphony* in *Symphony*, series D, vol. I (The Symphony in France, 1730–1790), pp. xxix, xliii, 217–41.

   Was practically unknown until work discovered in Basel. May be horn player Victor Pelissier who migrated to USA around 1790. Edited work's style typical of Mannheim-Paris blend (3 movements). Thematic index.

Ignaz Pleyel (1757–1831)[g,b]

638. Benton, Rita. *Ignaz Pleyel: a thematic catalog of his compositions.* New York: Pendragon, 1977. 484p. ISBN 0-918728-04-5   ML134 P74 A13

   Lists 6 *symphonies concertantes*, some with as many as 75 editions, versions and/or adaptations of original; 44 symphonies (with many adaptations) and 25 titles (from contemporary catalogs) impossible to locate. Several indices plus thematic locator.

639. Carse, Adam. "A Symphony by Pleyel." *MMR* 79 (1949): 231–36.

   Contains background and analysis of *Symphony in C*, possibly Benton 131.

640. Smith, Raymond R. "The Periodical Symphonies of Ignaz Pleyel." 2 vols. Ph.D. dissertation, Eastman School of Music of the Univ. of Rochester, 1967. 149, 314p.

   Summarizes symphonic history (1770–1795) with documentation from 18th century writings and comments from modern scholars. Covers all aspects of Pleyel's symphonic style. Presents scholarly editions of five works. Charles Warren Fox was adviser.

641. _____, and Douglas Townsend, editors. *Ignaz Pleyel: Four Symphonies, One Symphonie concertante* in *Symphony*, series D, vol. VI, 435p.

   Covers life, works and symphonic style (mostly in 3 movements, sonata-allegro first movements and rondo

finales; extended development sections; affection for
diminished seventh chord and similarities to Haydn
style). Thematic index: 42 symphonies and 6 *symphonies
concertantes*.

Jean-Féry Rebel (1666-1747)[g,b]

642. Rice, John A., and Dan George Saceanu, editors. *Jean-
      Féry Rebel: One Symphony* in *Symphony*, series D, vol.
      I (The Symphony in France, 1730-1790), pp. xvi-xvii,
      1-28.

      Symphony, *Les Elémens*, is ballet (written in 1737) in
      12 sections, depicting elements of earth, fire, water,
      etc.). Many movements are dances, supporting concept
      of pre-sinfonia French dance symphony as viable genre.

Henri-Joseph Rigel (1741-1799)[g,b]

643. Sondheimer, Robert. "Henri-Joseph Rigel." *MR* 17
      (1956): 221-28.

      Studies style of Rigel's preclassical works, including
      7 symphonies mentioned by Breitkopf. Known as one of
      France's symphonic pioneers.

644. Viano, Richard J., ed. *Henri-Joseph Rigel: Two Sym-
      phonic Works* in *Symphony*, series D, vol. II (Foreign
      Composers in France, 1750-1790), pp. xxvi-xxviii,
      161-214.

      A prolific composer (14 operas, 4 oratorios, 7 many
      chamber works and 20 orchestral works); edited examples
      show maturation from 1767 symphony to 1786 *symphonie
      concertante*, latter in high classic style. Explains
      both composer's popularity in Paris and nature of his
      symphonic style. Thematic index.

Valentin Roeser (ca. 1735-1782)[g,b]

645. Viano, Richard J., ed. *Valentin Roeser: One Symphony*
      in *Symphony*, series D, vol. II (Foreign Composers in
      France, 1750-1790), pp. xxiv-xxvi, xxxix-xlii, 141-
      60.

      Wrote over 120 instrumental works (sonatas, quartets,
      duos, trios, and 26 symphonies), some for clarinet,

Roeser's instrument. Explains style shift from Mannheim mode to more lyric French manner. Used both 3- and 4-movement symphonic forms. Thematic index lists 6 trios and 20 symphonies (1 doubtful and 1 lost).

Filippo Ruge (ca. 1725-after 1767)[g,b]

646. Pilat, Michael, and Richard J. Viano, editors. *Filippo Ruge: Two Symphonies* in *Symphony*, series D, vol. II (Foreign Composers in France, 1750-1790), pp. xix-xxi, xxxiii-xxxiv, 31-57.

    With singer wife helped establish popularity of Italian style in Paris. As flutist played *Concerts spirituel*. Symphonic style comes from Sammartini with little Mannheim influence. Thematic index of 12 symphonies.

Johann Schobert (ca. 1735-1767)[g,b]

647. Taxin, Ira, and Richard J. Viano, editors. *Johann Schobert: One Periodical Overture* in *Symphony*, series D, vol. II (Foreign Composers in France, 1750-1790), pp. xxiii-xxiv, xxxvii, 119-39.

    Recounts Mozart's admiration for Schobert and genesis of latter's six symphonies (arranged from keyboard *sinfonias* by F. Kotzwara). Surfaced ca. 1782 as periodical overtures (London: Bland). Edited work produced by another arranger and issued in 1781 or 1782 by Bremner. Thematic index confirms origins of 3 symphonies.

Joseph Boulogne, Chevalier de Saint-Georges (ca. 1739-1799)[g,b]

648. Braun, Melanie. "The Chevalier de Saint-Georges: an Exponent of the Parisian Symphonie Concertante." M.M. thesis, North Texas State Univ., 1982.

    Contains history of genre and composer's life. Examines symphonic style and edits 2 *symphonies concertantes*. Thesis available on microfiche and microfilm.

649. Brook, Barry S., and David Bain, editors. *Le Chevalier de Saint-Georges: Three Symphonic Works* in *Symphony*, series D, vol. IV, pp. xi-xxxi. xxxvii-xl, 195-305.

    Analyzes Saint-Georges' position in conflict between personal expression and catering to public taste. In-

cludes biography and brief study of works. Thematic
index lists 2 symphonies and 10 *symphonies concertantes*.

650. Lerma, Dominique-René de. "The Chevalier de Saint-
      Georges." *The Black Perspective in Music* 4 (1976):
      3-21.

      In part, discusses style of orchestral works, including
      2 symphonies. Augments coverage with complete list of
      works. Bibliography.

651. _____. *Chevalier de Saint-Georges: Symphonie concer-
      tante in G major (op. 13), Symphony No. 1 (Op. 11, No.
      1), scene from Ernestine, (and) String Quartet No. 1.*
      Columbia recording M-32781 (Black Composer Series, vol.
      1, 1974). Liner notes.

      Includes biography, discussion of style and analysis
      of works. Recording uses Brook's earlier edition of
      symphonie concertante.

Pierre Talon (1721-1785)[g,b]

652. Rice, John A., and Dan George Saceanu, editors. *Pierre
      Talon: One Symphony* in *Symphony*, series D, vol. I
      (The Symphony in France, 1730-1790), pp. xx-xi,
      xxxiii-xxxiv, 115-27.

      Stresses Talon's conservative style (orchestra of 3
      violin parts and bass, frequent imitation and excessive
      sequencing). Consistently uses 3-movement form in
      existing symphonies. Thematic index shows 12 extant
      and 6 lost works.

Jacques Widerkehr (1759-1823)[g,b]

653. La France, Albert, ed. *Jacques Widerkehr: One Symphonie
      concertante* in *Symphony*, series D, vol. VII. pp. xxix-
      xli, 145-72.

      Wrote mostly instrumental works, 1796-1804. Used
      various solo wind groups in *symphonies concertantes*,
      with "attractive and graceful melodies, brilliant vir-
      tuosic passages for solo instruments, and transparent
      orchestral sonorities." Thematic index notes 15 *sym-
      phonies concertantes* (7 lost) and 2 lost symphonies.

Germany

General

654. Carrow, Burton Stimson. "The relationship between the Mannheim School and the music of Franz Beck, Henri Blanchard, and Pierre Gaveaux." 2 vols. Ph.D. dissertation, New York Univ., 1956. 293, 152p.

First establishes style base in works of Stamitz and Cannabich (form, melody, rhythm, harmony and instrumentation), confirms Beck's faithfulness with style and examines nature of concurrence in Blanchard and Gaveaux. Finds both failed to react, aborting possible linkage to Mannheim. Illustrates Mannheim mannerisms. Includes 4 Beck symphonies in vol. 2.

655. Davis, Shelley. "The orchestra under Clemens Wenzeslaus: music at a late-eighteenth-century court." *JAMIS* 1 (1975): 86-112.

Surveys orchestral resources at court near Koblenz. Establishes size of ensembles (1783, 1787, 1790, 1791 and 1792), inventories court instruments and lists symphonic composers performed. Certifies high quality of court orchestras, explaining role in rapid growth of symphonic music. Valuable.

656. De Stwolinski, Gail B. "The Mannheim symphonists: their contributions to the technique of thematic development." 2 vols. Ph.D. dissertation, Eastman School of Music of Univ. of Rochester, 1966. 298, 88p.

Findings related to six types of sonata-allegro form used in 43 movements studied. Variant devices identified in works and composers assayed for developmental skills. Exploits every developmental facet in style. Summarizes research in various tables and diagrams each movement's development section (themes, tonality, techniques, etc.).

657. Durham, George D. "The development of the German concert overture." Ph.D. dissertation, Catholic Univ., 1957. 270p. (Also published by Catholic Univ. of America Press, Washington, 1957.)

Includes list of over 100 German composers who wrote in the genre. Studies 193 overtures from list.

658. Englander, Richard. *Die Dresdener Instrumentalmusik in der Zeit der Wiener Klassik.* Uppsala: Lundequist, 1956. 160p.

Covers period between Hasse and Weber, supplying names of musicians and works. Includes Frederick II court (pp. 29-33), identifying composers and music performed.

659. Flueler, Max. "Die norddeutsche Sinfonie zur Zeit Friedrichs des Grossen und besonders die Werke Ph. Em. Bachs." Ph.D. dissertation, Berlin, 1908. 75p. (Also published in Berlin by Eberling, 1908.)

Published version deletes chapter on Bach's symphonies.

660. Haberkamp, Gertraut. *Thematischer Katalog der Musik-handschriften der fürstlich Oettingen-Wallerstein'-schen Bibliothek Schloss Harburg.* Munich: G. Henle, 1976.

Compiles index of collection housed in Augsburg Univ. library. Collection is remains of holdings of one of most important centers of symphonic activity in late 18th century.

661. Helm, Ernest Eugene. *Music at the Court of Frederick the Great.* Norman: Univ. of Oklahoma Press, 1960. 268p. ML279 H4

Discusses symphonies, overtures and *sinfonias* of Frederick, C.P.E. Bach, J.G. Graun and K.H. Graun.

662. Heuss, Alfred. "Die Dynamik der Mannheimer Schule: die Detail-Dynamik." *ZfMw* 2 (1919/20): 44-54.

Discusses use of dynamics as developmental device with analysis of Mozart sonata (KV 309), projecting possible influence of Mannheim technique on Mozart.

663. _____. "Über die Dynamik der Mannheimer Schule." In *Festschrift Riemann*, pp. 435-55.

Surveys *crescendo* usage in Mannheim scores. Attempts to show influence of Mannheim *crescendo* on Haydn's symphonic style.

664. _____. "Zum Thema: 'Mannheimer Vorhalt'." *ZIMG* 9 (1907/8): 273-80.

Illustrates existence of "sigh" in earlier music and in scores after Stamitz's time. Suggests that "Mannheim taste" mentioned by Leopold Mozart might imply devices such as sigh.

665. Kamiénski, Lucian. "Mannheim und Italien." *SIMG* 10 (1908/9): 307-17.

Discusses Italian influence on German music of 18th century and especially on formation of Mannheim style.

666. Kirby, Frank Eugene. "The Germanic Symphony in the Eighteenth Century: Bridge to the Romantic Era." *JMR* 5 (1984): 51-83.

Surveys growth of 18th century symphony, covering "social-cultural mileu," forms "of and in" music, instrumentation, character and expression (includes study of key choices and 7 types of symphonies: pastoral, battle, hunt, intense emotional expression, national styles and literary and misc. effects). Extensive bibliography. Sums up much of recent research.

667. Komma, K.M. "Die Sudetendeutschen der 'Mannheimer Schule'." *ZfM* 106 (1939): 13-16.

An attempt during Nazi regime to establish Stamitz's German roots, Sudetenland being an area in Bohemia where large part of population spoke German. Attempt failed. See also Gradenwitz (entry 763) for outcome.

668. Larsen, Jens Peter. "Zur Bedeutung der 'Mannheim Schule'." In *Festschrift Fellerer/60th*, pp. 303-9.

Resume of scholarly thought on Mannheim (Riemann, Adler, Fischer, Sondheimer, Schökel, Tutenberg, Westphal, Tobel, Moser, Dommers and Wörner), advocating more realistic view since much of Mannheim manner was common practice by 1760. Strongly opposes Riemann's assertion that Stamitz was Haydn's predecessor and

stresses orchestral rather than compositional milestone
of school. For English translation, see Larsen: *Handel,
Haydn, and the Viennese Classical School*, Ann Arbor: UMI
Research Press, 1988, pp. 263-68.

669. McCredie, Andrew D. "Instrumentarium and instrumenta-
      tion in the north German Baroque opera." Ph.D. dis-
      sertation, Hamburg Univ., 1964. 339p.

      Describes emergence of north German opera orchestra.
      Materials on complement and balance (pp. 303-24) reveal
      ensembles of high quality.

670. _____. "Investigations into the Symphony of the Mozart-
      Haydn Era. The North German Manuscripts: An Interim
      Study." *MMASM* 2 (1967): 75-154.

      Studies sources for works of Louis Massonneau, Franz
      Neubauer, Christian Wilhelm Westerhoff, Andreas Jakob
      Romberg, Bernard Heinrich Romberg, Carl David Stegmann,
      Friedrich Herschel, J.G. Schwanenberger, Karl August
      Pesch, A.W.F. Mattern, Vincenz Maschek, Losenmeyer, J.W.
      Hertel, F.A. Rosetti, J.M. Sperger and Bendix Friedrich
      Zinck.

671. _____. "Symphonie concertante and Multiple Concerto
      in Germany (1780-1850): Some Problems and Perspectives
      for a Source-Repertory Study." *MMASM* 10 (1975): 115-
      47.

      Discusses nature of genre, orchestras' sizes in region,
      subscription concerts (with dates of foundings), catalogs
      listing works and library sources for manuscripts. Very
      broad coverage.

672. Münster, Robert. "Vier Musiker der Mannheimer Schule."
      Musica 14 (1960): 488-91.

      Briefly discusses J. Stamitz, Holzbauer, Richter and
      Filtz.

673. Murray, Sterling E. "Bohemian musicians in south German
      'Hofkapellen' during the late eighteenth century."
      Hudební Veda 15 (1978): 152-73.

      Describes migration from Bohemia to courts in western
      Europe (e.g., Mannheim, Koblenz, Regensburg, Donaue-

schingen, Mainz and Oettingen-Wallerstein). Lists 48
musicians in appendix with brief reference on each.

674. _____. "The double-horn Concerto: A Specialty of the
Oettingen-Wallerstein Court." *JM* 4 (1985/6): 507-34.

Focuses on composers, performers and repertoire, organized into three groups: before 1780, 1780-1794 and
after 1794. Provides insight into advanced nature of
court's symphonic activity. Appends list of works with
discography and excellent bibliography.

675. Piersol, Jon Ross. "The Oettingen-Wallerstein Hofkapelle
and Its Wind Music." 2 vols. Ph.D. dissertation,
Univ. of Iowa, 1972. 844p.

Describes court's instrumental resources as equal to
those in Paris and Mannheim. Documents music activities,
listing musicians and composers. Prepares inventory and
thematic index of wind music, almost all original compositions for five or more winds. Notes some transcrip-
tions (Act I of Mozart's *La Clemenza de Tito* and Paris
symphony and overtures by Paisiello and Rossini). Also
valuable in its detailing of music activities of court
and its orchestral resources.

676. Riemann, Hugo, ed. "Einleitung." in *DTB*, Jg. VIII/2,
II. Theil, II. Hälfte, pp. vii-xiv.

Riemann, discoverer of Mannheim School, championed
school's position as creator of early classical symphony.
Claimed Stamitz as Haydn's forerunner had created 4-move-
ment symphony and that mannerisms peculiar to Mannheim
(sigh, roll, dynamics, rocket themes, etc.) could be
traced in music by later composers, this insuring leadership of Mannheim. Later research tempered Riemann's conclusions as other centers of symphonic activity were un-
covered and as scholars often saw Mannheim devices as
common to other styles of era.

677. _____, ed. *The Mannheim Symphonists: a collection of
twenty-four orchestral works.* 2 vols. New York:
Broude Bros., n.d. 270, 285p. M2 R55

Extracts scores only from *DTB*. Vol. I contains works
by J. Stamitz, Richter, Filtz; vol. II, Filtz, Holzbauer,
Toeschi, C. Stamitz, Beck and Eichner.

678.   _____, ed. "Die Mannheimer Schule." In *DTB*, Jg. III/1,
        I. Theil (Sinfonien der Pfalzbayerischen Schule [Mann-
        heimer Symphoniker]), pp. ix-xxx, xxxix-xl.

        Introduction on pp. ix-xxx. Also includes thematic
        catalog of Stamitz's symphonies and orchestral trios on
        pp. xxxix-xl.

679.   _____. ed. "Der Stil und die Manieren der Mannheimer."
        In *DTB*, Jg. VII/2, II. Theil, I.Hälfte, pp. xv-xxvi,
        xxix.

        Second collection of scores and comments (see entry
        676). Additions to thematic catalog includes works by
        Eichner, Danzi, Earl of Kelly, J. Stamitz, Richter,
        Filtz, Holzbauer, Toeschi, Cannabich, C. Stamitz and
        Fränzl. Provides index for Beck's 19 symphonies,
        Eichner's 31, Early of Kelly's 14 and 8 by Danzi.

680.   Schubart, Christian Friedrich Daniel. *Ideen zu einer
        Ästhetik der Tonkunst.* Vienna: Degan, 1906. Reprint
        in 1969 by Olds in Wildeschein.

        Includes insightful comments on members of Mannheim
        School, evaluating overall style of each within frame-
        work of 18th century.

681.   Vogler, Georg Joseph. *Betrachtungen der Mannheimer
        Tonschule.* 3 vols. Mannheim, 1778-81. Facsimile
        reprint in 1974 by Olds of Hildesheim, 4 vols.

        Executed as monthly serial publication to assist
        music-lover in gaining tools to make value judgements
        on new music. Contained music, reviews and summaries
        of Vogler's teachings. Vogler was chaplain and, later,
        vice-Kapellmeister in Mannheim court, founding his Mann-
        heim Tonschule for teaching of music. In *Betrachtungen*
        comments on activities of Mannheim composers.

682.   Waldkirch, Franz. *Die konzertanten Sinfonien der Mann-
        heimer im 18. Jahrhundert.* Ludwigshafen: Julius
        Waldkirk, 1931. 139p. ML1255 W16 K6

Established concept of genre in first chapter, providing subjective definition of melodic style which may
relate to onset of *Sturm und Drang* period. Analyzes one
complete work each by Holzbauer, Toeschi, Cannabich, K.
Stamitz, A. Stamitz and Danzi. Riemann's influence
possibly at root of excessive attribution to Mannheim in
development of form.

683. Wolf, Eugene K. "Fulda, Franklin, and the Library of
Congress." *JAMS* 24 (1971): 286-91.

Offers genealogy of Henkel collection in Library of
Congress. Michael Henkel was teacher, organist and com-
poser in Fulda in late 18th century and helped found col-
lection of priceless manuscripts in the Landsbibliotek in
Fulda. Included sets of symphony parts by Johann and
Carl Stamitz and over 40 Mozart manuscripts.

684. _____. "Mannheim style." *NGDMM*, 10, 629-30.

Attributes to Italian influence dynamic effects, the
roll (from Jommelli), the sigh, *Bebung* (tremolo) and the
rocket theme. Illustrates each device with musical
example. Refutes many of Riemann's assertions.

685. _____. "The Music Collection of the Hessische Landes-
bibliothek Fulda and its Relationship with Collections
in Frankfurt, Washington, and Elsewhere." In *Festschrift Fulda/200th*, pp. 361-70.

Considered one of largest collections of 18th and 19th
century music in Europe, undiscovered until 1967. Symphonic holdings include works of Cannabich, Filtz and
Stamitz (both). Major portion of collection (orchestra
parts) now in Library of Congress. Feels other parts of
collection scattered to libraries elsewhere. Traces
history of holdings. See entry 683.

686. _____. "On the origins of the Mannheim symphonic
style." In *Festschrift Albrecht*, pp. 197-239

Shows convincingly Italian connections to Mannheim
style (esp. Johann Stamitz). Cites popularity of Italian style in Mannheim court and musical evidence of melodic style, use of *crescendo*, thematic style in expositions and orchestral style. Excellent illustrations.

687.   _____, and Jean K. Wolf. "A newly identified complex
         of manuscripts from Mannheim." *JAMS* 27 (1974): 379-
         437.

         Located about 125 manuscripts in Mannheim, Munich,
         Kassel, Donaueschingen and Regensburg. Lists variety
         of sacred works and over 50 symphonic works by Cannabich,
         Filtz (2), Johann Stamitz (10) and Holzbauer. Adds data
         on copyists, paper and watermarks.

German Composers

Johan Joachim Agrell (1701-1765)[g,b]

688.   Lindfors, Per. "En studie över Johan Agrells liv och
         musikaliska stil." *SvTMf* 19 (1937): 99-112.

         Based in part on study of symphonies, especially opus
         1 set dated 1746. Defines Baroque aspect of style.

689.   Sheerin, Jeannette Morgenroth, ed. *Johan Agrell: Five
         Symphonies* in *Symphony*, series C, vol. I, pp. xiii-
         xliii, 1-99.

         Covers Agrell's career and cultural background (Lin-
         köping, Uppsala, Kassel, Darmstadt and Nürnburg); his
         works; and extended treatment of symphonies with percep-
         tive stylistic summary. Analyzes edited works. Thematic
         index of 28 authentic, 5 questionable and 4 spurious sym-
         phonies. See also entry 904.

Carl Philipp Emanuel Bach (1714-1788)[g,b]

690.   Gallagher, Charles C., and E. Eugene Helm, editors.
         Carl Philipp Emanuel Bach: Six Symphonies in *Symphony*,
         series C, vol. VIII. 275p.

         Volume completes publication in modern edition of all
         symphonies. Covers biography, symphonic style (3 move-
         ments, avoidance of Classical phraseology, lack of con-
         cern for thematic contrast, importance of *Affekte*, dis-
         dain for Classical perception of sonata-allegro as hi-
         erarchy of two keys and linkage between polyphony and
         orchestration) and analysis of edited works. Thematic
         index of 18 symphonies with discography.

691. Newman, William S. "Emanuel Bach's Autobiography." *MQ* 51 (1965): 363-72.

     Lists works chronologically by date of printing. Mentions unpublished works including "couple of dozen sinfonias."

692. Schulenberg, David. *The Instrumental Music of Carl Philipp Emanuel Bach*. Ann Arbor: UMI Research Press, 1984. 202p. ISBN 8357-1564-7 ML410 B16 S35 1984

     Concentrates on style, using illustrations from symphonies in some instances. Establishes excellent style definition which would also encompass many aspects of Bach's symphonic approach.

693. Suchalla, Ernst. *Die Orchestersinfonien Carl Philipp Emanuel Bachs nebst einem thematischen Verzeichnis seiner Orchesterwerke*. Augsburg: Blasaditsch, 1968. 295p. ML410 B16 S8

     Analyzes symphonies and provides thematic index of all orchestral works with bibliography for each work. Analysis covers movement forms, variation technique, harmony, rhythm, dynamics and instrumentation. Printed version of 1968 dissertation from Johannes-Gutenberg Univ. in Mainz. Only major symphony study to date. Worthy of translation.

694. Wade, Rachel W., ed. *The catalog of Carl Philipp Emanuel Bach's estate*. New York: Garland, 1981.

     Facsimile of original edition by Schiebe (Hamburg), 1790. Original supposedly based on efforts of Bach's wife, Bach's own lists, Johann Jacob Westphal's lists, Breitkopf's lists and records of others not identified. Locates reprint of original in *Bach-Jahrbuch* (1938, pp. 101-36; 1939, 81-112; and 1940-48, 161-81), with commentary by Heinrich Miesner.

695. _____. *The Keyboard Concertos of Carl Philipp Emanuel Bach*. Ann Arbor: UMI Research Press, 1981. 360p. ISBN 0-8357-1207-9 ML13662 W3

     Chapter 4 (Compositional Process) gives insight into process in transitional period in which mature classical style evolved. Especially pertinent: comments on phrase structure (pp. 76-80). Based on author's dissertation (New York Univ., 1979).

696. Wotquenne, Alfred. *Thematisches Verzeichnis der Werke von Carl Philipp Emanuel Bach (1714-1788)*. Wiesbaden: Breitkopf & Härtel, 1964. 161p. ML134 B08 W63

Reprint of original 1905 edition (Leipzig: Breitkopf & Härtel). Lists 19 symphonies.

Johann Christoph Friedrich Bach (1732-1795)[g,b]

697. Geiringer, Karl. "Unbeachtete Kompositionen des Bückeburger Bach." In *Festschrift Fischer/70th*, pp. 99-107.

Wrote 5 symphonies, 3 of which are in Moravian archives in Bethlehem, Penn., and Winston Salem, N.C. Discusses these symphonies briefly.

William (Wilhelm) Friedmann Bach (1710-1784)[g,b]

698. Haas, Patricia Rose. "William Friedmann Bach by Dr. Martin Falck. Translated from the German." M.A. thesis, Univ. of Louisville, 1969. 119p.

Provides information on environmental factors related to growth of symphony. Section on style (pp. 27-30) mentions orchestral works (wrote 10 *sinfonias*). Covers biography only, with discussion of works to follow.

Franz Ignaz von Beeke (1733-1803)[g,b]

699. Murray, Sterling E., ed. *Franz Ignaz von Beeke: Symphony Cm1* in *Symphony*, series C, vol. VI (Seven Symphonies from the Court of Oettingen-Wallerstein), pp. xi-xlvi, lxv, 255-388.

Covers activities of school, its symphonic and orchestral styles and lives of composers (Fiala, Rosetti, Reicha, Wineberger and von Beeke). Analyzes edited von Beeke work, asserting its anticipation of early Beethoven symphonies (romantic elements and formal maturity). Thematic index of 27 authentic symphonies (25 in 4 movements) and 3 *symphonies concertante*.

Joseph Camerloher (1710-1743)[b]
Placidus von Camerloher (1718-1782)[g,b]

700. Forsberg, Susan, ed. *Joseph Camerloher, Placidus von Camerloher: Three Symphonies* in *Symphony*, series C, vol. II, pp. xxix-lv, 97-140.

Covers lives and works of both composers (were brothers) and comments on symphonic style, drawing upon editor's dissertation, "The symphonies of Placidus von Camerloher (1718-1782) and Joseph Camerloher (1710-1743): toward a determination of style and authorship" (New York Univ., in progress). Adds definitive analysis of edited scores. Thematic lists 29 symphonies by Placidus, 12 by Joseph and 49 by "Camerloher" (35 probably by Joseph, 6 by Placidus, 4 lost, 1 questionable and 3 spurious). Will establish method for determining correct attribution.

Bartolomeo Campagnoli (1751-1827)[g,b]

701. Garner, Bradley A., ed. *Bartolomeo Campagnoli: One Symphonie concertante* in *Symphony*, series D, vol. V, pp. xxxix-xlvi, 195-235.

Loosely paraphrases biographical parts of *New Grove* article. Served as leader of Gewendhaus orchestra, 1797-1818. Wrote superb pedagogical works for violin and viola. Notes sparse orchestral output: 3 flute concerti and edited work (solo violin and flute). Provides cogent analysis of latter. Thematic index.

Christian Cannabich (1741-1798)[g,b]

702. Beck, Rudolf L. "Geschichte und Genealogie der Hofmusikerfamilie Cannabich, 1707-1806." *AfMw* 34 (1977): 298-309.

Remains best and most accurate data available on Cannabich's life. Notes study with Jommelli, reinforcing concept of Italian influences in Mannheim. Was orchestra director when Mozart visited Mannheim in 1777.

703. Groman, Mary Alyce. "The Mannheim orchestra under the leadership of Christian Cannabich." Ph.D. dissertation, Univ. of California (Berkeley), 1979. 316p.

Details group's history (1720-1800), its members and leaders. Assesses orchestra's quality by examining works written, accenting demands on violinists. Concentrates on Cannabich's works, conducting and violin skills. Reviews bowing, pre- and post-Tourte.

704. Wolf, Jean K., ed. *Christian Cannabich: Symphonies 22, 23, 57, 73* in *Symphony*, series C, vol. III (The Symphony in Mannheim), pp. xxxix-lxxxiii, 197-339.

Offers biography that corrects flaws in *New Grove* entry with impressive documentation and contemporary quotes both entertaining and enlightening. Formulates symphony chronology by decades and carefully analyzes edited works. Lists 56 sources in bibliography. Thematic index shows 76 authentic, 13 spurious and 2 lost symphonies; 3 extant pastorales and 1 lost pastorale.

705._____. "The Orchestral Works of Christian Cannabich: A Documentary Study." M.A. chapter, New York Univ., 1968. 95p.

A detailed documentary analysis of papers and copyists of Christian Cannabich's orchestral manuscripts now located in the Bayerische Staatsbibliothek, Munich. Evidence found proves that many sources are parts copied by the composer himself and numbered in chronological order; others were copied by scribes of the Mannheim court and brought to Munich in 1778. Appendices include information on papers and copyists of the two courts, Cannabich handwriting samples, and documentary details on each Cannabich MS in the Munich collection. (Provided by author. Available by contacting author at 114 St. Pauls Road, Ardmore, PA 19003.) See entry 687.

Franz Danzi (1873-1826)[g,b]

706. Alexander, Peter M., ed. *Franz Danzi: Three Symphonic Works* in *Symphony*, series C, vol. V, pp. xxiii-xxxviii, 55-194

Recounts early life in Mannheim court (cellist in orchestra at 15, student of Abbé Vogler and move to Munich to replace father as principal cellist) and on lengthy career that followed. Demonstrates in discussion of symphonies that Danzi underwent stylistic maturation. Thematic index has 5 symphonies (1790-1817) and 6 *symphonies concertantes* (1785-1820; 2 lost).

Ernst Dietrich Adolf Eichner (1740-1777)[g,b]

707. Van Boer, Bertil H., Jr., ed. *Ernst Dietrich Adolf Eichner: One Symphony* in *Symphony*, series C, vol. XIV, pp. xli-li, 83-100.

Prepares excellent biography and discussion of symphonies. Performed as solo bassoonist most of life. Contrary to Riemann, was not associated with Mannheim court or school. Worked in Zweibrücken, England (briefly) and Potsdam. Notes "bold individualism" of symphonies, with little Italian taint and even less Mannheim bent. Characterizes each movement style. No thematic index but identifies an index in entry 708.

708. Reissinger, Marianne. *Die Sinfonien Ernst Eichners (1740-1777)*. Wiesbaden: Breitkopf & Härtel, 1970. 270p.

Categorizes themes in relation to transition from Baroque to Classic. Places symphonies in periods: experimentation (nos. 1-12), formal stability and enhanced expressivity (14-24) and synthesis of earlier periods (25-31). Sees style as blend of Italian form, middle-Germany harmony, Mannheim expression, French periodicity and *cantabile* and North German melodic tunefulness. Provides *incipits* for all movements of symphonies. Impressive bibliography. Represents published version of dissertation (Frankfurt, 1970).

Johann Samuel Endler (1694-1762)[g,b]

709. Biermann, Joanna Cobb, ed. *Johann Samuel Endler: Three Symphonies* in *Symphony*, series C, vol. II, pp. lvii-lxxiv, 141-254.

Worked most of life in Darmstadt. Designed symphonies in 3-to-7 movements, with an opening *Allegro* using one of many forms and frequent pairs of dances in middle movements, all seemingly unaffected by *sinfonia* style. Thematic index lists 30 symphonies (1748-1761).

Johann Friedrich Fasch (1688-1758)[g,b]

710. Sheldon, D.A. "Johann Friedrich Fasch: Problems in
      Style Classification." *MQ* 58 (1972): 92-116.

      Wrote many instrumental works, including 96 overtures
      (suites opening with French overtures) and 19 symphonies.
      Employs modified binary form (with double bar) in symphony
      and sonata movements, anticipating Classical sonata
      form. Covers symphonies on pp. 105-12. Employed transi-
      tional style with many attributes of preclassicism in
      evidence. See also P. Tryphon: "Die Symphonien von
      Johann Friedrich Fasch" (diss., Free Univ. of Berlin,
      1954); not examined.

Joseph Fiala (ca. 1750-1816)[g,b]

711. Murray, Sterling E., ed. *Joseph Fiala: Symphony C1* in
      Symphony, series C, vol. VI (Seven Symphonies from
      the Court of Oettingen-Wallerstein), pp. xi-l, 1-38.

      Features narrative on court, its orchestra, composers
      and symphonic style. Presents Fiala's life in some de-
      tail, indicating large output of instrumental music.
      Employs demanding *clarino* horn and trumpet parts, indi-
      cative of "extraordinary brass writing" at court. The-
      matic index shows 11 authentic and 1 spurious symphony
      and 4 *symphonies concertantes*.

Johann Anton Filtz (1733-1760)[g,b]

712. Agee, Richard J., ed. *Johann Anton Filtz: Two Symphonies*
      in *Symphony*, series C, vol. IV, pp. ix-xii, xvi-xvii,
      125-74.

      Joined Mannheim orchestra as cellist in 1754. Notes
      positive contemporary comments on Filtz. Schubart
      claimed Filtz was best of his time. Indicates progres-
      sive handling of form in analysis of edited works.
      Riemann's thematic index (entries 678, 679) indicates
      39 symphonies, adding several more later.

Ferdinand Fränzl (1767-1833)[g]

713. Pickett, Susan Ellen. "Ferdinand Fraenzel's symphonie
      concertante, opus 4: a performing edition with histori-

cal and editorial notes." Ph.D. dissertation, Texas Tech Univ., 1981. 309p.

Known as most important violinist of his time. Was native of Mannheim, succeeding Cannabich as court music director at Munich. While not a musicological project, does present full score in performing edition. Not included is piano reduction prepared by Pickett. Commentary and notes are 62 pages in length.

Ignaz Fränzl (1736-1811)[g,b]

714. Würtz, Roland, ed. *Ignaz Fränzl: Three Symphonies* in *Symphony*, series C, vol. XI, pp. xi-xxi, 1-87.

As leading musician in Mannheim in late 18th century wrote primarily instrumental music. Favorably compares style of works with that of Cannabich and Toeschi. Asserts that style matures from "quartet" symphony to mature Classical genre with edited scores supporting concept. Adds specific comments on orchestration and melody. Thematic index lists 5 authentic, 1 lost and 1 questionable symphony.

Carl Heinrich Graun (1704-1759)[g,b]

715. Bebbington, Warren A., ed. *Carl Heinrich Graun: Two Overtures* in *Symphony*, series C, vol. I, pp. xlv-lix, 163-98.

Combines discussion of brothers, covering lives (extended treatment, noting close association with Dresden and Berlin), works and symphonic works. Notes Carl's interest in vocal music and Johann's in instrumental. Thematic index (*Reference Volume* in *Symphony*, pp. 253-57) lists 32 opera overtures, most in *sinfonia* form and style. Edits two scores, one of which is French overture in all respects except for last movement in rondo form, the other more a true *sinfonia*.

716. Mennicke, Karl H. *Hasse und die Brüder Graun als Symphoniker; nebst Biographien und thematischen Katalogen.* Leipzig: Breitkopf & Härtel, 1906. 568p. ML1255 M52h

Remains in many ways definitive source for study of symphonies by Hasse and brothers Graun. Covers history

of instrumental style (pp. 26-98), French overture symphonies of composers (99-141), *sinfonia* symphonies (142-
249), connection between overture and drama (250-69) and
orchestration and dynamics. Thematic index (omitting
movement titles and tempos) includes symphonic works of
all three composers.

Johann Gottlieb Graun (1703-1771)[g,b]

717. Bebbington, Warren A., ed. *Johann Gottlieb Graun: Three
     Symphonic Works* in *Symphony*, series C, vol. I, pp. xlv-
     lix, 101-61.

     Notes greater interest (than his brother) in contra-
     puntal textures. Two of edited works (symphonies) ob-
     serve the outer dimensions of *sinfonia* while the overture
     follows French manner. Observes that melody tends toward
     spun-out Baroque style. See entry 715.

718. Mennicke, Karl H. See entry 716.

Johann Christoph Graupner (1683-1760)[g,b]

719. Rosenblum, Myron, ed. *Johann Christoph Graupner: Four
     Symphonies* in *Symphony*, series C, vol. II, pp. xiii-
     xxviii, 1-95.

     Points out composer's ability to absorb Italian, Mann-
     heim and French influences in music. Wrote 113 sympho-
     nies (52 *sinfonias*, 49 4-to-8 movement suite-like works
     and 12 *galant* style works in 4 movements), 87 overtures
     (suites), 44 concertos and 1,418 church cantatas. Edited
     scores include 2 4-movement *galant* works, 1 French over-
     ture and 1 concerto grosso clone. Thematic index derived
     from Nagel (entry 720).

720. Nagel, Wilibald. *Christoph Graupner als Sinfoniker*,
     Musikalische Magazin, No. 49. Langensalza: H. Beyer
     & Söhn, 1912.

     Not examined. Contains thematic catalog. Nagel felt
     Graupner may have influenced Mannheim composers. Was
     one of early pioneers of 4-movement symphonic form. See
     also Martin Witte: "Die Instrumentalkonzerte von Johann
     Christoph Graupner." Ph.D. dissertation, Georg-August
     Univ., Göttingen, 1963. Not examined.

Johann Adolph Hasse (1699-1783)[g,b]

Considered one of great *opera seria* composers of his
time. Wrote 60+ operas, most having *sinfonia* style overtures. *NGDMM* entry mentions at least 25 "additional"
sinfonias associated with operas, implying about 85 overtures available for concert performance. Breitkopf
(entry 116) contains 4 Hasse *sinfonias*, each identified
by source opera. See entries 70 and 448.

721. Mennicke, Karl H. See entry 716.

722. Schwartz, Judith Leah "Opening Themes in Opera Overtures
      of Johann Adolph Hasse: Some Aspects of Thematic Struc-
      tural Evolution in the Eighteenth Century." In *Bern-
      stein Festschrift*, pp. 243-59.

Based on concepts developed in dissertation (entry
68). Shows relationship between phrase structure and
style maturity. Uses as variables: phrase length,
"breaking-up of...Baroque homogeneous rhythm into dis-
cretely articulated motives," melodic contrast, "direc-
tional progression," melodic climax and others. Amply
illustrated with pertinent examples.

Johann David Heinichen (1683-1729)[g,b]

723. Ottenberg, Hans-Gunter, ed. *Johann David Heinichen:
      Symphony in D major* in *Symphony*, series C, vol. X
      (The Symphony in Dresden), pp. xi-xv, xix-xx, 39-50.

Provides summary of musical and symphonic activity in
18th century Dresden, brief biography of Heinichen and
analysis of edited symphony. Thematic catalog in *Reference Volume* of *Symphony* series, pp. 303-4, lists 9
symphonic works, 5 in *sinfonia* form. Edited work shows
transition from Baroque to Classic, with extended cadence
for second movement.

Ignaz Holzbauer (1711-1787)[g,b]

724. Agee, Richard J., ed. *Ignaz Holzbauer: Three Symphonic
      Works* in *Symphony*, series C, vol. 4, pp. ix-xxii, 1-
      124.

Contains translation of Holzbauer's autobiography he
provided for Carl F. Cramer's *Magazin der Musik* (1783)

but sparse stylistic comment by editor. Does note style
progression from earlier Baroque-like to later Mannheim-
oriented works. No thematic index provided for 65+ symphonies. See Hilgard Werner: "Die Sinfonien von Ignaz
Holzbauer (1711-1783): ein Beitrag zur Entwicklung der
vorklassischen Sinfonie," diss., Ludwig-Maximilians
Univ., Munich, 1942. Not examined.

725. Carse, Adam. "Ignaz Holzbauer." *MMR* 69 (1939): 208-9.

Includes discussion of composer's *Periodical Overture*,
opus 4, no. 3 (also in Riemann *DTB* edition, entries 676-
679). Titles finale "Tempesta del mare." Offers
valuable comments on orchestration.

Justin Heinrich Knecht (1752-1817)[g,b]

726. Höhnen, Heinz Werner, ed. *Justin Heinrich Knecht: One
Symphony* in *Symphony*, series C, vol. XIII, pp. xi-
xxiii, 1-71.

Cited as one of several composers of pastoral symphonies prior to Beethoven's sixth. Reviews life in Bibe-
rach and works (many church works). Summarizes other
earlier pastoral efforts for orchestra. Compares programs of Knecht ("Le portrait musical de nature") and
Beethoven pastoral symphonies. Edited work has 5 movements with choral finale. Thematic index lists 4 symphonies (3 lost), all with descriptive titles.

Georg Anton Kreusser (1746-1810)[g,b]

727. Klenck, Edith Peters, ed. *Georg Anton Kreusser: Two
Symphonies* in *Symphony*, series C, vol. XIV, pp. liii-
lx, 101-64.

Describes Mainz career and large output of symphonies.
Identifies four compositional periods, with most symphonies written in second and third periods. Notes dearth
of development in most scores. Used both 3 and 4-move-
ment form, favoring former in third period's 12 symphonies. Locates thematic index in author's earlier dissertation (entry 728).

728. Peters (Klenck), Edith. *Georg Anton Kreusser - Ein
Mainzer Instrumentalkomponist der Klassik.* Munich:

Katzbichler, 1975. ISBN 2-87397-104-6 ML410 K7368
P5

Represents publication (in typescript) of dissertation
(*Georg Anton Kreusser, Leben und Werk,* Mainz: Johannes
Gutenberg Univ.). Focuses primarily on style study of
composer's 54 symphonies (movement and overall form, instrumentation). Traces composer's style evolution in
final chapter. Appendix contains chronological work
list, family genealogy and list of works in court
library. Thematic index.

Johann Georg Lang (1722-1798)[g,b]

729. Davis, Shelley. "J.G. Lang and the early Classical
keyboard concerto." *MQ* 66 (1980): 21-52.

Somewhat related to symphonies. Delineates concerto
style and comments on performances of symphonies and
concertos in church services. See also author's dissertation, "The keyboard concertos of Johann Georg Lang
(1722-1798)," New York Univ., 1971. Not examined.

730. _____, and Gary L. Hill, editors. *Johann Georg Lang:
Three Symphonies* in *Symphony,* series C, vol. I, pp.
lxi-lxxvii, 199-311.

Born in Bohemia but worked in Augsburg and Coblenz area
(Ehrenbreitstien). Wrote most symphonies from late
1750's to early 1770's. Recounts in some detail use of
symphonies in church services but only summarizes style
matters. Favored 3-movement form and, internally, rudi-
mentary sonata-allegro (binary?). Thematic index of 40
symphonies, 27 in 3 and 3 in 4 movements. Does not identify movement content of 8 works.

Johann Gottlieb Naumann (1741-1801)[g,b]

731. Ottenberg, Hans-Günter, ed. *Johann Gottlieb Naumann:
Symphony in C major* in *Symphony,* series C, vol. X
(The Symphony in Dresden), pp. xxvii-xxix, 105-29.

Known as opera composer with overtures used as symphonies (see Breitkopf catalogs, entry 116). Offers
biography and summary of symphonies. Thematic index
(*Reference Volume,* 384-87) of 22 extant and 4 lost symphonies, all in *sinfonia* style.

Jan Křtitel Jiří (Johann Baptist Georg) Neruda (ca. 1706/1710–1776)[g,b]

732. Pilková, Zdeňka, ed. *Jan Křtitel Jiří: Symphony in A major* in *Symphony*, series C, vol. X (The Symphony in Dresden), pp. xxiv–xxvi, 87–103.

      Stresses transitional style of edited work (Baroque melodic features and bass lines, very immature first movement form and some imitative tendencies). Thematic index (*Reference Volume*, p. 391) shows 40 symphonies (13 extant, 18 lost, 1 spurious, 3 incomplete listings from Uppsala University library; most in 3 movements).

Johann Georg Pisendel (1687–1755)[g,b]

733. Landmann, Ortrun. "Johann Georg Pisendel und der 'deutsche Geschmack'." *SAI* 13 (1980): 20–34.

      Concentrates on Pisendel's concertmaster role in Dresden court orchestra in broadening German style with French and Italian elements. Relates court's high quality of musical activity to development of early classic style. Reveals German court rosters of composers with Dresden most popular. Lists orchestral component for Dresden, Mannheim, Berlin, London, Paris opera, Stuttgart, San Carlo in Naples and others.

734. Ottenberg, Hans-Günter, ed.. *Johann Georg Pisendel: Symphony in B-flat major* in *Symphony*, series C, vol. X (The Symphony in Dresden), pp. xx–xxii, 51–74.

      Recognized as distinguished concertmaster of Dresden opera orchestra and acquaintance of Bach and Vivaldi. Wrote mostly concertos. Thematic index notes sole symphony (*Reference Volume*, p. 426) in 3 movements, dated 1745–50. See also Hans Rudolf Jung, "Johann Georg Pisendel (1687–1755): Leben und Werk" (Ph.D. diss., Jena Univ., 1956); not examined.

Franz Xaver Pokorny (1728–1794)[g,b]

735. Angerer, Hugo, ed. *Franz Xaver Pokorny: Three Symphonies* in *Symphony*, series C, vol. VII (Seven Symphonies from the Court of Thurn und Taxis), pp. xi–xxii, xxxi–xlvi, 65–185.

Includes introduction to court and its music. Cites
Pokorny's studies with Stamitz, Richter and Holzbauer.
Documents impressive instrumental output (includes 100+
symphonies and 60 concertos), noting his rival's attempt
to reduce Pokorny's offerings by assigning them to other
composers. Thematic index lists 145 authentic and 3
questionable symphonies. Edited work (facsimile of autograph) analyzed by Robert Holzer.

736. Barbour, J. Murray. "Pokorny vindicated." *MQ* 49 (1963):
      38-58.

Represents part of research re-establishing Pokorny
as composer of many disputed works in Thurn und Taxis
library. Includes thematic index of some of 60+ disputed works. See also entries 121 and 735.

Joseph Reicha (ca. 1750-1795)[g,b]

737. Murray, Sterling E., ed. *Joseph Reicha: Symphony D1* in
      Symphony, series C, vol. VI (Seven Symphonies from
      the Court of Oettingen-Wallerstein), pp. xxix-xxxi,
      lxi-lxii, 169-214.

Introduced with account of Wallerstein school and overall symphonic and orchestral style of composers in group.
Notes Reicha's fine talent as cellist. Emphasized concerted works as composer. Thematic index contains 3 symphonies and 2 *symphonies concertantes*. See entries 660,
673-75.

Johann Friedrich Reichardt (1752-1814)[g]

738. Salmen, Walter. *Johann Friedrich Reichardt: Komponist,
      Schriftsteller, Kapellmeister und Verwaltungsbeamter
      der Goethezeit*. Freiburg: Atlantis, 1963. 363p.
      ML410 R3515

Covers Reichardt's many writings and influence of
folk music on his style. Discusses symphonies and
concertos with selected analysis (all 7 symphonies).

Franz Xaver Richter (1709-1789)[g,b]

739. Lebermann, Walter. "Zu Franz Xaver Richters Sinfonien."
      Mf 25 (1972): 471-80.

Comprises further effort to establish chronology and exact output of symphonies. Lists locations of known mss. of symphonies.

740. Van Boer, Bertil H., Jr., ed. *Franz Xaver Richter: Five Symphonies* in *Symphony*, series C, vol. XIV, pp. xiii-xl, 1-81.

Summarizes life (mainly in Mannheim). Deplores lack of systematic catalog of works. Notes style as "blend of old and new," often favoring *Fortspinnung* melodic style and contrapuntal writing. Discusses symphonies, offering one of best English-language sources on genre. Notes changing style (under varying influences) and retention of some older values in symphonies. Thematic index contains 83 authentic, 1 questionable and 4 spurious works. Identifies modern editions and discography through 1984. See entry 122.

Joseph Riepel (1709-1782)[g,b]

741. Emmerig, Thomas. *Joseph Riepel (1709-1782), Hofkapellmeister der Fürsten von Thurn und Taxis: Biographie, Thematisches Werkverzeichnis, Schriftenverzeichnis.* Kallmünz: Lassleben, 1984. ISBN 3-7847-1516-8 D107.9 T3T5 Bd. 14

Includes thematic index with listing of 18 symphonies, extensive bibliography and two indices (works, persons). Thurn und Taxis court was located in Regensburg, seat of Holy Roman Empire diet in 18th century.

742. _____, ed. *Joseph Riepel: One Symphony* in *Symphony*, series C, vol. VII (Seven Symphonies from the Court of Thurn und Taxis), pp. xvii-xviii, 1-31.

Prefaces study with short history of court and its music. Minimizes style in short discussion of symphonies. Notes 4-movement format in 4 of 18 symphonies. Refers to entry 741 for thematic catalog.

Giovanni Alberto Ristori (1692-1753)[g,b]

743. Ottenberg, Hans-Günter, ed. *Giovanni Alberto Ristori: Symphony in F major* in *Symphony*, series C, vol. X (The Symphony in Dresden), pp. xxii-xxiv, 75-85.

Opens with commentary on Dresden court's music and Dresden symphony. Notes Ristori's strength as opera composer and his adherence to Italian style except in church works where Viennese polyphony intrudes. Offers substantial analysis of edited work (originally overture to 1736 cantata). See *Reference Volume* (p. 476) for thematic index.

Andreas Romberg (1767-1821)[g,b]

744. Berrett, Joshua, ed. *Andreas Romberg: One Symphony* in *Symphony*, series C, vol. XIV, pp. lxi-lxxiii, 165-210.

Notes lack of primary sources, most lost in bombing of Hamburg and Münster in World War II. Cites dependence on Stephenson's study (entry 745) and his essays in *MGG* and *NGDMM*. Mentions Stephenson's listing of 10 symphonies but here lists only the 4 published, most of the latter written before 1800.

745. Stephenson, Kurt. *Andreas Romberg: ein Beitrag zur Hamburger Musikgeschichte*. Hamburg: Hans Christian, 1938.

Based on sources later lost in fire bombing of World War II. Notes composer's list of works in establishing output and chronology. Comments on symphonies and their overall style. Not examined. Annotation derived from entry 744.

Anton Rosetti (Franz Anton Rössler or Rösler) (ca. 1750-1792)[g,b]

746. Fitzpatrick, Horace. "Antonio Rosetti." *ML* 43 (1962): 234-47.

Makes Kaul's earlier research (entry 747) available in English. Explains Haydn-Rosetti connection that resulted in performance of several Rosetti symphonies as Haydn works at Salomon concerts in London. Asserts works embody two traditions: Italian opera-related classical instrumental style and Bohemian nationalism.

747. Kaul. Oskar, ed. *Anton Rosetti (1750-1792): Ausgewählte Sinfonien*. In *DTB* XII/1 (1912).

Offers biographical material in introduction and stylistic study of 34 symphonies listed in thematic index
of entire instrumental output. Includes Kaul's edition
of 5 symphonies in full score. See entry 746.

748. Murray, Sterling Ellis. "Antonio Rosetti (1750-1792)
      and His Symphonies." Ph.D. dissertation, Univ. of
      Michigan, 1973. 531p.

      Active in court music at Oettingen-Wallerstein (south
      Germany) and Mecklenburg-Schwerin (north Germany),
      spending most of life in these minor courts. Explains
      in great detail role of smaller courts in development
      of 18th century music and studies in depth Rosetti's
      symphonies. Concludes works were within period's style
      norm, based primarily on extensive study of form.

749. _____, ed. *Antonio Rosetti: (Three Symphonies)* in
      Symphony, series C, vol. VI (Seven Symphonies from
      the Court of Oettingen-Wallerstein), pp. xxvi-xxix,
      li-lx, 39-168.

      Prefaces Rosetti comments with discussion of Waller-
      stein school and orchestral style of works from school.
      Notes composer's adoption of Italian name. Gained con-
      siderable stature throughout life, even being commis-
      sioned to write and conduct requiem mass for Mozart
      commemorative ceremony in Prague on December 14, 1791.
      Cites Rosetti as leading figure in music of small courts
      in Germany. Includes analysis of edited works and the-
      matic index of 59 symphonies (43 authentic, 8 question-
      able and 8 spurious). Supplies concordance of his and
      Kaul's thematic indices. Impressive annotations for each
      entry.

750. _____. "The Rösler-Rosetti Problem: A Confusion of
      Mistaken Identity and Pseudonym." *ML* 57 (1976): 130-
      43.

      Identifies seven musicians who shared names with either
      Rösler or Rosetti (Rösler's name after 1770).

Theodor von Schacht (1748-1823)[g,b]

751. Angerer, Hugo, and Robert Holder, editors. *Theodor von
      Schacht: Two Symphonies* in *Symphony*, series C, vol.

VII (Seven Symphonies from the Court of Thurn und Taxis), pp. xxii-xxiv, xlvii-li, 187-255.

Provides summary of court and its music, short biography of Schacht (studied 5 years with Jommelli) and style summary of works. Was principal Italian opera advocate in Regensburg. Notes strong Italian influence in symphonies, many traits linked to Jommelli's mannerisms. Index shows 3-movement form in 10 of 33 authentic symphonies.

Johann Georg Christoph Schetky (1737-1824)[g,b]

752. Johnson, David, ed. *Johann Georg Christoph Schetky: One Quartetto* in *Symphony*, series C, vol. II, pp. lxxv-lxxxvi, 255-73.

Reveals career as cellist in Darmstadt, Hamburg, London and Edinburgh. Most of symphonies (or *quartetti*) written in 1777 for Edinburgh audiences. Notes more advanced style of *quartetti* and existence of several late symphonies now lost. Thematic index shows 3 symphonies and 6 *quartetti*, all in 3 movements.

Johann Christoph Schmidt (1664-1728)[g,b]

753. Ottenberg, Hans-Günter, ed. *Johann Christoph Schmidt: Overture in F major* in *Symphony*, series C, vol. X (The Symphony in Dresden), pp. xv-xvii, 1-15.

Covers generic style of Dresden symphonies in introduction, adding short biography of Schmidt (respected teacher and *Kapellmeister*). Thematic index (p. 513 in series' *Reference Volume*) shows four symphonic works, all multi-movement suites with French overture first movements. Comments briefly on style of edited work.

Franz Anton Schubert (1768-1827)[g,b]

754. _____, ed. *Franz Anton Schubert: Symphony in D major* in *Symphony*, series C, vol. X (The Symphony in Dresden), pp. xxxiii-xxxvii, 197-227.

Describes Schubert's main symphonic interest in church genre, writing only 1 *sinfonia da camera*. Describes in great detail church symphony style. Comments on style of edited *sinfonia da camera*. Thematic index (*Reference*

Volume, p. 516) also shows 1 three-movement and 41 single-movement church symphonies.

Joseph Schubert (1757-1833)[g,b]

755. _____, ed. *Joseph Schubert: Symphony in C major* in *Symphony*, series C, vol. X (The Symphony in Dresden), pp. xxxi-xxxii, 153-96.

Wrote 4 operas and many instrumental works: 49? concerti, 17 sonatas and one symphony (listed as written ca. 1788 in *Reference Volume's* thematic index, p. 521). Notes similarity to Haydn style in edited work.

Joseph Schuster (1748-1812)[g,b]

756. _____, ed. *Joseph Schuster: Symphony in D major* in *Symphony*, series C, vol. X (The Symphony in Dresden), pp. xxix-xxxi, 131-52.

Recounts gradual style evolution from *buffo* through South German and Viennese influences. Includes symphonic style and analysis of edited work, written during composer's 17th year. Thematic index (*Reference Volume*, p. 522) lists 1 lost and 17 extant works, mostly opera overtures (names source work); 6 written as church symphonies. Uses 3-movement form in 12 works.

Friedrich Schwindl (1737-1786)[g,b]

757. Downs, Anneliese. "The Symphonies of Friedrich Schwindl." Ph.D. dissertation, New York Univ., 1973. 240p.

Isolates 31 authentic works, 11 having later revisions (implying 42 differing examples?). Asserts that symphonies represent growth of genre (1760-1780) due to composer's broad background. Sees some regional style traits (e.g., Mannheim-style orchestration). Dwells on first-movement form with insight and historical perspective. Indicates (correctly) greatest asset of research: study of revised works, showing "cogent evidence of stylistic change and personal maturation." Thematic index.

Carl Philipp Stamitz (1745-1801)[g,b]

758. Agee, Richard J., ed. *Carl Philipp Stamitz: Three Symphonic Works* in *Symphony*, series C, vol. IV, pp. xii-xxii, 175-271.

Presents biography, detailing travels, fame, decline and eventual death as near-pauper. Comments on output of 51 symphonies, 60 concertos, 38 *symphonies concertantes* and many chamber works. Injects brief style discussion of symphonies, augmented by analysis of edited works (including 1 *symphonie concertante*). Notes preference for 3-movement format. Locates thematic catalog in Friedrich Carl Kaiser's dissertation, "Carl Stamitz (1745-1801): biographische Beiträge; das symphonische Werk; thematischer Katalog der Orchesterwerk" (Philipps Univ., Marburg, 1962), not examined.

759. Dickinson, A.E.F. "A Stamitz Symphony." *ML* 33 (1952): 282.

Asks for information on 7 parts "recently acquired" of work by Carl Stamitz.

760. _____. "A Symphony by Karl Stamitz." *MMR* 83 (1953): 116-21.

Analyzes E minor symphony found in 1953(?). Dwells on horn scoring in minor keys (crooks for relative major?). Paris version located in Basel Univ. library.

Johann Stamitz (1717-1757)[g,b]

761. Dürrenmatt, Hans-Rudolf. *Die Durchführung bei Johann Stamitz (1717-1757); Beiträge zum Problem der Durchführung und analytische Untersuchung von ersten Sinfoniensätzen.* Publikationen der Schweizerischen Musikforschenden Gesellschaft. ser. 2, vol. 19. Bern: Paul Haupt, 1969. 155p. MT130 S75 D8

Findings: all of 30 developments studied start in dominant; 20 treat principal theme first; only 12 begin recapitulation with principal theme; identifies thematic types, development treatments, formal aspects in development and tonal structure. Notes traditional nature of most development sections. Tables reveal order of events and relative size of three sections of movement. No musical examples, a substantial handicap. See Eugene Wolf's review in *Notes* 27 (1970), 42-44.

762. Gradenwitz, Peter. *Johann Stamitz. Vol. I: Das Leben.* Veröffentlichungen des musikwissenschaftlichen Institutes der Deutschen Universität in Prag, 8. Brno: Rudolf M. Rohrer, 1936. 56p. ML410 S811 G7 v.1 Vol. 2 (*Thematische Katalog*), unpublished microfilm in New York Public Library.

Valuable in its documentation of sources and 18th century events related to Stamitz's life. Index.

763. _____. "The Stamitz Family; Some Errors, Omissions and Falsifications Corrected." *Notes* 7 (1949/50): 54-64.

Gradenwitz's original biography (entry 762) was discredited by German historians during Nazi regime as being inaccurate on Stamitz's "Germanness." This article restates important family data, replanting family roots in Czech soil with supporting data. Explains why second volume never published: ownership of press in Brno (Brünn) was transferred from Czech to German owners in 1938 during Nazi annexation of Sudentenland.

764. _____. "Die Steinmetz-Manuskripte der Landes- und Hochschulbibliothek Darmstadt." *Mf* 14 (1961): 214.

Clarifies identity of works by Steinmetz (alternate spelling for Stamitz). Refers to unpublished thematic index (entry 762) for authentication. See entry 768.

765. _____. "The Symphonies of Johann Stamitz." *MR* 1 (1940): 354-63.

Asserts that foundation of Stamitz's symphonic form derives from Italian sources, particularly Tessarini. Discusses nature of first themes and of development process. Defines mature style and adds list of works.

766. Keillor, Elaine. "Communication." *JAMS* 28 (1975): 567.

Presents evidence that J. Stamitz and Valentin Roeser did indeed meet during Stamitz's Paris visit. Brook disagrees in *NGDMM* Roeser article. See entry 645.

767. Korte, Werner. "Darstellung eines Satzes von Johann
     Stamitz." In *Festschrift Fellerer/60th*, pp. 283-93.

     Supports Stamitz as excellent manipulator of form,
     especially developmental movements. Includes analysis
     of E-flat major symphony (La Melodia Germanica No. 3).

768. Noack, Friedrich. "Die Steinmetz-Manuskripte der Landes-
     und Hochschulbibliothek Darmstadt." *Mf* 13 (1960): 314-
     17.

     List 19 symphonies in manuscript parts by Johann Erhard
     Steinmetz (fl. ca. 1750), a *Jagdpfeifer* in hunt band of
     Dresden court. Works generally acknowledged to be by J.
     Stamitz.

769. Noske, Frits. "Zum Strukturverfahren in den Sinfonien
     von Johann Stamitz." In *Festschrift Fellerer/70th*,
     pp. 415-21.

     Studies form (especially motivic unity) in three
     Stamitz symphonies.

770. Pestelli, Giorgio. "Il cammino stilistico de Johann
     Stamitz." *Chigiana* 24 (1967): 97-110.

     Reviews all important literature, tracing development
     of style through examination of several works and noting
     strong Italian roots of that style.

771. Riemann, Hugo. "Stamitz oder Monn?" *Blätter für Haus-
     und Kirchenmusik* 12 (1907/8): 97-99, 113-17.

     Reimann's response to Adler's nomination of Monn as
     an earlier master of the symphony than Stamitz.

772. Scharschuch, Horst. "Johann Stamitz." *AfMw* 33 (1976):
     189-212.

     Emphasizes composer's life and family, his rebuilding
     of Mannheim orchestra. Adds brief commentary on works.

773. Volek, Tomislav. "Der Verhältnis von Rhythmus und Metrum
     bei J.W. Stamitz." In *Kongress Bonn, 1970*, pp. 53-58.

Argues that Stamitz's understanding of importance of
rhythmic motive as part of phrase construction may be
just as significant in his style as other features
heralded previously (*crescendo*, etc.).

774. Wolf, Eugene K., ed. *Johann Stamitz: (Five Symphonies)*
in *Symphony*, series C, vol. III (The Symphony in Mannheim), pp. xxi-xxxvii, 1-196.

Summarizes Stamitz's life while presenting extended
discussion of works and symphonic output (58 extant symphonies and 10 orchestral trios). Describes diversity of
output, identifying works in relation to life chronology.
Divides works into three periods: to ca. 1745-1748 (20
works), to ca. 1752-1754 (29 works) and to 1757 (9 symphonies and 10 orchestral trios), defining each period.
Notes beginning of Italian influence in second period.
Adds analysis of 5 edited works. Thematic index in
editor's dissertation (entry 776).

775. _____. "The orchestral trios, Op. 1, of Johann Stamitz." In *Festschrift Brook*, pp. 297-322.

Discloses genealogy and style of trios, works considered by author as non-symphonic. Depicts trios as being
"a mean between the symphonies and the chamber styles."
Stresses differing trio and symphonic styles.

776. _____. *The Symphonies of Johann Stamitz: a Study in the
Formation of the Classic Style*. Utrecht/Antwerp: Bohn,
Scheltema & Holkema and The Hague/Boston: Martinus
Nishoff, 1981. 500p. ISBN 90-313-0346-1 ML410 S811
W6

Must be described as one of most important contributions to study of symphony. Focuses on style matters
(overall form, phrase structure, movement forms) while
giving detailed study of style periods. Concludes that
Mannheim strongly influenced by *sinfonia* style (Galuppi,
Jommelli *et al.*) and that Stamitz adapted *sinfonia* style
to new symphonic style by infusing changes that enhanced
symphonic quality of works. Attributes Mannheim *crescendo* to Italian operas heard in Mannheim. Appends thematic
index and bibliography, both of splendid quality. Should
be noted as more than worthy of support afforded it by
Guggenheim and University of Pennsylvania foundations.

Represents up-date of author's dissertation (New York Univ., 1972).

777. _____, ed. *The Symphony in Mannheim: Johann Stamitz and Christian Cannabich* in *Symphony*, series C, vol. III. 339p.

Surveys in introduction (pp. xiii-xx) music of Mannheim court (1720-1778) and the nature of the court's symphonic activity. Isolates mannerisms in mature Mannheim style that distinguish it from that of the earlier *sinfonia*.

Joseph Touchemoulin (1727-1814)[g,b]

778. Angerer, Hugo, ed. *Joseph Touchemoulin: One Symphony* in *Symphony*, series C, vol. VII (Seven Symphonies from the Court of Thurn und Taxis), pp. xviii-xx, xxvii-xxix, 33-64.

Summarizes life as violinist-composer and notes in thematic index output of 18 symphonies (half in 4 movements). Edited work analyzed by Robert Holzer.

Georg Joseph Vogler (1749-1814)[g,b]

779. Van Boer, Bertil H., Jr., ed. *Georg Joseph Vogler: One Symphony* in *Symphony*, series C, vol. V, pp. xi-xxi, 1-53.

Evaluates Abbé Vogler's 4 symphonies as minor part of composer's creative output, adding lengthy biography and discussion of symphonies (3 written during Mannheim stay). Observes grand flourish of fourth and final symphony (edited for volume) and its contrapuntal finale. Thematic index.

Paul Wineberger (1758-1821)[g,b]

780. Murray, Sterling E., ed. *Paul Wineberger: Symphony F1* in *Symphony*, series C, vol. VI (Seven Symphonies from the Court of Oettingen-Wallerstein), pp. xxxi-xxxiii, lxiii-lxiv, 215-53.

Contains short summary of life and analysis of edited work. Cites skills in writing for winds in symphonies

and in wind *partitas*. Thematic index lists 9 symphonies
and 2 *symphonies concertantes*.

Jan Dismas Zelenka (1679-1745)[g,b]

781. Ottenberg, Hans-Günter, ed. *Jan Dismas Zelenka: Overture
      in A major* in *Symphony*, series C, vol. X (The Symphony
      in Dresden), pp. xvii-xix, 17-38.

      Cited as representative of learned style, quickly
      forgotten in rush of *galant* style that followed. Edited
      overture subtitled *Hipocondrie*, a programmatic reference
      to composer's hypochondria. Thematic index (*Reference
      Volume*, p. 597) lists 8 works, many with multiple (5+)
      movements.

                              Holland

Joseph Schmitt (1734-1791)[g,b]

782. Dunning, Albert. *Joseph Schmitt; Leben und Kompositionen
      des Eberbacher Zisterziensers und Amsterdamer Musikver-
      legers (1734-1791)*. Amsterdam: Heuwerkemeyer, 1962.
      135p. ML410 S2617 D8

      Known as Cistercian monk in Eberbach monastery before
      moving to Amsterdam in 1780. Had studied with Abel and
      become part of Mannheim symphonic tradition. Opened
      music press in Amsterdam, at times issuing own sympho-
      nies. Feels print activity acquainted him with Viennese
      classical works, leading to a maturation in style. The-
      matic index lists 19 symphonies (12 in 3 movements, 5 in
      4 movements, 1 pastoral symphony and 1 single-movement
      work). Studies two symphonies in Mannheim period.
      Anhang adds 4 more works.

                              Hungary

Ferenc Novotny (ca. 1749-1806)[g,b]

783. Somorjay, Dorottya, ed. *Ferenc Novotny: (Two Sympho-
      nies)* in *Symphony*, series B, vol. XII (The Symphony
      in Hungary, The Symphony in Bohemia), pp. xiii-xix,
      1-67.

      Presents short discourse on life and works (primarily
      sacred music composer), noting his musical gifts but

lack of "further" education. Places edited works in
Viennese style. Thematic index estimates his only two
symphonies written between 1782 and 1806.

Anton Zimmermann (1741-1781)[g,b]

784. Biondi, Michael, ed. *Anton Zimmermann: One Symphony* in
Symphony, series B, vol. XIV, pp. xxv-xxxiv, 45-69.

Focuses on symphonic style and establishment of a
reliable instrumental ensemble for archbishop of Hun-
gary. Notes composer's fondness for chromatic colora-
tion. Indicates Viennese aspect of style while showing
12 of 30 symphonies in 3 movements. Thematic index
contains 30 authentic and 1 questionable symphony.
Cites files of Angela Evans as a source for index.

Italy

General

785. Arnold, Denis. "Orchestras in Eighteenth Century
Venice." *GaSJ* 19 (1966): 3-19.

Studies orchestral resources at St. Marks, observing
certain phases of development. Notes large orchestra
in 1766 (strings, 12/5/6/4; oboes and flutes, 4; horns
and trumpets, 4). Dates recorded: 1700, 1714, 1732,
1735, 1744, 1765 and 1766. Stresses how events relate
to ensemble size, minimizing study of orchestral style.

786. Barblan, Guglielmo. "Le Orchestre in Lombardia all'-
epoca di Mozart." In *Kongress Vienna/1956*, pp. 18-21.

Provides data on Filharmonica di Mantova, Accademico
Filharmonico (Cremona), Teatro Ducale (Milan), and Ac-
cademia Filharmonica (Milan). Reveals large ensemble
in 1776 at Teatro Ducale of 28 violins, 6 violas, 2
cellos, 6 basses, 2 flutes, 2 oboes, 2 clarinets, 2
bassoons and 4 horns. Shows smaller group in 1748:
strings 11/11/6/2/5 with pairs of oboes and bassoons
and 5 trumpets. Most had at least 1 *cembalo* player.

787. Berger, J. "Notes on some Seventeenth-Century Compositions for Trumpets and Strings in Bologna." *MQ* 37
(1951): 354-67.

Studies San Petronio basilica archives, examining
trumpet-string ensemble repertory by Torelli and others
and written before 1695 when basilica's large orchestra
disbanded. Notes many *sinfonia concerti* of period
"abandon imitative writing" in *allegro* movements.

788. Della Corte, Andrea, and G. Pannain. *Storia della
      musica.* Vol. II. Torino: Tipografia sociale Torinese,
      1964. 690p. ML193 C6 1964 v.2

      Covers (pp. 290-344) symphony in 18th century, includ-
      ing discussion of works of Pergolesi (sonatas), A. Scar-
      latti (overtures, with musical examples to define model),
      Valentini, Locatelli, Geminiani, Vivaldi, Boccherini
      (with analysis of *Sinfonia in D major*) and Sammartini.
      Notes briefly genre in France and Mannheim.

789. Delage, Joseph Ovide, Jr. "The overture in seventeenth
      century Italian opera." Ph.D. dissertation, Florida
      State Univ., 1961. 231p.

      Encompasses Roman opera overtures, Venetian opera over-
      tures of Cavalli and Monteverdi, overtures of later Vene-
      tian opera by Cesti and others and early *sinfonias* of A.
      Scarlatti. Stresses emergence from two-part design to
      three-part form. Studies factors in new style (tonality,
      tempo and shift to homophonic texture). Lists 150+ ex-
      tant overtures from period. Prepares critical editions
      of 15 overtures: *Il Sant' Alessio* (Stefano Landi); *Ermi-
      nia sul Giordano* (Michelangelo Rossi); *La Vita humana*
      (Marco Marazolli); *Egisto* and *Eritrea* (Francesco Caval-
      li); *La Magnanimità d'Alessandro, Il Tito, Alessandro
      vincitor* and *La Semirami* (Antonio Cesti); *Ercole in Tebe*
      (Jacopo Melani); *Il Numa Pompilio* (Giovanni Maria Pag-
      liardi); *L'Orfeo* (Antonio Sartorio); *La Galatea* (Pietro
      Andrea Ziani); *L'amor volubile e tiranno* and *Il Pompeo*
      (A. Scarlatti).

790. Dent, Edward J. "Italian Opera in the Eighteenth Cen-
      tury and Its Influence on the Music of the Classical
      Period." *SIMG* 14 (1912/13): 500-509.

      Stresses relationship between evolving instrumental
      forms (including symphony) and Italian opera and cantata
      (texture, phrase structure, etc.)

791. Green, Douglass M., and Gordana Lazarevich, editors. *Antecedents of the Symphony: The Eighteenth-Century Overture in Naples* in *Symphony*, series A, vol. I, pp.xxxi-xlvi, 39-257.

Includes overtures of Provenzale, della Torre, A. Scarlatti, Sarro, Feo, Vinci, Pergolesi, Sellitto, Leo, Jommelli, Paisiello, Cimarosa and an anonymous composer. Studies influence of overture on symphony, rise of sonata form and late 18th century overture. Considered one of best chronicles of genre's history. Edits 20 scores by above composers. Thematic index for Sarro only. See entry 793 for best thematic index of genre.

792. Hansell, S.V. "Orchestral Practice at the Court of Cardinal Pietro Ottoboni." *JAMS* 19 (1966): 398-403.

Studies orchestral resources available. Identifies performers and works performed (mostly sacred or operatic with orchestral accompaniment). As vice-chancellor of Catholic Church (1689-1740) employed many notable musicians, including A. Scarlatti and Corelli.

793. Hell, Helmut. *Die Neapolitanische Opernsinfonie in der ersten Hälfte des 18. Jahrhunderts: N. Porpora - L. Vinci - G.B. Pergolesi - L. Leo - N. Jommelli.* Tutzing: H. Schneider, 1971. 623p. ISBN 3-7952-0111-X ML1261 H44

Establishes definition of genre and devotes chapter each to study of composers' works. Thematic index lists 220 works and their locations in most instances. Reinforces linkage between *sinfonia* (especially those of Jommelli) and concert symphony. Argues convincingly that early *sinfonia* is closer in style to Baroque concerto than to preclassical symphony while latter seems closer to dance form (binary form, repeats, etc.). Finds, however, later works of Leo and Jommelli more directly connected to early symphony. Detects that many "Mannheim mannerisms" can be traced to Jommelli. See Landon's review, *HYb IX* (1975), 366.

794. Lazarevich, Gordana. "The Neapolitan Intermezzo and Its Influence on the Symphonic Idiom." *MQ* 57 (1971): 294-313.

Shows that the "classic concept of phrase structure can be traced in four aspects of the early 18th century Neapolitan intermezzo: melody, harmony, cadences and orchestral texture."

795. Lippmann, Friedrich. "Die Sinfonie Manuskripte der Bibliothek Doria Pamphilj in Rom." *AnM* 5 (1968): 201-47.

Contains *incipits* of 119 symphonies by 36 composers.

796. Livingston, Herbert Stanton. "The Italian Overture from A. Scarlatti to Mozart." 2 vols. Ph.D. dissertation, Univ. of North Carolina, 1952. 343, 198p.

Examined over 500 works, mostly from Library of Congress. Notes three periods in genre's growth (1695-1730, 1730-1760 and 1760-1790). Comments on manuscripts, scoring practices of composers and copyists (abbreviated figures, etc.) and printed editions available. Prepared scores of overtures to *La Statira* (1690) and *Il prigioniero fortunato* (1698, Scarlatti), *Pirro e demetrio* (ca. 1708, Haym), *Elpidia* (1725, Vinci), *Cajo Mario* (1746, Jommelli), *Il geloso in cimento* (1774, Anfossi), Love in a Village (1762, Abel) and *Der Aerndtekranz* (1771, Hiller).

797. Longyear, Rey M., ed. *The Northern Italian Symphony, 1800-1840* in *Symphony*, series A, vol. VI. 427p.

Some of composers and works, in part, fall within 18th century style parameters and are included in this *Guide*: Rolla and Asioli (entries follow). Establishes data on performance history and practices, style, form and sources. Defines two paths Italian symphony took after 1770: 3-movement form quite similar to older *sinfonia* and 1-movement church form.

798. Wolf, Eugene K., ed. *Antecedents of the Symphony: The Ripieno Concerto* in *Symphony*, series A, vol. I, pp. xiii-xxix, 1-38.

Defines *ripieno* concerto (concerto without soloists, orchestral concerto, concerto-sonata, etc.). Affirms 2 types: *sonata da chiesa* (trio sonata played by orchestra) and *sinfonia* (follows general 3-movement plan in homo-

phonic texture). Proposes that *ripieno* concerto created
"an idiomatic style for nontheatrical orchestral works
...dependent on neither imitative techniques nor
solo/tutti opposition for purposes of construction."
Asserts that early concert symphonies "were in fact heirs
to the over three decades of stylistic and formal
development embodied in the *ripieno* concerto."

Italian Composers

Tomaso Albinoni (1671-1750)[g,b]

799. Wolf, Eugene K., ed. *Tomaso Albinoni: Concerto in B-flat
      major* in *Symphony*, series A, vol. I (Antecedents of the
      Symphony), pp. xix-xx, xxv, 23-25.

      Preceded by discussion of *ripieno* concerto. Notes
      early appearance of first movement binary form in con-
      certo (Albinoni's 3rd concerto in his opus 2 set of six;
      Sala, 1700). Includes example as edited score.

Pasquale Anfossi (1727-1797)[g,b]

800. Johnson, Joyce L., ed. *Pasquale Anfossi: Two Sinfonie*
      in *Symphony*, series A, vol. IV, pp. xli-lviii, 155-
      204.

      Opens with long account of life and works (opera,
      primarily), noting use of his opera *sinfonias* as con-
      cert symphonies. Thematic index lists 67 *sinfonie*,
      listing sources (opera, cantata, etc.) for only 40.

Anonymous (fl. after 1750)

801. Green, Douglass M., and Gordana Lazarevich, editors.
      Anonymous: Sinfonia to S. Geneviefa in *Symphony*,
      series A, vol. I (Antecedents of the Symphony), pp.
      lv-lvi, 207-26.

      Notes initial attributions to Leonardo Leo (died in
      1744) or Giacomo Sellito, the latter discounted later
      by Hell (entry 793). Notes similarity to style of
      Jommelli. Estimates work written after 1760.

Bonifazio Asioli (1769-1832)[g,b]

802. Longyear, Rey M., ed. *Bonifazio Asioli: Sinfonia Azi-
     one teatrale campestre* in *Symphony*, series A, vol. VI
     (The Northern Italian Symphony, 1800-1840), pp. xxvi-
     xxvii, xliii-xliv, 151-206.

     Editor's coverage of style period begins on p. xv.
     Presents major events in life, revealing composer's
     high esteem (taught Mozart's elder son) in Napoleonic
     Italy. Little provided on his symphonic style. Thema-
     tic index lists 7 extant and 2 lost symphonies, with 6
     of 9 written before 1800. Only 2 symphonies have more
     than 2 movements, with only 1 four-movement example.

Luigi Boccherini (1743-1805)[g,b]

803. Almeida, Antonio de, ed. *Luigi Boccherini: Six Sinfonie*
     in *Symphony*, series A, vol. IV, pp. lix-lxvi, 205-334.

     Recounts details of composer's far-ranging life (Spain,
     Potsdam, Paris, Italy, Vienna), summarizes his style and
     evaluates composer's stature ("...one of greatest Rococo
     composers" who "would have been a symphonist of the first
     rank had he not been Italian...."). Offers facsimiles of
     autograph scores. See entries 804 (includes thematic
     index) and 887.

804. Gérard, Ives. *Thematic, bibliographical and critical
     catalog of the works of Luigi Boccherini*. Translated
     by A. Major. London: Oxford Univ. Press, 1969. 716p.
     ML134 B63 G5

     Lists 8 symphonies and 1 *symphonie concertante* for
     small orchestra and 21 symphonies for large orchestra.
     Shows additional work in appendix. Contains chronolo-
     gical list of works and 3 indices: discography, publi-
     shers of Boccherini's works and general index.

Antonio Brioschi (fl. ca. 1725-ca. 1750)[g,b]

805. Churgin, Bathia, and Tilden A. Russell, editors.
     Antonio Brioschi: Three Symphonies in *Symphony*,
     series A, vol. III, pp. ix-xxii, 1-60.

     Offers extended biography and discussion of work (major
     emphasis on style and 18th century sources). Notes

Brioschi's 1733 work as one of earliest known symphonies
(originated as overture to Hebrew cantata). Defines in
great detail Brioschi's symphonic style (favors 3 movements, uses strings only, first movements in well-defined
sonata-allegro outlines, fond of counterpoint, etc.),
contrasting it with that of Sammartini. Includes extensive analysis of edited works. Excellent contribution.
Churgin has compiled thematic index of Brioschi's works,
unpublished at this time.

Fortunato Chelleri (ca. 1690-1757)[g,b]

806. Churgin, Bathia, ed. *Fortunato Chelleri: One Symphony*
in *Symphony*, series A, vol. III, pp. xxiii-xxxii, 61-
74.

Comments on life and 21 extant symphonies (18 as 3-
movement *sinfonias* and 3 as suite symphonies of 4, 6 or
8 movements). Notes most written for strings alone, had
bipartite first movements (tending toward the Baroque),
showed poor definition of subordinate materials and often
used single rhythmic motive to unify a movement (another
Baroque trait). Later works show greater clarity in
sonata-allegro form. No thematic index existed at time
volume published. Identifies other thematic catalogs
listing Chelleri works.

Domenico Cimaroso (1749-1801)[g,b]

807. Green, Douglass M., and Gordana Lazarevich, editors.
Domenico Cimarosa: Il mercato di Malmantile sinfonia
in *Symphony*, series A, vol. I (Antecedents of the
Symphony), pp. lviii-lxii, 243-57.

Presented as part of "Eighteenth-Century Overture in
Naples," treating 13 composers in process. Describes
route of opera overture in late 18th century (became
one-movement work in binary form, little development but
with several themes of great appeal and "verve") to contrast with more complex first-movement form in symphony.
Describes Cimarosa's great success in opera. While wrote
very little instrumental music, overtures often played in
symphony concerts. No thematic index.

Evaristo Felice dall'Abaco (1675-1742)[g,b]

808. Wolf, Eugene K., ed. *Felice dall'Abaco: Concerto in F
      major* in *Symphony*, series A, vol. I (Antecedents of
      the Symphony),pp. xxvii, 27-38.

      Describes in lengthy introduction (xv-xxi) nature and
      history of *ripieno concerto* as a predecessor of symphony.
      Notes in analysis of edited work appearance of binary
      form in two of four movements. Dates work from 1717-1720
      or earlier.

Francesco della Torre? (fl. ca. 1675)

809. Green, Douglass M, and Gordana Lazarevich, editors.
      *Francesco Della Torre?: Chi tal nasce tal vive,
      introduzione* in *Symphony*, series A, vol. I (Antece-
      dents of the Symphony), pp. xxxiii-xxxiv, 43-44.

      Includes precise discussion of early *sinfonia* (pp.
      xxxv-xlvi) and identity of edited work's composer.
      Della Torre, who was manager of Naples theater, may have
      written above opera work. Analyzes short overture (three
      sections, homophonic in texture and finale in rounded
      binary).

Francesco Feo (1692-1761)[g,b]

810. Green, Douglass M., and Gordana Lazarevich, editors.
      Francesco Feo: Siface, introduzione, in *Symphony*,
      series A, vol, I (Antecedents of the Symphony), pp.
      1-li, 111-14.

      Opens with review of genre (pp. xxxv-xlvi), adding very
      short summary of Feo's life and works and succinct analy-
      sis of edited work (3 movements, use of binary form and
      free of concerto influence). Written in 1742.

Giorgio Giulini (1716-1780)

811. Cesare, Gaetano. "Giorgio Giulini, musicista: contri-
      buto alla storia della sinfonia in Milano." *RMI* 24
      (1917): 1-34, 210-71.

      Count Giulini was Sammartini pupil and wrote in style
      approximating that of teacher. Focuses on life and study
      of symphonies and those of Chiesa and Monza. Includes

full score of Giulini's *Sinfonia in F.* Cesare was one of
early 20th century music historians to study Italian
symphony.

Niccolò Jommelli (1714-1774)[g,b]

812. Inglefield, Kenley Paul. "The Sinfonias of Niccolò
     Jommelli." D.M.A. document, Univ. of Cincinnati, 1971.
     50p.

     Offers concise biography and generalized analysis of
     symphonies. Reconstructs 9 Jommelli sinfonias but fails
     to include these in final draft. Studies only form and
     orchestration. Available only from Cincinnati on inter-
     library loan. See also entry 793.

813. Green, Douglass M., and Gordana Lazarevich, editors.
     Niccolò Jommelli: Bajazette, sinfonia in *Symphony*,
     series A, vol. I (Antecedents of the Symphony), pp.
     liv-lv, 185-206.

     Opens with extended history of 18th century Neapolitan
     overture (pp. xxxiii-xlvi). Notes Jommelli's influence
     on Dittersdorf and Wagenseil and his successes as *Ober-
     Kapellmeister* at Ludwigsburg (orchestra of 47, best
     singers, etc.). Discloses Jommelli's lack of popularity
     upon his return to Naples was due to changing public
     taste. Identifies Jommelli's *sinfonia* trademark, a
     prominent orchestral *crescendo*.

Giovanni Battista Lampugnani (ca. 1708-ca. 1788)[g,b]

814. Vitali, Carlo, and Michele Girardi, editors. *Giovanni
     Battista Lampugnani: Five Sinfonie* in *Symphony*, series
     A, vol. IV, pp. xxvii-xxxix, 43-153.

     Starts career as opera composer (1732). Later worked
     as harpsichordist (second director) in Milan opera
     houses, conducting an early Mozart opera in 1770.
     Speaks to style of overtures (poor thematic definition,
     little development and lack of thematic dualism in first
     movements). Includes brief comments on edited works.
     Thematic index contains 10 extant (4 from operas), 4
     lost, 2 questionable and 2 spurious works.

Leonardo Leo (1694-1744)[g,b]

815.   Green, Douglass Marshall.   "The instrumental ensemble
        music of Leonardo Leo against the background of con-
        temporary Neapolitan music."   Ph.D. dissertation,
        Boston Univ., 1958.   274p.

        Presents excellent analysis of Leo's *sinfonia* style,
        stressing form and orchestration and including profuse
        examples (some in reduced score) by Leo and other com-
        posers (Pergolesi, Porpora, Scarlatti, Durante, etc.).
        Scope of research broader than title implies.   Added
        validity realized from author's interests and skills in
        music theory.   Thesis adviser: Geiringer.

816.   _____, and Gordana Lazarevich, editors.   *Leonardo Leo:*
        (Four Sinfonie) in *Symphony*, series A, vol. I (Antece-
        dents of the Symphony), pp. liii-lvi, 147-83.

        Remarks on history of *sinfonia* (pp. xxxiii-xlvi) while
        noting Leo's opera career and his approach to *sinfonia*.
        Emphasizes maturity of style of four edited works (1736-
        1742), especially greater contrast of second themes in
        opening movements.   Finales are all dance movements in
        triple meter.   See also entry 793.

817.   _____.   "Progressive and Conservative Tendencies in the
        Violoncello Concertos of Leonardo Leo."   In *Festschrift
        Geiringer/70th*, pp. 261-71.

        Emphasizes concertos but frequently mentions style of
        Leo's *sinfonias* in process.

(Padre) Giovanni Battista Martini (1706-1784)[g,b]

818.   Brofsky, Howard, ed.   *Padre Giovanni Battista Martini:*
        Four Sinfonie in *Symphony*, series A, vol. IV, pp. xii-
        xxvi, 1-42.

        Recounts Martini's illustrious teaching career (J.C.
        Bach, Grétry, Jommelli and Mozart) while explaining his
        pedagogical style (study of Renaissance and Baroque
        scores).   Notes huge output but scant style progress
        into *galant* era.   Includes impressive discussion of
        symphonic style, identifying 8 concerto-symphonies from
        output of 24 *sinfonie*.   Edited examples include 2 of
        former.   Thematic index also contains 6 incomplete one-

movement (fast) symphonies, possibly church symphonies. *Reference Volume* also has same index.

819. _____. "The instrumental music of Padre Martini." Ph.D. dissertation, New York Univ., 1963. 357p.

Covers symphonies on pp. 82-152. Concludes Martini was extremely conservative in embracing evolving pre-classic style. Wrote 2 kinds of symphonies: concerto-symphonies (in style of Baroque concerto) and symphonies (Italian *sinfonie*). Observes that only 4 of 8 *sinfonia* first movements exhibit "primitive sonata form." Thematic index and extensive bibliography.

820. _____. "The Symphonies of Padre Martini." *MQ* 51 (1965): 649-73.

Comments on conservative handling of form while in-jecting good overall style analysis. Concludes was one of "transitional composers in whose music early Classi-cal features appear; at same time we can witness in it the disintegration of Baroque style." Thematic index.

Stanislao Mattei (1750-1825)[g,b]

821. Longyear, Rey M., ed. *Stanislao Mattei: Five Symphonies* in *Symphony*, series A, vol. VIII, pp. ix-xi, xxi-xxiv, 1-161.

Defines style evolution from 18th to 19th century in Italian symphony with predominance of one-movement genre, a marked contrast to four-movement examples in other countries. Most were church symphonies with a similarity to opera overtures. Adds perceptive comments on Mattei's transitional style and sees some expressive elements in edited works. Of 27 symphonies in thematic index, only 2 were written after 1800. Four have a multi-movement format (3 to 6).

Simone Mayr (1763-1845)[g,b]

822. Facoetti, Fausto, ed. *Simone Mayr: One Sinfonia* in *Symphony*, series A, vol. IV, pp. lxvii-lxxii, 335-57.

Known as one of greatest opera composers in early 19th century Italy. Notes lack of research into sym-phonic style while locating 9 works in score and 11

others in parts in Bergamo's Donizetti Institute, some
possibly written before 1800. Edited work (written ca.
1800) is set of variations (analyzed in above).

Giovanni Paisiello (1740-1816)[g,b]

823. Green, Douglass M., and Gordana Lazarevich, editors.
      Giovanni Paisiello: La serva padrona, sinfonia in
      Symphony, series A, vol. I (Antecedents of the Sym-
      phony), pp. lvi-lviii, 229-42.

      Opens section with short history of 18th century Nea-
      politan overture (pp. xxxiii-xlvi), adding discussion
      of Paisiello's life and works (over 100 operas and
      "several symphonies"). Explains simple form of edited
      work as "six different ideas presented in alternation."

Giovanni Battista Pergolesi (1710-1736)[g,b]

824. Claydon, Humphrey. "Three string quartets attributed
      to Pergolesi." *ML* 19 (1938): 453-59.

      Studies 3 manuscripts found in 1936: *Simphonia* (B-
      flat major), *Simphonia* (f minor/major) and *Simphonia* (G
      major). Analyzes each, adding movement *incipits*.

825. Cudworth, Charles L. "Notes on the instrumental works
      attributed to Pergolesi." *ML* 30 (1949): 321-28.

      Comments on *sinfonia* to *Il geloso schernito* (by Galup-
      pi), two *sinfonie di apertura* arranged for keyboard
      (first probably North German chamber symphony; second, by
      Pergolesi), 6 concerti and another *sinfonia*.

826. Green, Douglass M., and Gordana Lazarevich. editors.
      Giovanni Battista Pergolesi: S. Guglielmo, sinfonia
      in *Symphony*, series A, vol. I (Antecedents of the
      Symphony), pp. li-lii, 125-36.

      After covering history of genre (pp. xxxiii-xlvi),
      presents summary of Pergolesi's short life and brief
      discussion of works. Composer used edited work (1731)
      in three different operas. Also analyzed in entry 25.

827. Paymer, Marvin E. *Giovanni Battista Pergolesi (1710-
      1736): a Thematic Catalog of the Opera Omnia with an
      Appendix Listing Omitted Compositions.* New York:

Pendragon, 1977. 99p. ISBN 0-918728-01-0 ML134
P613 A35

Encodes *incipits* in Brook's *Simplified Plaine and
Easie Code*, a numerical-letter notation system. Does
not include 5 symphonies attributed to Pergolesi (see
p. 81). Omits *incipits* for all work not in *Opera Omnia*.
Index and bibliography.

828. _____. "The instrumental music of Giovanni Battista
Pergolesi; a study in authenticity." Ph.D. dissertation, City Univ. of New York, 1977. 513p.

Based on establishment of style norm for *sinfonias*
written by other composers during Pergolesi's life (control group A) and comparing latter's works to that norm,
using 30 factors (phrasing, orchestration, key range,
cadence types, etc.) in style profile. Develops control
group B from sinfonias written after Pergolesi's death.
Finds authentic works more faithful to control group A.
Relates questionable works to both groups for levels of
authenticity.

Nicolò Porpora (1686-1768)[g,b]

829. Degrada, Francesco. "Le musiche strumentali di Nicolò
Porpora." *Chigiana (Sienna)* 25 (1968): 99-125.

Contains thematic index of Porpora's instrumental
works. Includes analysis of *Sinfonie da camera a tre
istromenti* (London, 1736), noting Baroque style of church
and chamber sonatas in group.

Francesco Provenzale (ca. 1626-1704)[g,b]

830. Wolf, Eugene K., ed. *Francesco Provenzale: Il schiavo
di sua moglie, introduzione* in *Symphony*, series A,
vol. I (Antecedents of the Symphony), pp. xxxiii-
xxxiv, 41-42.

Resembles Venetian *canzona* overture (two sections of
contrasting tempos, homophonic in one section and poly-
phonic in other). Work dates from 1671. Provenzale
was a precursor of Neapolitan school.

Gaetano Pugnani (1731-1798)[g,b]

831. Johnson, Joyce L., ed. *Gaetano Pugnani: Six Symphonies*
      in *Symphony*, series A, vol. III, pp. xxxix-xlv, 117-
      239.

      Recounts Pugnani's European successes as violinist.
      Comments on symphonic style (40+ works, 4 movements,
      first movements in embryonic sonata form) and on 6
      edited works. Locates thematic index in Zschinsky-
      Trotzler, *Gaetano Pugnani 1731-1798*, Berlin (Atlantis),
      1939; not examined. Müry updates catalog in entry 832.

832. Müry, Albert. *Die Instrumentalwerke Gaetano Pugnani*.
      Basel: Krebs, 1941. 109p.

      Appears to be only book on subject, originating as
      author's Ph.D. dissertation (Basel, 1940). Covers sym-
      phonies and overtures on pp. 49-59, concentrating on
      movement forms as primary style element. Adjusts some
      entries in earlier thematic catalog (see 831 above).

Rinaldo di Capua (ca. 1705-ca. 1780)[g,b]

833. Bostian, Richard Lee. "The Works of Rinaldo di Capua."
      Ph.D. dissertation, Univ. of North Carolina, 1961.
      257p. (plus supplement)

      Stresses composer's connection between Italian opera
      and emerging symphony (pp. 173-200). Analyzes 9 *sinfonie*
      and overtures, some dated as early as 1730. Concentrates
      on adequacy of second themes and on orchestration. In-
      cludes full scores of two overtures: *Cantata per la nati-
      vita della beata virgine* and *La donna vendicativa* (inter-
      mezzo).

Alessandro Rolla (1757-1841)[g,b]

834. Longyear, Rey M., ed. *Alessandro Rolla: (Two Symphonies)*
      in *Symphony*, series A, vol. VI (The Northern Italian
      Symphony, 1800-1840), pp. xxii-xxiii, xxxvii-xxxviii,
      1-34.

      Prefaces discussion of composers with general history
      of symphony in Italy from 1770 to 1840, noting two types
      (3 movements and single movement with slow introduction)
      and increasing prominence of woodwinds. Mentions

"undatable" nature of Rolla's symphonies, all in classic style. Estimates that 2 of 12 symphonies were written in 18th century. Thematic index.

Antonio Sacchini (1730-1786)[g,b]

835. Johnson, Joyce L., and Derek Moore, editors. *Antonio Sacchini: Two Symphonies* in *Symphony*, series A, vol. III, pp. xxxiii-xxxvii, 75-116.

Speaks to composer's colorful life, adding brief segment on two edited works (complete output; one is two-movement concert symphony while other is three-movement oratorio overture). Latter is facsimile of 18th century manuscript score of part of oratorio.

Giovanni Battista Sammartini (1700 or 1701-1775)[g,b]

836. Barblan, Guglielmo. "Sammartini e la scuola sinfonica milanese." *Musicisti lombardi ed emiliani* 15 (1958): 21-40.

Traces chronology of works, notes 18th century writings on composer but minimizes matters of style.

837. Churgin, Bathia. "G.B. Sammartini and the Symphony." *MT* 116 (1975): 26-29.

Comprises concise and valuable summary of Churgin's research, including biography and symphonic style. Evidences admirable insight in matters of style.

838. _____. "The Recapitulation in Sonata-form Movements of Sammartini and Early Haydn Symphonies." In *Kongress Vienna/1982*, pp. 135-40.

Studies 35 early Haydn and 50 Sammartini symphonies in establishing Haydn's trend toward greater variety in recapitulations (mostly related to principal themes) and Sammartini's "reformulation" of section into characteristicaly irregular pattern. Feels latter represents Sammartini's artistic preferences rather than his formal immaturity. Examples.

839. _____. "The Symphonies of G.B. Sammartini." 2 vols. Ph.D. dissertation, Harvard Univ., 1963. 555, 318p.

Describes arena (Milan) in which composer flourished
(pp. 36-65). Divides symphonies into 3 periods: ca. 1740
(works transitional in style), 1740-1760 (works in classical idiom, emphasizing more lyric second movement) and
1760-1775 (continuation of mature classic style but
marked by several innovations such as textural variety).
Vol. 2 contains thematic index and scores of 5 movements
from 3 symphonies (76a, 43, 65).

840.   _____. *The Symphonies of G.B. Sammartini: Volume I -
The Early Symphonies.* Cambridge (Mass.): Harvard
Univ. Press, 1968. 213p.

Contains scores of symphonies 1-19 and opera (*Memet*)
overture and short discussion of symphonic style, latter
differing from chamber style by being less ornamental,
less figural in melody, richer in thematic substance and
more complex in formal design. Notes preference for two
and three movement symphonies, always starting with fast
movement. Adds comments on sources, chronology, performance practice, editorial procedures and notes on each
edited work. See Wolf's review in *JAMS* 26 (1973), 164-
67.

841.   _____, ed. *Giovanni Battista Sammartini: Ten Symphonies
in Symphony,* series A, vol. II, lviii, 190p.

Includes in introduction (pp. xiii-lviii) summary of
life and works, sources and chronology of symphonies
and their style, stylistic sources of early classic
symphony, performance practices and analysis of edited
works (nos. J-C *7, *38, *39, 44, 57, 46, 4, 62, 52 and
26; *works also in entry 840). Represents author's most
recent (1984) efforts.

842.   Jenkins, Newell, and Bathia Churgin. *Thematic catalogue
of the works of Giovanni Battista Sammartini: Orchestral and vocal music.* Cambridge (Mass.): Harvard Univ.
Press, 1976. 315p. ISBN 0-674-87735-7 ML134 S16 A2

Biography (pp. 1-21), style (pp. 21-23), catalog of
symphonies (pp. 45-94).

843.   Mishkin, Henry G. "The Published Instrumental Works of
Giovanni Battista Sammartini: A Bibliographical
Appraisal." *MQ* 45 (1959): 361-74.

Challenges Saint-Foix's belief that some of Giuseppe Sammartini's works were written by Giovanni Battista. Asserts that only Giuseppe's French opus can be attributed to Giovanni.

844. Saint-Foix, Georges de. "La chronologie de l'oeuvre instrumentale de Jean Baptiste Sammartini." *SIMG* 15 (1913/1914): 308-24.

Determines lineage of works with subsequent exceptions noted in entries 842 and 843. Based on study of 18th century catalogs and editions printed in England and France.

845. Sondheimer, Robert. "Giovanni Battista Sammartini." *ZfMw* 3 (1920/1921): 83-110.

Supports chamber works as most important instrumental works since they supposedly showed composer's early efforts to establish strong secondary themes in sonata-allegro movements, this somewhat in contrast to treatment of form in early symphonies. Results are uneven since did not have access to many symphonies and was unsure of the chronology of many of works studied.

846. Torrefranco, Fausto. "Le Origini della Sinfonia. Le Sinfonie dell'imbrattacarte (G.B. Sammartini)." *RMI* 20 (1913), 291-346; 21 (1914), 97-121; 22 (1915), 431-46.

Responds to Riemann's overlooking Italian predecessors of Mannheim School by stressing foundation of new instrumental style in works of Tartini, Locatelli and Sammartini. Underscores importance of Sammartini's strong rhythmic organization in evolving classical style. Proposes chronology of works through study of early catalogs. Lists (in final article) other composers whose works might fit into this early development.

Domenico Sarro (Sarri) (1679-1744)[g]

847. Green, Douglass M., and Gordana Lazarevich, editors. *Domenico Sarro (Sarri): Five Introduzioni* in *Symphony*, series A, vol. I (The Antecedents of the Symphony), pp. xlvi-1, 51-107.

Opens introduction with detailed history of *sinfonia*
and Neapolitan *sinfonia* (pp. xxxiii-xlvi). Explains
Sarro's importance as one of leading exponents of *buffo*
style in Naples, noting "cross influences between Sarro's
comic-vocal and instrumental styles" as important in
derivation of new classical instrumental idiom. Observes
concerto grosso roots of Sarro's opera "overtures."
Includes 13 *introduzioni* in thematic index.

Alessandro Scarlatti (1660-1725)[g,b]

848. Wolf, Eugene K., ed. *Alessandro Scarlatti: Cambise,
      introduzione* in *Symphony*, series A, vol. I (The Ante-
      cedents of the Symphony), pp. xxxv-xxxvi, 45-50.

      Opens with Italian *sinfonia* history, emphasizing Nea-
      politan activities (pp. xxxiii-xlvi) and Scarlatti's
      evolving *sinfonia* style. Notes his change to three-
      movement form in 1695, tracing roots of first movement
      to concerto. Characterizes style of typical Scarlatti
      sinfonia. Includes analysis of edited work.

Giuseppe Sellitto (1700-1777)[g,b]

849. Green, Douglass M., and Gordana Lazarevich, editors.
      Giuseppe Sellitto: Siface, sinfonia in *Symphony*,
      series A, vol. I (The Antecedents of the Symphony),
      pp. liii, 137-45.

      Presents summary of history of *sinfonia* (pp. xxxiii-
      xlvi), gives brief account of Sellitto's life and works
      and analyzes form of edited work (three movements, slow
      movement interrupted by *presto* section, concerto-like
      opening of first movement).

Michele Stratico (ca. 1721-ca. 1782)[g,b]

850. Roeder, Michael Thomas. "Sonatas, concertos and sym-
      phonies of Michele Stratico." 2 vols. Ph.D. disser-
      tation, Univ. of California (Santa Barbara), 1971.
      183, 247p.

      In style study of symphonies, concludes works were
      typical Italian *sinfonie*, "simple and insipid." Notes
      that most works, written in 1740s and 1750s, show little
      of mature classic style. Edits 10 works in vol. 2,
      including 3 *sinfonie*. Thesis adviser: Geiringer.

Giulio Taglietti (ca. 1660-1718)[g]

851. Wolf, Eugene K. *Giulio Taglietti: Concerto in D major*
      in *Symphony*, series A, vol. I (The Antecedents of the
      Symphony), pp. xxv, 17-22.

      Offers resume of history of *ripieno* concerto, one of
      symphony's ancestors and brief summary of composer's life
      and works. Indicates edited example is typical *sinfonia*
      type *ripieno* concerto.

Giuseppe Torelli (1658-1709)[g,b]

852. Enrico, Eugene Joseph. "Giuseppe Torelli's music for
      instrumental ensemble with trumpet." Ph.D. disserta-
      tion, Univ. of Michigan, 1970. 263p.

      Has some sections peripherally related to growth of
      symphony: orchestral resources at San Petronio basilica
      in Bologna and form and style of trumpet chamber works
      (sonatas, *sinfonie* and concertos). Adviser: Cuyler.

853. Wolf, Eugene K., ed. *Giuseppe Torelli: (Two Ripieno
      Concertos)* in *Symphony*, series A, vol. I (The Antece-
      dents of the Symphony), pp. xxii-xxiv, 3-15.

      Presents summary (pp. xv-xxi) of *ripieno* concerto's
      history, describing that form's role as one of sympho-
      ny's ancestors. Explains Torelli's role in introducing
      more modern type (*sinfonia* species) of concerto. Notes
      similarity in style between *ripieno* concerto and the
      true *sinfonia*. Includes analysis of edited works.

Leonardo Vinci (ca. 1696-1730)[g,b]

854. Green, Douglass M., and Gordana Lazarevich, editors.
      Leonardo Vinci: Artaserse, sinfonia in *Symphony*,
      series A, vol. I (The Antecedents of the Symphony),
      pp. li, 115-23.

      After extended introduction to Neapolitan overture in
      18th century, presents very brief discussion of Vinci's
      life and works. Little comment made on specific style
      of edited work except for references in introduction.
      Work in three movements (fast-slow-fast), first and
      second movements in through-composed binary and finale
      approximating minuet form (no trio).

Giovanni Battista Viotti (1755-1824)[g,b]

855. White, Chappell, ed. *Giovanni Battista Viotti: One Sym-
      phonie concertante* in *Symphony*, series D, vol. X, pp.
      liii-lxii, 291-353.

      Divides life between Italy, France and England, with
      more productive years in latter two. More noted for 29
      violin concertos, almost all written prior to 1800.
      Wrote only 2 *symphonies concertantes*, both around 1787
      for Paris audiences. Adds thoughtful analysis of edited
      work (2 movements, 2 solo violins, first movement in
      sonata form, second in rondo and little development in
      either movement). Thematic index.

Niccolò Antonio Zingarelli (1752-1837)[g,b]

856. Longyear, Rey M., ed. *Niccolò Zingarelli: Seven Sym-
      phonies* in *Symphony*, series A, vol. VIII, pp. xi-xx,
      xxv-xxxiii, 163-382.

      Explains highly productive life and duality in sympho-
      nic style: early works (1780s) in traditional three-move-
      ment form, later works (1791-1836) in one movement (only
      2 without slow introduction) and certainly designed as
      church symphonies. Provides edited examples of each
      genre. Estimates 30% of later works were fugal sympho-
      nies with fast section featuring contrapuntal settings of
      parts of the first thematic group. Thematic index lists
      69 authentic works (12 three-movement and 57 one-move-
      ment). Cites editor's article on symphonies in future
      issue of *Analecta Musicologica* and his "The Instrumental
      Music of Niccolò Zingarelli" in Robert L. Weaver, ed.
      American Musicological Society, South Central Chapter:
      Abstracts of Papers Read at the Annual Meetings, 1971-73
      (Nashville: George Peabody College for Teachers, 1973)
      30-31; not examined.

Norway

Johan Daniel Berlin (1714-1787)[g,b]

857. Kortsen, Bjarne, ed. *The Collected Works of Johan Daniel
      Berlin (1714-1787)*. Bergen: Edition Norvegica, 1977.
      247 p. M3 B488

Contains full scores of composer's 3 symphonies with short commentary on each (pp. xxix-xxvi). Includes biographical sketch. Text in English and Norwegian. Editor added list of his writings, many in English.

858.   _____, ed. *Johan Daniel Berlin: Symphony in D major* in *Symphony*, series F, vol. I (The Symphony in Norway), pp. xv-xvii, xxii, 1-17.

Covers entire history of Norwegian symphony in introduction (pp.xi-xv). Details transplanted German composer's career (47 years as organist in Trondheim) and works, noting preclassical style of symphonies. Used three-movement form exclusively, each movement being a variation of binary form. Recognized as Norway's first symphonist. Thematic index lists 3 symphonies. See entry 857 for complete edition of symphonies.

Johan Henrich Berlin (1741-1807)

859.   Kortsen, Bjarne, ed. *Johan Henrich Berlin: Symphony in C major* in *Symphony*, series F, vol. I (The Symphony in Norway), pp. xvii-xix, xxv, 19-149.

After summarizing Norwegian symphonic history (pp. xi-xv), discusses life and accomplishments (wrote first Norwegian horn and piano concertos). Notes both Rococo and Classic aspects in music. Edited symphony manifests some Mannheim influences. Emphasizes extended length of edited work, its strong Haydn influence and its first movement's "primitive" sonata form style. Thematic index.

Poland

General

860.   Abraham, Gerald. "Some Eighteenth-century Polish Symphonies." In *Festschrift Geiringer/70th*, pp. 13-22. (Reprint in Gerald Abraham, *Essays on Russian and East European Music*, New York: Oxford, 1985.)

Surveys works of A. Haczewski, Karol Pietrowski, Antoni Milwid, Jakub Gołąbek, Jan Wanski, Wojciech Dankowski, Namieyski and Bazyli Bohdanowicz. Analyzes several scores (all except Milwid), adding numerous examples. Bibliography.

861. Muchenberg, Bohdan. "Z zagadnień dokumentacji symfonii
     polskiej drugiej połowy XVIII wieku." [The problems
     of documentation of Polish symphonies from the second
     half of the eighteenth century] *Z dziejów muzyki
     polskiej* 14 (1969): 65-86.

     Uses Breitkopf catalogs to identify anonymous works
     in Polish archives and shows earliest printed Polish
     symphony to be by Marcin Josef Żebrowski. (Summarized
     from materials provided by William Smialek.)

862. Opieński, Henryk. "La symphonie polonaise au XVIIIe
     siècle." *RMl* 15 (1934): 193-96.

     Based on study of holdings of library of Cistercian
     Fathers at Obra (maintained excellent orchestra). Li-
     brary had 150 sets of symphonic parts written by most
     of representative composers of 18th century, including
     4 Polish symphonies (2 by Albert Dankowski and 1 each
     by Wański and an anonymous composer). One Dankowski
     example uses Polonaise for introduction to first move-
     ment while trio of anonymous symphony's minuet employs
     melody based on old Polish folk tune.

863. Prosnak, Jan. *Kultura muzyczna Warszawy XVIII wieku.*
     [The music culture of eighteenth-century Warsaw.]
     Kraków: Polskie Wydawnictwo Muzyczne, 1955.

     Indirectly covers symphony in few pages devoted to
     concerts in Warsaw. Lists inventory of symphonies,
     mostly by foreign composers, and discusses orchestral
     resources during period. Notes references to symphonies
     in actual programs. Index of names includes foreign
     composers known in Poland. (Abstracted from materials
     prepared by William Smialek.)

864. Reiss, Josef. "Dzieje symfonii w Polsce." [History of
     the symphony in Poland.] *Muzyka polska: monografia
     zbiorowa*, ed. Mateusz Gliński. Warsaw: Muzyka, 1927,
     pp. 131-41.

     Outlines history of Polish orchestral music (symphony
     included) of 18th and 19th centuries based on works known
     at that time (1927). Identifies *Symphony in B-flat* by
     Antoni Milwid as earliest Polish symphony. Outdated by
     later research. (Based on materials prepared by William
     Smialek.)

865. Sledzinski, Stefan. "Outline history of Polish symphonic music (part 1)." *Polish Music* 15 (1980): 35-41.

Explains why Poland did not support major symphonic activity during 19th century after having experienced significant development in 18th century. Emphasizes social and historical factors related to decline. Includes analysis of 18th century works by Haczewski, Lentz and Lessel. Planned a final second article but was unable to finish project prior to his death.

866. Smialek, William, and Bohdan Muchenberg, Jan Prosnak, Jacek Berwaldt, Wendelin Swierczek and Florian Dąbrowski, editors. *The Symphony in Poland* in *Symphony*, series F, vol. I. 358p.

Covers in introduction history of both 18th and 19th centuries and includes brief biographies for 7 composers with an edited work for each inserted. Translates into English all Polish titles in bibliography. Composers: Orłowski, Pawłowski, Pietrowski, Bohdanowicz, Gołąbek, Wański and Dobrzyński. See those entries below. Introduction prepared by Smialek.

867. Sowinski, Albert. *Les musiciens polonais et slaves*. Paris: Libraire Adrien Le Clerc, 1857. 599p. SBN 306-701-66-9 ML106 P7 S7 1971 (Reprint by Da Capo, 1971.)

Divided in two sections: resume of Poland's music history organized by genre (court music, folk music, etc.) and biographical dictionary of musicians (lacks adequate lists of works). In French.

868. Strumillo, Tadeusz. "Do dziejów symfonii polskiej." [Towards a history of the Polish symphony.] *Muzyka* 5 (1953): 26-45.

Describes role of symphonic music in 18th century Poland, identifying church as most important center of symphonic music. Discusses use of word *sinfonia* in 18th century Polish sources, listing each known work with relevant historiography. Groups works chronologically by style, drawing conclusions on Polish and German symphonies of same period. (Based on materials prepared by William Smialek.)

869. Węcowski, Jan. "La musique symphonique polonaise du
      XVIIIe siècle." In *Musica Antiqua Europae Orientalis*,
      ed. Zofia Lissa, pp. 334-53. Warsaw: Państwowe
      Wydawnictwo Naukowe, 1966.

      Discusses 20 known Polish symphonists, summarizing
      information on each composer and his works. Maintains
      view that churches were centers for 18th century Polish
      symphony. Provides catalog of symphonies by non-Polish
      composers found in Polish archives.

                      Polish Composers

Bazyli Bohdanowicz (1740-1817)[g]

870. Swierczek, Wendelin, and William Smialek, editors.
      Bazyli Bohdanowicz: Symphony in D major in *Symphony*,
      series F, vol. VII (The Symphony in Poland), pp. xviii,
      xxxi, 49-60.

      Opens with Smialek's review of 18th and 19th century
      Polish symphony, followed by his summary of composer's
      life and works. Was famed for his family's (8 children)
      circus-like concerts (3 children on 1 violin, witty text-
      less vocal works) in Vienna where he moved in 1779.
      Edited work (before 1780) is in 4 movements, finale being
      a *Polonese*, evidence of importance of national character-
      istics in early Polish symphony. Thematic index lists
      only single work.

Adalbert (Wojciech) Dankowski (ca. 1760-after 1800)[g]

871. Opieński, Henryk. "Symfonie A. Dankowskiego i J. Wań-
      skiego." [The symphonies of A. Dankowski and J. Wań-
      ski.] *Kwalrtalnik muzyczny* 16 (1932): 685-92.

      More specific version of entry 862, explaining in
      greater detail style features of Dankowski and Wański
      symphonies and role of symphonic music in the Polish
      mass. Provides *incipits* for each movement, identifying
      instrumentation. *NGDMM* indicates that Dankowski's 2
      symphonies are available in modern editions.

Jakub Gołąbek (ca. 1739-1789)[g]

872. Muchenberg, Bohdan, ed. *Jakub Gołąbek: Symphony in D
      major* in *Symphony*, series F, vol. VII (The Symphony
      in Poland), pp. xviii-xix, xxxiii, 61-70.

      Discussion by William Smialek covers both composer's
      life (p. xviii-xix) and symphonic style (p. xiii). The-
      matic index lists 3 works, all in 3 movements and all
      available in modern editions. Notes incomplete recapitu-
      lation in edited work's first movement and tendency of
      Polish symphonists of period to place two themes in tonic
      key in exposition.

Michal Orłowski (fl. 1750-1800)

873. Muchenberg, Bohdan, ed. *Michal Orłowski: Symphony in F
      major* in *Symphony*, series F, vol. VII (The Symphony
      in Poland), pp. xvii, xxv, 1-13.

      Short comments by William Smialek establish what few
      facts known about Orłowski's life and works. Explains
      discovery of edited work's manuscript in Pauline monas-
      tery near Czestochowa, noting its listing in the clois-
      ter's music catalog dated 1819. Recounts finding of list
      of 117 symphonies on cover of one of archive's volumes,
      one of which was Orłowski's lost E-flat symphony. Edited
      work has 3 movements, the latter 2 in rondo form.
      Thematic index lists 2 works mentioned.

Jakub Pawłowski (fl. 1750-1800)

874. Prosnak, Jan, ed. *Jakub Pawłowski: Symphony in B-flat
      major* in *Symphony*, series F, vol. VII (The Symphony
      in Poland), pp. xvii-xviii, xxvii, 15-25.

      Opens with general introduction to Polish symphony by
      William Smialek (pp. xi-xvii), followed by discussions
      of individual composers in which discovery of Pawłowski's
      3 symphonies in Neuchâtel (Switzerland) municipal library
      is recounted. Lists these in thematic index, noting only
      1 movement in each. Form of edited work loosely approxi-
      mates sonata-allegro while also resembling *ripieno* con-
      certo in its frequent *soli* passages. Orchestrated for
      strings and oboes, clarinets and horns. Generally
      assigns melodic woodwind *soli* to clarinets.

Karol Pietrowski (fl. 1750-1800)[g]

875. Berwaldt, Jacek, ed. *Karol Pietrowski: Symphony in D major* in *Symphony*, series F, vol. VII (The Symphony in Poland), pp. xviii, xxix, 27-48.

    Presents in introduction prepared by William Smialek (pp. xi-xvii) general survey of Polish symphony's history in 18th and 19th centuries. Comments on similarity between edited work and Haydn's *Symphony No. 70* (e.g., finale) and on composer's adoption of Viennese classic style in his symphonies. Editor has published critical scores of composer's two symphonies, one of which is reprinted in this collection. Thematic index.

Jan Wański (1762-1821)[g,b]

876. Opienski, Henryk. "Symfonie A. Dankowskiego i J. Wańskiego" [The symphonies of A. Dankowski and J. Wański]. *Kwartalnik Muzyczny* 16 (1932): 685-94.

    See entry 871.

877. Sabrowski, Florian, ed. *Jan Wański: Symphony in D major* in *Symphony*, series F, vol. VII (The Symphony in Poland), pp. xix, xxxv, 71-84.

    Introductory materials (pp. xi-xvii) by William Smialek recount Polish symphonic history in 18th and 19th centuries, adding short biography and analysis of edited work. Thematic index list 3 symphonies, placing their dates of composition between 1790 and 1800. All are in 4 movements with minuets as third movements. Two employ themes from Wański's operas (identified but lost).

Portugal and Brazil

General

878. Brito, Manuel Carlos de, ed. "Symphonic music in Portugal." In *Symphony*, series F, vol. V (The Symphony in Portugal), pp. xiii-xvi.

    Describes low level of symphonic activity in Portugal, ascribing condition to: lack of royal court during Spanish occupation (1580-1640), bad economic conditions caused by subsequent war of independence and dominance of church music. Notes establishment of first court orchestra in 1728 and beginning of two strong traditions: Italian opera and orchestrally accompanied church music. Lists symphonists active in 18th century: José António Carlos Seixas, Pedro António Avandano, João Cordeiro da Silva, António Cláudio da Silva Pereira, Antonio Puzzi, Luciano Xaver dos Santos, Marcos Portugal, João José Baldi, Leal Moreira and João Domingos Bomtempo. (All except Silva Pereira and Puzzi are included in *NGDMM.*) Observes Italian, French and two-movement overture models in works of above composers. Decries lack of thematic development in all works except those by Bomtempo. Bibliography.

Portuguese and Brazilian Composers

João Domingos Bomtempo (1775–1842)[g]

879. Sarrautte, Jean-Paul. *Catalogue des oeuvres de João Domingos Bomtempo.* Lisbon: Foundation Calouste Gulbenkian, 1970. 127p. ML134 B76 S24

Includes biographical sketch of composer's activities in Paris and London (1801–1814). Structures catalog into 2 parts: printed works and manuscript works, adding brief comment on each. Lists symphonies on pp. 56 and 90–94. In French.

880. Sousa, Filipe de, Christopher Bochmann, and Maria Fernanda Cidrais, editors. *João Domingos Bomtempo: Symphony No. 2 in D major* in *Symphony*, series F, vol. V (The Symphony in Portugal), pp. xx–xxv, xxix–xxx, 69–270.

Earlier discussion by Manuel Carlos de Brito (pp. xiii–xvi) covers nature of genre in Portugal. Described as 19th century composer by Cidrais, style evaluated as pre-Romantic and reflective of Viennese classic school. Recounts Bomtempo's Paris and London successes before return to Lisbon (1821). Includes Bochmann's extended analysis of edited work, latter reinforcing admirable quality of Portugal's music at turn of century. While composer completed 7 symphonies, only 2 are extant (as noted in thematic index).

António Leal Moreira (1750-1819)[g,b]

881. Salzmann, Pierre, Christopher Bochmann, and Maria Fer-
      nanda Cidrais, editors. *António Leal Moreira: Sinfo-
      nia a due orchestre in D major* in *Symphony*, series F,
      vol. V (The Symphony in Portugal), pp. xvi-xx, xxvii,
      1-68.

      Cidrais describes Moreira's notoriety as opera composer
      in Italian style and his fame as Portugal's great compo-
      ser of that age. Notes (in Bochmann's analysis) emerging
      classical style of edited work and its *pasticcio* final
      third movement that consists of extended sections from
      earlier movements. Two-orchestra format defined as
      violins, cellos, basses, trumpets, flutes and bassoons in
      orchestra I and violins, cellos, basses, horns, oboes and
      violas in orchestra II. Thematic index contains 3 works,
      with 2 in single movements as possible church symphonies
      were written after began devoting efforts to church music
      in 1801.

José Maurício Nunes Garcia (1767-1830)[g]

882. Person de Mattos, Cleofe. *Catálogo temático das obras
      do Padre José Maurício Nunes Garcia.* Rio de Janiero:
      Conselho Federal de Cultura, 1970. 413p. ML134 N85
      M2

      Lists instrumental works starting on page 327, in-
      cluding *Sinfonia Funebre* (in 1 movement), *Zemira* opera
      overture, an overture in D major and *Sinfonia Tempestade*
      (overture). Comments on instrumental works (pp. 376-77).
      In Portuguese.

883. _____, ed. *José Maurício Nunes Garcia: Two Symphonies*
      in *Symphony*, series F, vol. VIII (The Symphony in the
      New World), pp. xxix-xxxi, 55-108.

      Termed "most important Brazilian composer of his time"
      (Behague, *NGDMM* 7, 153). Parents were Portuguese lieu-
      tenant and Brazilian black woman. Known as church com-
      poser primarily (19 masses, 4 requiems, motets, vespers,
      etc.). Notes that most of instrumental works related to
      church. Both edited works (*Sinfonia funebre*, 1798;

Zemira overture, 1803) are in one movement, reflecting
their church function. *Zemira* score is a reconstruction
of an earlier 19th century edition by Leopoldo Miguéz.
Omits any analysis of either work.

Russia

General

884. Mooser, R. Aloys. *Annales de la Musique et des Musiciens
en Russie en XVIIIe Siècle.* 3 vols. Geneva: Mont
Blanc, 1948-51.

Documents in great detail importation of western European music into Russia, especially Italian opera.
Coverage: vol. I, beginnings through 1761; vol. II, 1762-
1796; vol. III, 1796-1801. Mentions few Russian composers since most were Italian in early years. Includes in
appendix (vol. III) discussion of *orchestres de cors
russes.* Emphasizes breadth and depth of Italian musical
invasion. According to Vassiliades (entry 885), no
independent symphonic tradition existed in 18th century
Russia, only opera overtures in Italian style. Includes
extensive bibliography in each volume.

885. Vassiliades, Evangeline. "Overture and symphony in
eighteenth-century Russia." Ph.D. dissertation, New
York Univ., 1977. 307p.

Contributions: expanded history of Russian music in
18th century, extended discussion of Russian folk song
style and generational analysis of 18th century Russian
overture. Composers included: V.A. Pashkevich, E.I.
Fomin, D.S. Bortniansky, D.A. Zorin, P.A. Skokov, N.P.
Iakhontov, Hermann Raupach, I.B. Kerzelli, Franz Kerzelli, I.F. Kerzelli, Anton Biulandt, Ferdinand Tietz, Otto
Tewes, Ernst Wanzura, Franz Blyma, A.N. Titov, S.I. Davy-
dov, A.A. Pleshcheev, Osip Kozlovsky, Catterino Cavos and
one anonymous composer. Adds analytical notes on each
work studied (see appendix). Evaluates and analyzes
holdings of major Soviet libraries used in research.
Lists extensive sources in bibliography. Explains
association of Russian folk song with maturing classical
idiom in Russian music.

Spain

General

886. Climent, José. *Fondos musicales de la región Valenciana
      I; Catedral metropolitana de Valencia*. Valencia:
      Institución Alfonso Magnánimo, 1979. ISBN 84-500-
      31902-3

      Divulges cathedral's holdings of symphonic works by
      José Pons (1768-1818), Spain's major church symphonist
      (perhaps country's only such composer): 4 *oberaturas*
      (one dated 1806) and 4 *sinfonie*. Notes 2 overtures for
      gran orquesta by Blas Vicente (dates unknown) in hold-
      ings. Describes library's contents as primarily sacred
      with exception of instrumental works noted. Observes
      also in inventory manuscripts parts of 6 Boccherini quar-
      tets. Notes integration of instrumental performances
      into celebrations of mass and presentations also in
      special afternoon concerts (*siestas*).

887. Hamilton, Mary Neal. *Music in Eighteenth Century Spain*.
      Urbana: Univ. of Illinois Press, 1937. ML315.3 H21 M98

      Focuses on both sacred and secular music. Mentions
      symphonic activity tangentially (pp. 137-39) in discus-
      sion of Opera Concerts, 1787-1790 (an imitation of Paris'
      Concerts spirituels), at which performances of symphonies
      by Haydn, Cimarosa, Salieri, Pleyel and Rosetti occurred.
      Notes use of 54-member orchestra for Rosetti work.
      Offers (p. 171) Francisco de Almeyra as possibly first
      Spanish symphonist, with some works published by Pleyel.
      Valuable in its portrayal of 18th century Spanish musical
      life. Bibliography.

888. Shadko, Jacqueline Andrea. "The Spanish symphony in
      Madrid from 1790 to 1840: a study of the music in its
      cultural context." 2 vols. Ph.D. dissertation, Yale
      Univ., 1981. 664p.

      Studies origins and development of Madrid symphony as
      performed in Royal Palace, salons of wealthy patrons
      and theaters (opera houses). Discusses performance of
      symphonies before theatrical performances and between
      acts of operas. Notes use of symphonies in Spiritual
      Concerts in Lent. Traces, identifies foreign models:

Italian opera and works of Boccherini, Brunetti and those of Haydn promoted by Boccherini. Presents editions of 7 symphonies: Balado, Mayo, Moral, Moreno (3) and Nono. See also entry 889.

889. _____, ed. *The Symphony in Madrid* in *Symphony*, series F, vol. IV. 394p.

Preface includes discussion of musical environment of Madrid, non-Spanish composers active there and other evidence supporting Madrid's position as an 18th century music center. Includes five symphonists in study: Francisco Javier Moreno (1748-1836), Pablo del Moral (fl. 1765-1805), Juan Balado (?-1832), Felipe de Mayo (1789-?) and José Nonó (1776-1845). Notes dearth of Spanish symphonies in period and, conversely, strong Italian presence (and influence) at same time. Isolates 3 areas of symphonic activity: theaters, *Palacio Real* and private salons. Impressive bibliography included. See entries below on each composer.

890. Subirá. José. "Conciertos espirituales españoles en el siglo XVIII." In *Festschrift Fellerer/60th*, pp. 519-29.

Describes Spanish version of *concerts spirituels* held during Lenten season. Details contents of notices in *Diario de Madrid* of frequent orchestral programs, showing performances of symphonies by Rosetti, Haydn, Kozeluch, Miguel Mortelari, Salieri, Prati, Janebencks, Pablo Moral, Pleyel and other unidentified composers. Suggests a more frequent performance of concertos. Relates same tradition being established in other locations (Barcelona, Valencia, Cadiz and Palma).

891. _____. *Temas musicales madrileños*. Madrid: Instituto de Estudios Madrileños, 1971. 323p. ML315.8 M13 S9

Scope: music in Madrid in 18th and 19th centuries. Contains (in first section, *La musica instrumental*) valuable data on 18th century concerts in Madrid and Barcelona and inventories of important music libraries (*Biblioteca Nacional* and *Palacio Real*). Relates extensive holdings of 18th century symphonists (Abel, etc.) to level of symphonic activity in Spain's music centers. Also includes 19th century concerts. Notes definite

influence of both Brunetti and Boccherini. See also
entry 803.

Spanish Composers

Juan Balado (?-1832)

892. Shadko, Jacqueline A., ed. *Juan Balado: Sinfonía a*
      toda orquesta in D minor in *Symphony*, series F, vol.
      IV (The Symphony in Madrid), pp. xvi, xxvii, 239-80.

      Notes only 3 extant works, including 1 symphony (1
      movement with slow introduction, monothematic, Italian
      in style, and possibly written in early 19th century).
      Describes Balado as violist in Royal Palace, the archives
      of which contained his symphony. One-movement symphony
      might be related to church activities.

Gaetano Brunetti (1744-1798)[g,b]

893. Belgray, Alice Bunzl. "Gaetano Brunetti, an exploratory
      bio-bibliographical study." Ph.D. dissertation, Univ.
      of Michigan, 1970. 264p.

      Could be evaluated as definitive biographical sketch
      in English (pp. 1-107) on composer. Includes summary
      of 18th century musical life in Madrid (pp. 108-11) and
      discussion of music (117-24), latter based on study of
      trio sonatas but dealing with some authority on general
      style. Edits complete sonata and single movement from
      another. Co-authored (with Newell Jenkins) Brunetti
      NGDMM entry, detailing in part symphonic style.

894. Jenkins, Newell, ed. *Gaetano Brunetti: Nine Symphonies*
      in *Symphony*, series A, vol. V. 635p.

      Dedicates entire volume to works of Brunetti, includ-
      ing insightful and rewarding description of symphonic
      style, analyses of edited works and thematic index of 37
      symphonies and 4 *symphonies concertantes*. Identifies
      important early 19th century thematic catalog by Louis
      Labitte (see entry 895) as vital source for studies. Of
      37 symphonies only 5 are in 3 movements and 1 in single
      movement, remaining in 4 movements. Notes Labitte's
      dating of most works between 1769 and 1792. See Landon's
      review in *HYb* XIII (1982), 244-49.

895. Labitte de Reims, Louis. "Catalogue themátique des oeuvres inédites, la plupart autographes de Gaëtano Brunetti, 1er violon du roi d'Espagne Charles IV. Cette précieuse collection fait part de la bibliothèque musicale de Louis Labitte de Reims." Manuscript, ca. 1810.

Contains listings of 34 of 37 Brunetti symphonies with *incipits* and tempos of first movements and dates of composition of most works. Compositions listed belonged to Labitte who prepared catalog. Owned by Aristide Wirsta, Bourg-la-Reine (Seine). Brook 197.

896. Subirá. José. "Dos madrileñizados músicos del siglo XVIII; Luigi Boccherini y Gaetano Brunetti." *Anales del instituto de Estudios Madrileños* 2 (1967): 323-31.

Documents both composers' presence in Madrid while reporting a festival in honor of Boccherini in 1960. Describes some of symphony holdings in National Library in Madrid, including 32 symphonies by Brunetti.

Felipe de Mayo (1789-?)

897. Shadko, Jacqueline A., ed. *Felipe de Mayo: Sinfonia in F major* in *Symphony*, series F, vol. IV (The Symphony in Spain), pp. xvi, xxix, 281-309.

Establishes single-symphony output by almost unknown composer after editor's general introduction to Madrid's role in 18th century music (pp. xi-xii). Shows "outmoded" style of edited work (in *sinfonia* style similar to that employed by Sammartini, with movements in binary form, no development and a melodic style more to the Baroque taste). Thematic index.

Pablo del Moral (fl. 1765-1845)[g,b]

898. Shadko, Jacqueline A., ed. *Pablo del Moral: Sinfonia in C major-C minor* in *Symphony*, series F, vol. IV (The Symphony in Spain), pp. xiv-xv, xxv, 195-237.

Enjoyed considerable fame as dramatic composer (132 *tonadillas*, 8 *sainetes*, 29 *comedias*, 3 *loas* and 1 opera). Studies edited work (3 movements, using unorthodox tonal schemes, with somewhat immature second and third move-

ments). Employs Spanish tempo marking *despacio* in two
movements. Indicates first recorded performance of work
in 1790. Thematic index.

Francisco Javier Moreno (1748-1836)

899. Shadko, Jacqueline A., ed. *Francisco Javier Moreno:
      (Three Sinfonie)* in *Symphony*, series F, vol. IV (The
      Symphony in Spain), pp. xiii-xiv, xxiii, 1-194.

      Discusses symphonic form perhaps unique to Spain,
      sinfonias de argumento (argument symphonies). Replaced
      traditional *tonadillas* as *entr'act* offerings in perfor-
      mances of operas and plays. Tended to be programmatic
      in portraying conflicts suggested in titles: *Sinfonia...
      le due opposti caratteri Superbia ed Umiltà* (Symphony
      [of]...the two opposing characters: Pride and Humility)
      and *Sinfonia...titolata la sala di scherma* (Symphony ...
      entitled the Fencing School). Categorized latter as
      programmatic single-movement overture (with slow intro-
      duction), using transitions in work for descriptive
      passages. Includes one traditional four-movement sympho-
      ny in editions. Thematic index lists 3 works, ca. 1801-
      1805.

José Nonó (1776-1845)[g,b]

900. Shadko, Jacqueline A., ed. *José Nonó: Sinfonía in F
      major-C major* in *Symphony*, series F, vol. IV (The
      Symphony in Spain), pp. xvii-xviii, xxxi, 311-94.

      Suggests dual tonality caused by loss of manuscript of
      first movement (in C major). Wrote over 30 operas, none
      surviving. Evaluates style of existing first movement as
      being influenced by Rossini but that of remaining move-
      ments as like "mature Haydn symphony." Dates work around
      1814. Thematic index lists symphony as Nonó's sole sur-
      viving work. Includes summary of Spain's 18th century
      symphonic history (pp. xi-xii).

José Pons (ca. 1768-1818)[g,b]

901. López-Calo, José, and Joám Trillo, editors. *José Pons:
      Three Symphonies* in *Symphony*, series F, vol. V (The
      Symphony in Spain), pp. xxxi-xlii, 271-364.

Summarizes his (López-Calo) *NGDMM* article in discussion of Pons' life and symphonies. Pons was primarily church musician who wrote church symphonies to be performed during *siestas* (afternoon concerts) on feast days. Cast in single movements with changes of tempos and materials implying multi-movement overall form. Employs French overture-like slow introductions in 6 of 9 works. Notes works' lack of sophistication in both style and form usually exhibited in Italian-style symphonies. Offers Pons as only known Spanish composer of church symphonies, remarking on church holdings of symphonies by Haydn, Pleyel and others as indication of enterprising concert activity under *fiesta* rubric. Dates works between 1793 and 1818. Thematic index.

Sweden

General

902. Nisser, Carl. *Svensk Instrumentalkomposition, 1770-1830* [Swedish Instrumental Composition, 1770-1830]. Stockholm: Bokförlager Gothia, 1943. ML120 S9 N5

Presents master listing in alphabetical order of composers whose works appeared in Sweden between 1770 and 1830 with brief description (generally) of number of movements, tempos, lengths of movements, meters, sources and publication data. Prefaced by list of catalogs used to assemble Nisser's volume. In Swedish.

903. Van Boer, Bertil H., Jr., ed. *The Symphony in Sweden, Part 2* in *Symphony*, series F, vol. III. 328p.

Contains well-documented discussion of Swedish concert life (1720-1840), summary of Swedish symphony in that period and resumes of lives and works of 15 symphonic composers, including a thematic index for each. Covers works of Ferdinand Zellbell, Sr.; Arvid Niclas friherr von Höpkin; Hinrich Philip Johnsen; Ferdinand Zellbell, Jr.; Anders Wesström; Jonas Åman; Francesco Antonio Baldassare Uttini; Anders Piscator; Pehr Frigel; Johan David Zander; Johann Friedrich Grenser; Johann Christian Friedrich Haeffner; Joachim Nikolas Eggert; Johan Fredrick Berwald and Johan Wikmanson. Notes first orchestral concerts in 1745 and the preponderance of "imported" works on those programs (only 29 of 280 by Swedish composers). Perceives Swedish symphonic history as parallel of that of central Europe.

904. Walin, Stig. *Beiträge zur Geschichte der schwedischen Sinfonik; Studien aus dem Musikleben des 18. und des beginnenden 19. Jahrhunderts.* Stockholm: P.A. Norstedt, 1941. xxiv, 431p.

Covers 18th and 19th century symphonists, Swedish archives holding early scores and literary sources and their locations. Studies symphony's history in 3 divisions: aspirations and education, performing organizations and history of performances (public concerts more significant than court concerts) and style study of 92 works by Roman, Zellbell, von Höpkin, Brant, Johnsen, Zellbell (Jr.), Wesström, Lindström, Zetterwall, Åman, Piscator, Kraus, Zander, Struve, Eggert and J.F. Berwald. Bengtsson (see Roman entries below) feels many works studied might be attributed to other composers. Van Boer later (in letter of June 23, 1987) mentions new genre history (Lennart Hedwall, *Den svenska symfonin*, Stockholm: Awe/Gebers [Almqvist och Wiksell], 1983, ISBN 91-20-06932-4; not examined) as successor to Walin, covering "development of the Swedish symphony from the late 17th century through the present." Entry 904 was Walin's dissertation (Uppsala, 1941).

Swedish Composers

Johan Joachim Agrell (1701-1765)[g,b]

905. Sheerin, Jeannette Morgenroth. "The Symphonies of Johan Agrell (1701-1765): Sources, Style, Context." 2 vols. Ph.D. dissertation, Univ. of North Carolina, 1986. 665, 186p.

Studies symphonies of Swedish composer, incorporating biography, spread of symphonies (sources, paper and copyists), authenticity, status in 18th century and Agrell's symphonic style. Inserts extremely detailed thematic catalog of 37 symphonies (28 authentic, 5 doubtful, 4 spurious). Provides insight into preclassical style since half of composer's works written before 1750. Includes thorough style study, noting importance of orchestral suite in formation of early symphony. Bibliography stresses sources for study of 18th century paper and copyists and sources for study of Swedish music. See also entries 688 and 689.

Jonas Åman (fl. 1750-1770)

906. Van Boer, Bertil H., Jr., ed. *Jonas Åman: Symphony in C major* in *Symphony*, series F, vol. III (The Symphony in Sweden), pp. xxix-xxxi, lxi, 59-64.

Classifies Åman as "prolific amateur composer of symphonies," noting his somewhat primitive symphonic style, his preference for 3 movements and the *galant* orientation of most works. Thematic index lists 6 authentic works and 1 spurious.

Johan Fredrik Berwald (1787-1861)[g,b]

907. Van Boer, Bertil H., Jr., ed. *Johan Fredrik Berwald: Symphony in E-flat major* in *Symphony*, series F, vol. III (The Symphony in Sweden). pp. xliv, lxxvii, 301-27.

Acknowledged as cousin of Franz Berwald, lacking musical sophistication of latter. Debuted as concert violinist at age of six and mounted esteemed career as soloist and conductor. Notes great promise of early compositions, unfulfilled in later works. Thematic index lists 1 symphony (4 movements, with minuet by Johan Wikmanson, his teacher) and 1 overture (3 movements with slow introduction), both from 1797 (age 10), and a later overture (ca. 1813).

Joachim (Georg) Nikolas Eggert (1779-1813)[g]

908. Van Boer, Bertil H., Jr., ed. *Joachim (Georg) Nikolas Eggert: Symphony in E-flat major* in *Symphony*, series F, vol. III (The Symphony in Sweden), pp. xli-xliv, lxxv, 235-300.

Includes detailed biography and discussion of symphonic style; anticipates Romantic style with innovative orchestration and exaggerated dynamics. Thematic index identifies 4 complete symphonies (half in 3 movements, half in 4) and 1 unfinished work, all written between 1800 and 1813.

Gustaf Frederici (Fredrici)(1779-1801)[g]

909. Svensson, Sven E. "Gustaf Frederici; En svensky Wienklassiker." *SvTMf* 20 (1938): 5-29.

Represents Svenson's original article on now-considered fictional composer, supposedly student of both Haydn and Mozart. Offers elaborate historical and stylistic study of fictional composer and his works. *NGDMM* mentions Svenson's "lively sense of humor" and his "skillful stylistic arrangements." Author edited all of the non-existent Frederici's "works."

Pehr Frigel (Frigelius) (1750-1842)

910. Van Boer, Bertil H., Jr., ed. *Pehr Frigel: Overture in C minor* in *Symphony*, series F, vol. III (The Symphony in Sweden), pp. xxxiv-xxxvi, lxvii, 107-20.

More famed for his Herculean effort of cataloging holdings of library of Royal Academy of Music (was repository for music manuscripts), completed impressive quantity of music, most in conservative style. Considers edited overture a hybrid of overture and symphony (two movements, a binary section followed by a fugato). Includes detailed analysis of edited score. Thematic index discloses 4 overtures, with 3 in single-movement form.

Johann Friedrich Grenser (1758-1795)[b]

911. Van Boer, Bertil H., Jr., ed. *Johann Friedrich Grenser Sinfonia alla posta in E-flat major* in *Symphony*, series F, vol. III (The Symphony in Sweden), pp. xxxviii-xl, lxxi, 151-93.

Although Dresden native, concentrated career in Stockholm. Composed numerous works for winds (was oboist) and 2 known symphonies (1 lost). Features *corno piccolo* in E-flat alto, "small, tightly-wound horn" as both *concertante* and *tutti* instrument in edited score (orginally completed in 1783). Uses as opening theme version of post horn call that announced arrival of mail coaches in Sweden. Thematic index.

Johann Christian Friedrich Haeffner (1759-1833)[g,b]

912. Van Boer, Bertil H., Jr., ed. *Johann Christian Friedrich Haeffner: Overture in E-flat major* in *Symphony*, series F, vol. III (The Symphony in Sweden), pp. xl-xli, lxxiii, 195-234.

Moved from native Germany to Stockholm for organ position. Later served as head of Uppsala's *Akamemiska
Kapell*, raising standards of university orchestra's performance significantly. Notes diversity of Haeffner's
works (from opera to occasional music, including 4 overtures dated 1795-1822). Comments on edited work's pre-
Romantic style. Thematic index.

Hinrich Philip Johnsen (1716-1779)[g,b]

913. Van Boer, Bertil H., Jr., ed. *Hinrich Philip Johnsen:
Symphony in F major* in *Symphony*, series F, vol. III
(The Symphony in Sweden), pp. xxv-xxvi, lv, 19-28.

Summarizes life and works, mentioning skills as keyboard teacher and performer. Used *sinfonia* form in 2
symphonies (both ca. 1755), one edited for this volume.
Comments on limited harmonic vocabulary and use of Baroque *Fortspinnung* in melodic writing. Describes overall
style as "faintly bizarre." Thematic index.

Joseph Martin Kraus (1756-1794)[g,b]

914. Eppstein, Hans. "Über Kraus' Instrumentalmusik." In
Kongress Stockholm, 1978, pp. 52-63.

Focuses primarily on overall style rather than specific
genre. Mentions symphonies (pp. 55-56). Identified as
German composer whose career evolved in Sweden. Extensive bibliography.

915. Kaiser, Fritz. "Die konzertante Symphonie des 18. Jahrhunderts und die Sinfonia concertante von Joseph Martin
Kraus." In *Kongress Buchen/1980*, pp. 139-53.

Summarizes history of genre (especially with regard to
18th century Parisian activities). Adds careful analysis
of composer's work for solo violin, flute, viola and
cello, establishing comparisons with works by C. Stamitz,
A. Stamitz, Mozart, Haydn, J.C. Bach, Breval and Saint-
Georges, especially on basis of extended use of solo
passages. Excellent bibliography.

916. Riedel, Friedrich W., ed. "Die Trauerkompositionen von
Joseph Martin Kraus. Ihre geistes- und musikgeschicht-
liche Stellung." In *Kongress Buchen/1980*, pp. 154-69.

Includes listing of works composed (ca. 1770-1780)
memorializing outstanding persons' deaths. Compares
style of these works with that of Kraus' *Trauerkantate*
and *Trauersinfonie* for King Gustaf III of Sweden. Sees
latter style a blend of learned church and theater
styles.

917. Van Boer, Bertil H., Jr., ed. *Joseph Martin Kraus:
      Six Symphonies* in *Symphony*, series F, vol. II (The
      Symphony in Sweden), pp. xxix-xlviii, 117-359.

Born in Germany, educated in law, emigrated to Sweden
1778 and gradually rose to prominence. Details output,
feeling many works lost, particularly symphonies. Divides works into groups (suggested by Kraus' travels):
Mannheim, 1769-1773; Buchen, 1775-1776; Paris, 1784-1786.
Describes symphonic style (early affinity for Italian
sinfonia, slow introductions to first movements, fondness
for the programmatic and flexibility in use of sonata-
allegro form). Analyzes edited works. Thematic index
lists 18 authentic symphonies and 1 questionable (including 3 in 4 movements and a church symphony in 1 movement). Mentions editor's forthcoming book, *Die Werke von
Joseph Martin Kraus. Erste Teil: Systematisch-thema-
tisches Werkverzeichnis*, possibly based on dissertation
(Uppsala, in progress in 1982).

Anders Piscator (1736-1804)

918. Van Boer, Bertil H., Jr., ed. *Anders Piscator: Symphony
      in F major* in *Symphony*, series F, vol. III (The Sym-
      phony in Sweden), pp. xxxiii-xxxiv, lxv, 87-105.

Identifies Piscator as native-born Swedish composer who
served as organist at Karlstad cathedral. May have considered himself to be an amateur composer (small output
of only 3 extant works). Thematic index lists just two
of the surviving symphonies, both in four movements and
influenced by C.P.E. Bach and second generation Mannheim
composers. Provides modest stylistic analysis of edited
work.

Johan Helmich Roman (1694-1758)[g,b]

919. Bengtsson, Ingmar. "Instrumentale Gattungen im Schmelz-
      tiegel; Beispiel: Die Orchestermusik von Johan Helmich
      Roman (1694-1758)." In *Gattung und Werk in der Musik-*

geschichte *Norddeutchlands und Skandinaviens*, edited by
Friedhelm Krummacher and Heinrich Schwab, pp. 97-106.
Kieler Schriften zur Musikwissenschaft 26. Kassel:
Bärenreiter, 1982. ISBN 3-7618-0677-9

Discusses Roman's output and symphonic style and, more
importantly, lists the orchestral works in a table that
provides meters, keys, overall form (3 movements, etc.)
and individual movement forms of each work. Includes
thematic index that supplements thematic index in entry
920.

920. _____. *J.H. Roman och hans Instrumentalmusik; käll-
och stilkritiska studier* (J.H. Roman and his instrumental music; a critical survey of sources of style).
Studia Musicologica Upsaaliensia, 4. Uppsala: Almqvist
& Wiksell, 1955. xxiv, 476p.

Presents summary in English on earlier research, life,
musical environment and sources, historical background of
sources, extended section on sources (method, source
description, problems with title and medium, critical
study of sources) and a third major section on style
(method and aim of style analysis, authenticity criteria,
authenticity of attributed works, chronology considera-
tions and summary of life and works). Establishes style
description without comparison to models then available.
Lacks specific discourse of Roman's symphonic style.
Adds details on instrumental style useful in understanding symphonies. Summaries detail general rather than
exact findings of each chapter. Bibliography and
thematic index.

921. _____, ed. *Johan Helmich Roman: Six Symphonies* in *Symphony*, series F, vol. II (The Symphony in Sweden), pp.
xi-xxviii, 1-116.

Summarizes life and state of research, stressing
authenticity problems. Discusses symphonic style
(genres, thematic contrast in sonata-allegro, transitional nature of style, little influence of *sinfonia*,
development skills and influences of suite and *ouverture*). Analyzes 6 edited works, isolating several
concepts, including *ouverture* rhythm, suite influence,
Handel's influence and *Fortspinnung*. Proposes phases
in symphonic development: 1730-1737, overture sympho-

nies; 1738-1745, suite and concerto symphonies; 1737-
1752, remaining symphonies. Thematic index of 20
authentic works.

922. _____. *Mr. Roman's spuriosity shop; a thematic catalog
      of 503 works from ca. 1680-1760 by more than sixty
      composers.* Stockholm: Swedish Music History Archives,
      1976.

      Comprised of *incipits* from over 450 manuscripts col-
      lected by Roman and circulated by editor to attract
      attention of scholars who might identify anonymous works,
      many originally attributed to Roman.

923. _____. *Supplement No. 1 to Mr. Roman's spuriosity
      shop; list of identifications Dec. 1976-March 1980.*
      Stockholm: Swedish Music History Archive, 1980.

      Upgrades entry 922 with identifications of some anony-
      mous and questionable works.

Francesco Antonio Baldassare Uttini (1723-1795)[g,b]

924. Van Boer, Bertil H., Jr., ed. *Francesco Antonio Baldas-
      sare Uttini: (Two Symphonies)* in *Symphony*, series F,
      vol. III (The Symphony in Sweden), pp. xxxi-xxxiii,
      lxiii, 65-85.

      Denotes Uttini as one of founders of Italian opera
      tradition in Sweden, noting his move from Italy to
      Stockholm in 1755. Presented his first opera in Swedish
      language in 1773, demonstrating his support of Gustav
      III's plans for Swedish national opera. Thematic index
      lists 4 symphonies (ca. 1753-before 1770), one identified
      as opera *sinfonia*. Explains symphonic style as *sinfonia*-
      based , Mannheim-influenced (slightly) but subsequently
      gradually maturing in its handling of first-movement
      form.

Arvid Niclas friherr von Höpkin (Höpken)(1710-1778)[g]

925. Van Boer, Bertil H., Jr., ed. *Arvid Niclas friherr von
      Höpkin: Sinfonia da chiesa in E-flat major* in *Symphony*,
      series F, vol. III (The Symphony in Sweden), pp. xxiii-
      xxiv, liii, 3-18.

      Of German ancestry but himself a native of Sweden,

received first formal music training while on military
assignment in Kassel. Remained an active Swedish army
officer for rest of life. Wrote mostly dramatic works,
including 2 Italian-style operas. Thematic index shows
3 symphonies, one a church symphony (edited and in style
and form of French *ouverture*) and 2 *sinfonie* (latter
possibly spurious according to *NGDMM*).

Anders Wesström (ca. 1720-1781)[g,b]

926. Van Boer, Bertil H., Jr., ed. *Anders Wesström: Symphony
     in D major* in *Symphony*, series F, vol. III (The Sym-
     phony in Sweden), pp. xxviii-xxix, lix, 41-57.

     Born in Sweden, served as lawyer part of his life.
     Studied violin with Tartini in Padua. In instrumental
     works reflects strong Mannheim influence, especially in
     2 surviving three-movement symphonies. Thematic index.

Johan Wikmanson (1753-1800)[g,b]

927. Van Boer, Bertil H., Jr., ed. *Johan Wikmanson: Minuet
     and Trio* in *Johan Fredrik Berwald: Symphony in E-flat
     major* in *Symphony*, series F, vol. III (The Symphony
     in Sweden), pp. xliv-xlvi, 316-18.

     Recounts Wikmanson's reputation as organist and his
     failure to establish himself primarily as composer.
     While serving as Berwald's teacher may have given child
     (10 years old) score of minuet to study, the work later
     incorporated into his student's symphony. See entry 907.

Johan David Zander (1753-1796)[g,b]

928. Van Boer, Bertil H., Jr., ed. *Johan David Zander:
     Symphony in B-flat major* in *Symphony*, series F, vol.
     III (The Symphony in Sweden), pp. xxxvi-xxxviii,
     lxix, 121-49.

     Recounts Zander's professional career (violinist,
     musical director, violin teacher and composer). Thema-
     tic index indicates only 1 surviving symphony (4 move-
     ments with slow introduction, using mature sonata-alle-
     gro form in first and fourth movements). Influenced
     both by Haydn (formal structure and style and lyric

themes) and French composers (dramatic impact of some
passages, contrasting dynamics and operatic phrasing).

Ferdinand Zellbell, Jr. (1719-1780)[g,b]

929. Van Boer, Bertil H., Jr., ed. *Ferdinand Zellbell, Jr.:*
      Symphony in d minor in *Symphony*, series F, vol. III
      (The Symphony in Sweden), pp. xxvi-xxviii. lvii-lviii,
      29-39.

      Studied with father, Roman and Telemann (with latter
      for 2 years in Hamburg). Traces carefully style matu-
      ration from Baroque to Rococo to early Classical and
      notes influences of Telemann, Graun and Hasse. Thematic
      index contains 7 works, all except 1 in 3 movements and
      written ca. 1750 or earlier. Likens edited work more to
      French suite than to *sinfonia* (*ouverture* first movement,
      followed by 2 dance movements).

Ferdinand Zellbell, Sr. (1689-1765)[g]

930. Van Boer, Bertil H., Jr., ed. *Ferdinand Zellbell, Sr.:*
      Symphony in C major in *Symphony*, series F, vol. III
      (The Symphony in Sweden), pp. xxii-xxiii, li, 1-8.

      Remarks on composer's good reputation as organist and
      composer in the Protestant tradition of Buxtehude, rein-
      forced by his 30 organ preludes. Wrote only single sym-
      phony, an early setting in *sinfonia* style (essentially
      in three-voice texture not unlike early Sammartini sym-
      phonies, using fairly clear forms and cast somewhat in
      early *galant* style). Thematic index.

Switzerland

General

931. Sondheimer, Robert. "Sinfonien aus dem 18. Jahrhundert
      in den basler Sammlungen Lucas Sarasin und Collegium
      musicum; Ein Beitrag zur Geschichte und Auffassung
      der Sinfonie im 18. Jahrhundert." In *Kongress*
      Basel/1924, pp. 321-25.

      Lucas Sarasin (1730-1802) was wealthy silk manufacturer
      in Basel who collected a variety of musical works,
      including many symphonies and overtures written during
      his life. He had a thematic catalog of the collection

prepared, this becoming one of the better sources of
information on the early symphony. Composers in collec-
tion: Sammartini, Rinaldo da Capua, Chiesa, Monza,
Bernasconi, Spourni, Polaci, Jomelli, Nardini, Piccinni,
Pugnani, Cammerlocher, Wagenseil, Stamitz, Filz, Beck, J.
Chr. Bach, Schwindl, Gassmann, Gossec, Cannabich,
Toeschi, Eichner, Rigel, Vanhall, Boccherini and
Kotzeluch (spelling as per source).

AUTHOR INDEX

Abert, Anna Marie. "Stilistischer Befund und Quellenlage zu Mozarts Lambacher Sinfonie," 330

Abert, Hermann. "Mozart: Symphony in G minor - an Analysis," 331

Abraham, Gerald. "Eighteenth Century Music and the Problems of its History," 73; "Some Eighteenth-century Polish Symphonies," 860

Addams, Eugene Bayne. "Source and Treatment of Thematic Material in the Developments of Sonata-allegro Movements in the Symphonies of Wolfgang Amadeus Mozart," 332

Adler, Guido. "Haydn and the Viennese Classical School," 187; "Die weiner klassische Schule," 154

Agee, Richard J. *Carl Philipp Stamitz: Three Symphonic Works*, 758; *Ignaz Holzbauer: Three Symphonic Works*, 724; *Johann Anton Filtz: Two Symphonies*, 712

Alexander, Peter M. *Franz Danzi: Three Symphonic Works*, 706

Allroggen, Gerhard. "Zur Frage der Echtheit der Sinfonie KV Anh. 216=74g," 336; "Vorwort" (Mozart's symphonies), 334, 335; "Mozarts erste Sinfonien," 333

Almeida, Antonio de. *Luigi Boccherini: Six Sinfonie*, 803

Alston, Charlotte Lenora. "Recapitulation Procedures in the Mature Symphonies of Haydn and Mozart," 188

Altner, Vladimir. *František Xaver Dušek: (Four Symphonies)*, 462

Anderson, John. "Brass Scoring Techniques in the Symphonies of Mozart, Beethoven and Brahms," 337

Anderson, Otto. "The Introduction of Orchestral Music into Finland," 561

Andrews, Harold L. "The Submediant in Haydn's Development Sections," 189

Angerer, Hugo. *Franz Xaver Pokorny: Three Symphonies*, 735; *Joseph Touchemoulin: One Symphony*, 778

Angerer, Hugo, and Robert Holder. *Theodor von Schacht: Two Symphonies*, 751

works from ca. 1680-1760 by more than sixty composers, 922; Supplement No. 1 to Mr. Roman's spuriosity shop; list of identifications Dec. 1976-March 1970, 923; "The Symphony in Scandinavia," 7

Bennett, Clive. "Clementi as Symphonist," 540

Bennett, Lawrence. "The Italian Cantata in Vienna, ca. 1700-ca. 1711," 155

Benton, Rita. *Ignaz Pleyel: a thematic catalog of his compositions*, 638

Berger, J. "Notes on some Seventeenth-Century Compositions for Trumpets and Strings in Bologna," 787

Berrett, Joshua. *Andreas Romberg: One Symphony*, 744

Berwalt, Jacek. *Karol Pietrowski: Symphony in D major*, 875

Biancolli, Louis. *The Mozart Handbook*, 341

Biermann, Joanna Cobb. *Johann Samuel Endler: Three Symphonies*, 709

Biondi, Michael. *Anton Zimmermann: One Symphony*, 784

Blom, Eric. "The Minuet-Trio," 52; *Mozart*, 342; "Wolfgang Amadeus Mozart" (symphonies), 343

Blomstedt, Herbert T. "Till Kännedomen om J.C. Bachs Symfonier," 521

Blume, Friedrich. *Classic and Romantic Music*, 75; "Mozart's Style and Influence," 343

Bookspan, Martin. *101 Masterpieces of Music and Their Composers*, 43

Bostian, Richard Lee. "The Works of Rinaldo di Capua," 833

Botstiber, Hugo. *Geschichte der Ouverture und der freien Orchesterformen*, 8

Bowles, Edmund A. "Music Ensembles in Eighteenth-Century Festival Books in the New York Public Library," 124

Braun, Melanie. "The Chevalier de Saint-Georges: an Exponent of the Parisian Symphonie Concertante," 648

Breitkopf, Johann Gottlob Immanuel. *Raccolte delle megliore sinfonie di piu celebri compositori di nostro tempo, accomodate all'clavicembalo*, 116

Brenet, Michel (Marie Bobillier). *Les concerts en France sous l'ancien régime*, 562; *Histoire de la symphonie à orchestre depuis ses origines jusqu'à Beethoven inclusivement*, 563

Brito, Manuel Carlos de. "Symphonic music in Portugal," 878

Broder, Nathan. "The Beginnings of the Orchestra," 125; *Mozart: Symphony in G minor, KV 550*, 345; "The Wind Instruments in Mozart's Symphonies, 346

Brofsky, Howard. "The Instrumental Music of Padre Martini," 819; *Padre Giovanni Battista Martini: Four Sinfonie*, 818; "The Symphonies of Padre Martini," 820

Van Boer, Bertil H., Jr. *Arvid Niclas friherr von Höpkin: Sinfonia da chiesa in E-flat major*, 925; *Anders Wesström: Symphony in D major*, 926; *Anders Piscator: Symphony in F major*, 918; *Ernst Dietrich Adolf Eichner: One Symphony*, 707; *Francesco Antonio Baldassare Uttini: (Two Symphonies)*, 924; *Ferdinand Zellbell, Jr.: Symphony in d minor*, 929; *Ferdinand Zellbell, Sr.: Symphony in C major*, 930; *Franz Xaver Richter: Five Symphonies*, 740; *Georg Joseph Vogler: One Symphony*, 779; *Hinrich Philip Johnsen: Symphony in F major*, 913; *Joachim (Georg) Nikolas Eggert: Symphony in E-flat major*, 908; *Johan David Zander: Symphony in B-flat major*, 928; *Johan Fredrik Berwald: Symphony in E-flat major*, 907; *Johan Wikmanson: Minuet and Trio in Johan Fredrik Berwald: Symphony in E-flat major*, 927; *Johann Christian Friedrich Haeffner: Overture in E-flat major*, 912; *Johann Friedrich Grenser: Sinfonia alla posta in E-flat major*, 911; *Jonas Åman: Symphony*, 906; *Joseph Martin Krauss: Six Symphonies*, 917; *Pehr Frigel: Overture in C minor*, 910; *The Symphony in Sweden, Part 2*, 903

Van der Meer, John Henry. "Die Verwendung der Blasinstrumente im Orchester bei Haydn und seiner Zeitgenossen," 311

Vasseur, Jean Philippe. *Isidor Bertheaume: (One Symphonie concertante)*, 602

Vassiliades, Evangeline. "Overture and symphony in eighteenth-century Russia," 885

Verchaly, André. *Étrangères dans l'oeuvre de W.A. Mozart*, 424

Viano, Richard J. *Foreign Composers in France, 1750-1790*, 595; *Hébert Philippe Adrien Leemans: One Symphony*, 628; *Henri-Joseph Rigel: Two Symphonic Works, 644; Jean-Baptiste Mirolgio: One Symphony*, 633; *Jean-Baptiste Sébastien Bréval: (Two Symphonies concertantes)*, 604; *Valentin Roesser: One Symphony*, 645

Vinton, John. "The Development Section in Early Viennese Symphonies: A Re-valuation," 167

Vitali, Carlo, and Michele Girardi. *Giovanni Battista Lampugnani: Five Sinfonie*, 814

Vogler, Georg Joseph. *Betrachtungen der Mannheimer Tonschule*, 681

Volek, Tomislav. "Der Verhältnis von Rhythmus und Metrum bei J.W. Stamitz," 773

Wade, Rachel W. *The catalog of Carl Philipp Emanuel Bach's estate*, 694; *The Keyboard Concertos of Carl Philipp Emanuel Bach*, 695

TITLE INDEX

COMPOSER INDEX

290

SUBJECT INDEX

Abstracts
    Articles, 1
    Books, 1
    Catalogs, 1
    Dissertations, 1
    Essays, 1
    Iconographies, 1
    Reviews, 1
Analysis, aesthetic, Mozart, 401, 419
Analysis, affective, Mozart, 331, 374
Analysis, form, 27, 43, 51
    Bach, J.C., 107
    Dittersdorf, 176
    Haydn, 16, 44, 45, 286
    Mozart, 24, 25, 359, 363, 373, 415, 421
    Vanhall, 115
Analysis, Haydn, symphonies 85, 92, 94, 100, 101, 103, 104:
    entry 231; symphonies 103, 104 (by Momigny): entry 284
Analysis, historical, Mozart, 430
Analysis, metric, Mozart, 340
Analysis, musical task (Levarie), 276
Analysis, philosophical, Mozart, 419
Analysis, phrase treatment, Haydn, 269
Analysis, stylistic, 63, 122
    Dittersdorf, 176
    Gassmann, 182
    Haydn, 264
    Mozart, 391
    Ordonez, 438-39
    Paradeiser, 440
    Pergolesi, 828
    Sorkočević, 479
Anecdotes, musical, 18th century England, 491, 506
Antecedents, 70, 79, 80, 86, 87, 101, 103, 104, 112, 115, 163
    Italian, 787, 789, 791, 798-99, 801, 808-10, 813, 823,
        826, 830, 847-49, 853-54